PORTFOLIO / PENGUIN

CAR GUYS VS. BEAN COUNTERS

Bob Lutz held senior leadership positions at GM, Ford, Chrysler, and BMW over the course of an unparalleled forty-seven-year career, culminating in his vice chairmanship of General Motors from 2001 to 2010. He is the bestselling author of *Guts: 8 Laws of Business from One of the Most Innovative Business Leaders of Our Time.*

CAR GUYS

VS.

BEAN COUNTERS

The Battle for the Soul of American Business

BOB LUTZ

PORTFOLIO / PENGUIN

This book is dedicated to the hardworking men and women, at all levels, hourly and salaried, in the domestic U.S. automobile industry. The problems, mostly, were not your fault!

PORTFOLIO/PENGUIN

Published by the Penguin Group
Penguin Group (USA) Inc., 375 Hudson Street,
New York, New York 10014, USA

USA / Canada / UK / Ireland / Australia / New Zealand / India / South Africa / China
Penguin Books Ltd, Registered Offices: 80 Strand, London WC2R 0RL, England
For more information about the Penguin Group visit penguin.com

First published in the United States of America by Portfolio/Penguin, a member of Penguin Group
(USA) Inc., 2011
This paperback edition with a new preface published 2013

THE LIBRARY OF CONGRESS HAS CATALOGED THE HARDCOVER EDITION AS FOLLOWS:
Lutz, Robert A.
Car guys vs. bean counters : the battle for the soul of American business / Bob Lutz.
p. cm.
Includes index.
ISBN 978-1-59184-400-6 (hc.)
ISBN 978-1-59184-622-2 (pbk.)
1. Automobile industry and trade—United States. 2. New products—United States.
I. Title. II. Title: Car guys versus bean counters.
HD9710.U52L88 2011
338.7'6292220973—dc22
2011010720

Printed in the United States of America
1   3   5   7   9   10   8   6   4   2

Set in Bembo Std
Designed by Sabrina Bowers

Contents

Preface to the Paperback Edition

THE HARDCOVER EDITION OF CAR GUYS VS. BEAN COUNTERS quickly gained media accolades and pleasing sales numbers when it was published. I had always argued with potential publishers that good sales were guaranteed for a book about the transformation of General Motors from its decline, fall, and rebirth. Given the number of employees at GM alone—not to mention those at Ford and Chrysler, the Japanese transplants, and all the North American automotive suppliers—the potential for a book relating to the car business had to be huge.

Fortunately, I was not disappointed. I have personally signed thousands of copies at automotive events across the country.

What did surprise me, though, was the amount of letters and e-mails I received from readers far removed from the auto industry who found the "car guys vs. bean counters" paradigm (which I had naively assumed to be mainly an automotive phenomenon) equally present and equally frustrating in their fields of endeavor.

One successful eye surgeon told me that I could change a few words and the book would apply just as much to the field of ophthalmology, which, apparently, also pits the "doers" (ophthalmologists and surgeons) against the administrators, safety regulators, insurance companies, and other "non-eye guys" who nevertheless hold considerable sway in a field that should celebrate the maintenance and repair of vision. A vast bureaucracy that insists on "process" and "repeatability" creates many internal "metrics" designed to lead to greater efficiency, uniformity, and lower cost. All of that can be good and, in fact, is almost necessary. But it is only valuable if it doesn't inhibit the primary desired result of ophthalmology: better eye care for the patients.

On another occasion, a journalist at a major news magazine hosted me at her company's offices. Having been charged with reviewing my book, she asked what my main premise was, or what message I was trying to convey to the reader. As succinctly as I could, I explained that my book was about achieving in any organization the proper balance between the creators, change agents, and doers on one hand and the worriers and keepers of the status quo on the other. Having only "creators" without the stabilizing, cautionary guidance from the "bean counters" can, of course, lead to fun-filled chaos. The trouble, I said, is that I've found the imbalance to always be in favor of those who value order, stability, predictability, and short-term financial results above all else.

To my surprise, she stopped writing, put her pen aside, and stared silently out the window. After a long moment, she turned back to me and said, "You should try working in this place!" So, here we have a company selling a product (magazine) that should be pure, creative, informative entertainment, with no long-term durability, safety, or emissions requirements, produced and distributed at a predictable low cost—and yet, even in such a simple process, the "magazine guys" feel dominated by the bean counters!

Did my book actually change the plight of the ophthalmologist or journalist? Did it help the cause of those who, inspired by the likes of Sir Richard Branson, Elon Musk, and Steve Jobs, actually want to create, innovate, and provide superior value to customers and shareholders? I would love to say "Yes, it's helped liberate those who drive change, who accept intelligent risk, who can lead effectively in a rapidly evolving environment." Sadly, I would be deceiving myself and others.

Consider this recent jewel emanating from the mammoth human resources department of a large industrial company. Embedded in the near-endless text describing changes to the performance evaluation process is this bit of hard-hitting, value-creating prose:

> The Individual Business Goals feedback section expands to include total employee contribution to the company, shifting the focus from a task-oriented review to a total results or contribution perspective.

(Are you still with me?)
It continues:

> A new Behaviors section focuses on *how* work is completed in alignment with the five key elements of the Company's Global Leadership Framework—character, personal capability, focus on results, interpersonal skills, and leading change. This framework now applies to all employees, whether they are spearheading their own work, leading projects, or managing people. In short, how you go about achieving your results is just as important as the business performance you deliver.

Now, *there* is a call to dynamic, results-oriented performance if I ever read one! What these well-meaning HR professionals are really saying is: "Be considerate, be nice, fit in, don't rock the boat, don't intimidate with your superior intelligence, knowledge of the subject matter, or sense of urgency. Be popular! It's half your grade!"

Is it any wonder that individual initiative and drive for change is woefully absent in a behavioral metric system such as this one? Even more amazing is that many CEOs complain of a risk-averse corporate culture, yet tolerate culture anesthesia through company practices such as this.

No, the "counters and measurers" are not yet back in the rightful niche. This is why you, the buyer of the paperback edition of *Car Guys vs. Bean Counters*, must read and absorb the core message. Then, you must tirelessly battle the forces of darkness in your own company or organization. Further, I strongly recommend that you urge friends and acquaintances to buy *Car Guys vs. Bean Counters* and then behave similarly. If we can collectively do this five or six million times, we can have the bean counters on the run. Of course, then I'll have to hire one!

Preface

IT WAS IN 1979 IN THE UNITED KINGDOM. I HAD JUST BEEN ELEVATED TO president of Ford Europe and was conducting my first monthly quality meeting.

Ford's quality was about average for Europe at the time, but we were having a major problem with our UK-built four-cylinder engines: camshafts (an essential part that controls the valves) were wearing out at a totally unacceptable rate. Some camshafts failed after as little as 10,000 miles, few lasted more than 15,000 miles, and the bulk of the repeat failures occurred soon after the expiration of the then-prevalent 12,000-mile warranty.

I asked what we were going to do to achieve industry-standard durability on camshafts. Manufacturing and Engineering had a number of solutions, all requiring some increase in parts cost and a nominal investment in equipment. I authorized these on the spot, and emphasized the need for speed in incorporating the changes.

End of story? Not quite! The finance guys piped up and informed me that I had, by my hasty decision, just blown a roughly $50 million hole in the profit forecast. It seems that was the amount of profit the Parts and Service organization was reaping by shipping an endless stream of shoddy, soft camshafts to hundreds of thousands of customers who "had no other choice . . . they've got to buy them." Yes, they had no choice . . . until their next vehicle purchase.

I ultimately prevailed, but I paid for it the rest of my time at Ford, gaining the reputation as "a good product guy, but he's not bottom-line focused, not a sound businessman." This philosophy of treating the customer as a hapless victim to be exploited was endemic in American corporations, and it cost us dearly. I contend that I wasn't the lousy businessman. The MBA bean counters who were perfectly willing to sacrifice goodwill and reputation for a lousy $50 million in ill-gotten profit were the villains. And eventually the chickens came home to roost.

This book is about what happened to America's competitiveness, and why. Most of the examples and observations are from the automobile sector, for the simple reason that that's what I know best, and I was a participant in the decades-long decline of General Motors. But the creeping malignancy that transformed the once all-powerful, world-dominating American economy from one that produced and exported to one that trades and imports is now common to all or most sectors.

It really boils down to a matter of focus, priorities, and business philosophy. Leaders who are predominantly motivated by financial reward, who bake that reward into the business plan and then manipulate all other variables to "hit that number," will usually *not* hit the number, or, if they do, then only once. But the enterprise that is focused on excellence and on providing superior value will see revenue materialize and grow, and will be *rewarded* with good profit. Is profit an integral part of the business equation and a God-given right, no matter how compromised the product or service? *Or* is the financial result an unpredictable reward, bestowed upon the business by satisfied customers?

To some restaurant owners, people booking reservations weeks in advance is a sign that "we did something wrong." Perhaps the food is *too* good . . . best to back off a bit on the quality of the meat and produce. Ease off on the butter! We'll reduce cost, improve margins! And the customers, presumably, will keep coming, right?

But to other owners, the excess demand is a sign of success, of the formula working, of customers appreciating the value of their efforts. In this case, profit can be increased by selective higher pricing to keep the waiting times reasonable while gaining a premium reputation. Want to guess which restaurant will be in business longer, and be more successful?

There is a GM car, produced worldwide, which is hugely successful wherever it is produced and sold. It has great styling, is larger than its direct competitors, and generally exceeds customer expectations. It is profitable in a vehicle category in which that status is rarely achieved. A cause for celebration, of joy at having found the winning formula? Yes, but there are factions who complain that "we overachieved"; the car is "better and richer than it needs to be," so let's "correct back to the centerline with the next model." Listening to those voices would put GM back on the downward slope. The drive to reduce cost, skimp a bit on service, ruthlessly pursue quarterly earnings targets no matter what the negative consequences has hurt American business from automobiles to appliances, as well as the service industries.

My premise is that the trend is reversible. We don't have to be a nation of importers, bond traders, and venture capitalists who have no interest in the long-term viability of the company as long as they have a surefire, timely exit strategy.

As an industrial power, the United States has a historic window. Exchange rates are in our favor, labor rates are, by most standards, competitive. We still have ingenuity, initiative, and a deep well of technological innovation.

It's time to stop the dominance of the number crunchers,

living in their perfect, predictable, financially projected world (who fail, time and again), and give the reins to the "product guys" (of either gender), those with vision and passion for the customers and their product or service.

It applies in any business. Shoemakers should be run by shoe guys, and software firms by software guys, and supermarkets by supermarket guys. With the advice and support of their bean counters, absolutely, but with the final word going to those who live and breathe the customer experience. Passion and drive for excellence will win over the computer-like, dispassionate, analysis-driven philosophy every time.

The Beginning

A CHAUFFEUR-DRIVEN CADILLAC GLIDED SILENTLY TO THE CURB IN front of the Ann Arbor office of Exide Technologies, the world's largest producer of lead-acid batteries. I was CEO and had a good view of the front from my office with its cigar-friendly sliding glass door.

The chauffeur opened the passenger-side door, and a very tall man unfolded his six-foot-six-inch frame and walked toward the main entrance. Morning sun silhouetted his broad shoulders, and inside my office, we were ready for him: coffee brewed, muffins arrayed, orange juice poured.

This was important company, for the tall stranger was none other than former Duke University basketball player G. Richard (Rick) Wagoner, then president and CEO of General Motors. The scene of his arrival at my modest office complex is forever etched in my memory, for it marked the end of a long, convoluted rapprochement that had developed in fits and starts. It also signaled the beginning of a presumed three-year relationship with GM that was to last almost nine years and would prove to be both the most rewarding as well as the most frustrating epoch in my career.

I was, at this juncture in 2001, nearing seventy. After retiring at sixty-six as vice chairman of Chrysler in 1998, I'd written my book *Guts*, and was serving as CEO of troubled Exide Technologies. (Talk about troubled: my predecessor CEO, his president, and the CFO had been indicted, tried, convicted, and sentenced to hard time in federal penitentiaries for committing a veritable Chinese restaurant menu of state, local, and federal felonies. Trying to raise much-needed new capital or find new customers for a company this tarnished was near impossible. And all this took place before the larger, more publicized Enron scandal. I longed for the ethics and order I knew to be the hallmarks of all the Big Three Detroit OEMs. But, I digress; my Exide time would fill another book.) During those 1998–2000 post-Chrysler years, I encountered a curious phenomenon: journalists, analysts, and supplier executives would, at random intervals, contact me with basically the same question: "What's wrong with GM? Why can't they get it right? What would you do?"

This sentiment intensified to the point where the late Heinz Prechter, an influential Detroit resident and founder of American Sunroof Corporation (later just ASC), started hatching a coup: he would assemble a complete senior management team (essentially him, me, and Steve Miller, America's emergency-CEO for companies in Chapter 11), raise capital, buy GM shares, and then talk the GM board into cleaning out the existing top management. It was a grand scheme, and it consumed several afternoons and evenings at Prechter's estate on Grosse Ile. Prechter, in a manic phase of the bipolar disorder that would ultimately claim his life through suicide, rubbed his hands with glee over what he called "the big one." Sadly, or perhaps luckily, it came to naught.

And there were others. J. T. Battenberg, then CEO of Delphi, the parts and components spin-off from GM (and an Exide competitor in batteries), called me at work one day. His proposal: he would exert backdoor influence to have me elected CEO of GM because, despite his loyalty to the company (he was, prior to the spin-off, one of GM's most senior automotive executives), he was worried about the company's course, leadership style, and, above all, design direction. His fears were more than pure altruism: GM was Delphi's largest customer, by far. Lower GM sales would translate immediately into lower revenue for Delphi. I declined to make myself available.

In 2000, John Devine, GM's newly hired chief financial officer, invited me to dinner. Over a late supper in a dark booth in the restaurant at the Dearborn Ritz-Carlton, John outlined his plan: sensing disarray in GM's management structure and passenger-car creation, he wanted me to join the company as vice chairman for product development.

"Sounds good to me, John," I replied. "What does Rick think about it?" Ah, there was the rub! John hadn't discussed it with Rick yet, and this would have to await the right mood and moment. I wasn't expecting anything, and thus was neither surprised nor disappointed when that's exactly what I got.

Then, a few months later and quite out of the blue, I ran into François Castaing, formerly my chief of product development at Chrysler, now retired. A reformed Frenchman, Castaing had become a U.S. citizen but still spoke with a heavy accent. His reputation as a brilliant, fast-moving, troop-motivating leader was firmly established in the industry. His years of running Renault's Formula One racing team had honed his focus on speed and precision. A large measure of Chrysler's huge success in the 1990s can be ascribed to him.

What François wanted to convey to me was this: he had been asked to work for GM in a consulting capacity, to assess the product program and methods, and to provide ideas for improvement. He had seen all the future products, he told me. Naturally, I asked what he thought.

"*C'est une catastrophe!*" was his verdict. "If you think the Pontiac Aztek was bad, you don't want to see what's next. The stuff is awful! I can't change it; I declined the offer." Just what I wanted to hear to raise my level of enthusiasm for an offer which might or might not even come!

One or two more dinners with John Devine ensued at which he reaffirmed his desire to have me join GM, while adding that "Rick wasn't quite there yet." I began to discount the thought of ever working for GM . . . it sounded too much like John had changed his mind but hadn't gotten around to telling me.

Then came the dinner of the Harvard Business School Club, held at Oakland Hills Country Club in the summer of 2001. I was their guest speaker and honoree. Wagoner, a Harvard Business School graduate and officer of the club, gave the introduction. Rick, always witty, delivered the introduction in a mildly irreverent way, almost as a "roast," to which I responded by suggesting that any automotive CEO who bore even distant responsibility for the Aztek should perhaps be measured in his criticisms.

It was meant in jest, but it clearly stung. Speech done and trophy in hand, I shared a table with Rick.

"So, Bob, what's your candid opinion of where GM stands in terms of product, and what should we do?"

"How much time do you have," I replied, "and where do you want me to begin?"

The floodgates were open. Ignoring normal table etiquette and the others around us, Rick asked, and I replied to, countless questions. When the club was shutting down for the night, Rick asked if we could meet again to "continue this interesting conversation."

Thus, a few weeks later, the aforementioned modest breakfast at Exide headquarters took place. I had no conference table in the sparsely furnished office, so I sat behind my desk with Rick seated opposite me and leaning slightly forward. He soon allowed that he had come to the conclusion that GM could, in fact, use the services of a natural, intuitive, experienced car guy.

"Who do you know," Rick asked, "who is just like you, similar background, similar ability, but fifty years old?" A good, logical question, but I was stumped.

"He's probably out there somewhere," I responded, "but if he is, I sure haven't heard of him." Thoughtful pause on Rick's part.

"I see. Would you be willing to enter into a consulting arrangement with GM?"

I countered that with a resounding no, explaining that I'd have the frustration, the knowledge, the desire to do something, but no power to actually get it done. Besides, I would have the whole organization mobilized against me to "neutralize" the threat to the status quo.

This resulted in a long and somewhat painful silence, broken finally by Rick asking, in a painfully halting way, "I don't suppose . . . you know, at your age and all . . . that you'd be . . . willing to consider, conceivably . . . actually coming back to work at GM full time for a few years?" There—it was out! Title, compensation, and responsibilities were quickly sketched out, but would have to be blessed by the board.

I told Rick my value to the company would come in three distinct phases:

Phase One. Exert my influence to improve products already in the pipeline and use my communications skills and reputation with the media to have them seen in the best possible light.

Phase Two. Lead the creation of the future portfolio: cars and trucks of unsurpassed design excellence and characteristics. Cars and trucks so good, so desirable, that customers would pay full price and wait for delivery if necessary.

Phase Three. Permanently change the culture of the company, especially around design, planning, and engineering, in such a way that mediocrity (or the dreaded adjective "lackluster," so frequently applied to new GM cars) would be permanently banished.

How these three phases were accomplished over almost nine years instead of the originally envisaged three years is what the rest of this book is about.

An Unstoppable Force

TO FULLY APPRECIATE WHAT I WAS ABOUT TO WALK INTO, WE MUST FIRST understand the situation GM was in, and how it got there. So, a brief history lesson is in order. I won't delve into the detail that is readily available elsewhere—including at GM itself. In fact, ex-CEO Jack Smith used to teach an in-house course on "GM History" to young employees. While the intentions were no doubt noble, and the material no doubt fascinating, the whole idea was indicative of the culture of corporate infallibility and self-worship being fostered on the premises.

The GM we know today began to take shape in 1920, when Alfred P. Sloan took the wheel of the conglomeration of car companies collected in 1908 by Billy Durant and christened "General Motors."

Sloan brought order and managerial discipline to what Durant had cobbled together and established a visionary method for running what was even then a huge corporation. He believed in some centralized control, especially in the establishment of budgets, allocation of capital, and selection of key management. But he also displayed uncanny instincts for controls that were simultaneously "loose" and "tight."

"Tight" control was maintained on the overall vision for the company, and especially its brands. "A car for every purse and purpose" was a famous phrase attributed to Sloan. The brands were to form a hierarchy from the lowest price, with Chevrolet, Pontiac, Buick, and Oldsmobile serving as increasingly expensive, increasingly premium stepping-stones to the "Standard of the World," Cadillac, and its junior cousin, LaSalle.

The "looser" control manifested itself in the broad autonomy granted the divisions in what kinds of vehicles they produced and how they chose to market them. Sloan also displayed his visionary skill in recognizing the importance of automotive design, hiring the legendary and flamboyant designer Harley Earl and establishing the first "Art and Color" department, which was to assure that all of the products of the corporation would be as well proportioned and stunningly beautiful as the custom bodies Harley Earl created before his arrival at GM.

Recognizing early on the international potential of automotives, Sloan expanded the company through exports (Buick being especially successful with the Chinese moneyed class, paving the way for Buick's astounding success in that country in the most recent period), as well as through acquisitions. By 1931, GM had acquired Vauxhall in the United Kingdom, Adam Opel AG in Germany, and Holden in Australia.

The 1930s saw generation after generation of increasingly beautiful, well-crafted GM cars, all distinctive in appearance and performance while sharing common body engineering and construction through GM's body works, the Fisher Body division. This was an early example of the successful application of "economies of scale," achieved while maintaining the all-important separate character and role of each GM division.

While the 1930s were a struggle, the advent of World War II in 1941 brought a sudden halt to automobile production as U.S. industry as a whole turned to defense production, with GM at the forefront in the production of military vehicles—both amphibious and land—diesel engines, and even aircraft. It was a period when production skills, which GM already had in spades, mattered, and the only customer was the U.S. war machine.

In 1945, the atomic bomb ended World War II with an exclamation point, and the corporation returned rapidly to civilian production. The nation had been without a single new car since late 1941—the pent-up demand was huge; tooling of the 1942 models was dusted off, minor design changes were introduced to identify the cars as the "all-new, postwar cars," and the race for dominance in the U.S. car market was on.

GM's design and engineering prowess was all-conquering. While other Detroit companies gradually fell by the wayside or merged (Packard, Nash, and Hudson had all disappeared by the 1960s) and while the other "Big Two," Ford and Chrysler, produced some highly notable successes, there was simply no overcoming the sheer brilliance of the cars produced by GM. They were brash, exciting, chrome-laden, at times startling, as when Cadillac first introduced tail fins—inspired by the Lockheed P-38 Lightning fighter aircraft—on its 1948 models. All the GM vehicles of this era had beautiful proportions and simply radiated excellence. GM was the first, in the early 1940s, to introduce the fully automatic transmission, the Hydra-Matic, which Ford was forced to buy while Chrysler struggled with a less capable and less sophisticated semiautomatic unit.

Flaunting its sure grip on America's tastes, GM paraded new models and concept cars around the country in "Motoramas," live shows featuring music, talent, lights, motion, and chrome to rival any Hollywood production. By now, the Harley Earl baton had been passed to the even more talented (and flamboyant) Bill Mitchell, who, through talent, personality, and astonishing displays of expensive personal haberdashery, became the incarnation of the automotive designer: cocky, confident, disdainful of "marketing," resisting the constraints of "finance," scheming to overcome the dictates of the engineers. Mitchell and his team became the force that ran GM in the late 1950s through the '60s. Talented young designers sought jobs at GM Styling, because that's where the great stuff happened!

Audacious, seemingly impossible dreams made it through to production under Mitchell, from the monstrous lateral fins on the 1959 Chevrolet to the aerodynamically useless vertical fins on the 1961 Cadillac. Was everything in the best of taste, or with actual customer utility in mind? Of course not. Like Mitchell himself, who had a lovably insolent and profane side to him, his operations at times were greeted by headshaking among the country's intellectual elite. But it didn't matter: the public adored what GM produced and demanded more of the same.

GM launched ever more desirable products, like the legendary Pontiac GTO, the Oldsmobile 442, the Buick Riviera, a plethora of Cadillacs, and the sensational "tri-5" (1955, '56, '57) Chevrolets, the first of the brand with a V8, which sold in record volumes, and have now achieved high-value collectible status. Engines steadily became larger and more powerful. GM was usually triumphant in the horsepower race, and the fact that these ultraheavy, overly powerful land yachts got only nine or ten miles per gallon was of little concern with fuel prices at twenty-five cents per gallon— roughly, as today, one-fourth what the rest of the world was paying. (Is it any wonder that the Europeans, and later the Japanese, focused predominantly on smaller, more fuel-efficient vehicles when customers in their home markets were paying four times as much for fuel?) GM's overseas business was booming, too, as company resources were poured into Opel and Vauxhall in Europe, and Holden in Australia.

But the real GM domination took place here in the United States. One out of every two vehicles sold was produced by a GM division. GM's flashy designs, and equally flashy designers, became an intrinsic part of the American culture of consumption, newness, and "keeping up with the Joneses." Whether it was the economy, the customers, the dealers, or the suppliers, everyone benefited from GM's success. Sure, some voiced concern and resentment, and best-selling books, like Vance Packard's *The Waste Makers* and John Keats's *The Insolent Chariots*, reflected a small but growing nucleus of concern over whether all this arrogant opulence and the ever-shorter fashion cycle were really of benefit to society. But these books were written by intellectual elitists . . . so who cared what they said?

One incident that caused GM lasting harm was a 1965 book by a young lawyer and consumer advocate by the name of Ralph Nader. *Unsafe at Any Speed* accused the Corvair, different from other American cars with its rear-engine design, of being inherently unstable and accident-prone. Nader's work gained huge notoriety and effectively shut down Corvair sales in the mid-1960s.

Unaccustomed to being dented by a lone ideologue, GM hired investigators to delve into Nader's personal life, seeking any salacious information that would silence him. But news of the investigation leaked and caused a public outcry. In an effort at damage control, GM chairman Jim Roche (not the most charismatic of figures, even on a good day) delivered an abject apology to Nader. It was an epic low point in the company's history; GM, for perhaps the first time, was cast in the role of villain. This occurrence also lent credibility to the nascent "safety advocacy" movement, costing GM more of the American public's trust than the company realized at the time.

But it mattered not. GM still had 50 percent market share. In 1965 French national TV produced a one-hour special on the globe-spanning power of GM. They titled it "GM, Le Budget de la France" ("The budget of France")—at the time, GM's sales revenue exceeded the budget of the French Republic.

The unstoppable GM machine roared on, despite some increasingly strident criticism. As the 1970s approached, GM's top leadership spoke of the "60-60-60" plan, meaning that GM would have 60 percent market share and GM stock would rise to $60 per share, all by the time the core senior leadership turned sixty.

It was not to happen.

The Beginning of the End

IT'S HARD TO SAY EXACTLY WHEN, WHY, AND WHERE THINGS FIRST WENT wrong. The company changed, as did the climate in which it operated. Certainly government played a role, as did the media. Foreign competitors, a "fringe" at first, began growing at the base of the mighty GM oak, with companies like BMW, Jaguar, and Mercedes providing affluent American customers more prestige than the Cadillac, the erstwhile pinnacle of automotive achievement.

But, as a former employee (in the 1960s) and observer of the scene at the time, I often refer to one of the key factors using the movie title *The Empire Strikes Back*. At some point in the early to mid-1970s, power shifted within GM, both in terms of organization and in terms of geography. To understand how and why, we need a little more history.

In the heady days of the 1950s and '60s, the epicenter of power was in Warren, Michigan, in the GM Tech Center. This is where Design, Engineering, and Advanced Research were situated. This is where ideas were floated, radical designs were created, decisions to produce were made. Finance and the all-powerful "Treasurer's Office" (referred to as the "T.O." within GM) were not located in the Tech Center, nor even in the venerable GM Building in Detroit. Far from the real action, Finance and T.O. were in New York, America's financial capital. GM's chairmen were almost always alumni of the T.O.; they ran the finances and steered the (compliant) board of directors. But the president and chief operating officer were always selected from the "hardware" end, usually from Engineering. It would not be an exaggeration to say that the power to run the car business resided principally with the president, with the hierarchically senior chairman responding to the initiatives of the doers as well as counting and reallocating the vast sums of money that GM's successful product programs generated.

And then there was Design, first under Harley Earl, later under Bill Mitchell. These men were celebrities, as were their talented subordinates. Earl had the ear of Alfred P. Sloan, routinely calling him to plead the reversal of decisions deemed not in Styling's best interest. Mitchell, Earl's successor, further expanded the influence and power of GM Styling (now called "Design"). Whether it involved cars, trucks, office décor, building architecture, or corporate aircraft interiors, anything visible to the human eye and associated with GM required the involvement and approval of Design. The epic GM pavilion at the 1964 New York World's Fair, unequalled in razzle-dazzle opulence before or since, was a monument to the power of GM Design.

Design's amazing power was often wielded ruthlessly. Bill Mitchell once walked into a Buick studio (located in the Warren complex) and discovered the head of the Buick Division reviewing the full-scale clay model of one of "his" future Buicks. Furious, Mitchell demanded to know why the division head had dared venture into his, Mitchell's, domain! The Buick executive, apparently a courageous sort, responded, "This is my studio. It may be in your building, but the studio is mine. Buick pays all the expense; it comes out of my budget. I have every right to be here!" Mitchell, momentarily nonplussed, stomped out, called his finance guy, and asked if this was true. The keeper of the budgets told him that, yes, the production studios, whether Chevrolet, Pontiac, Buick, Oldsmobile, or Cadillac, were all funded by the divisions themselves. The so-called advanced studios, on the other hand, were on the budget of GM Design and, therefore, Mitchell's.

Mitchell had a solution: he ordered the removal of all work in progress from the division-financed production studios, and had the "clays," with the attendant designers and modelers, moved into the advanced areas. The next time the general manager of the Buick Division showed up to review "his" Buick clay model, he found a cavernous, empty room. Access to "Advanced" was, of course, denied. (Behavior like this did not endear Design to the rest of the company.)

In another act of naked hubris, Mitchell decided that the Camaro, Firebird, and Corvette, the company's trio of sports cars, did not "sound right." They were equipped with the company's V8s, powerful and reliable, still revered to this day, but to Mitchell's discerning ear they didn't sound as good as a Ferrari or Lamborghini V12. Unlike the V8's rumble, those engines produced a sound much like the rending of expensive fabric, transitioning into a wonderful high-pitched wail at higher RPMs. Ferraris had the sound of expensive hardware, and Mitchell wanted it. He talked to Engineering, who didn't fully understand, or want to understand, what Mitchell was saying.

Mitchell, knowing all too well the styling axiom "I hear you talking, but my ears can't see," decided that only a demonstration would suffice. He dispatched an emissary to Maranello, Italy, to purchase a factory-fresh Ferrari V12 at a cost, in today's terms, of roughly $100,000. Upon its arrival, Mitchell's small engineering staff—yes, Design had engineers for just such purposes—set to removing the offending, vulgarly low-class GM V8 from a Pontiac Firebird and replacing it with the carefully transplanted Ferrari engine, by itself worth a multiple of the receiving car. This lucky Firebird, which exists to this day, received some garish stylistic modifications and was dubbed "Pegasus."

Mitchell gathered his peers from Engineering, triumphantly started the engine, and blipped the throttle, resulting in decidedly un-Pontiac-like shrieks of high-pitched Euro-power. "That, gentlemen," spoke Mitchell, "is how a goddamn sports car is supposed to sound!" Point made—but Camaros and Firebirds never did get V12s. Still, "Pegasus" was arguably Mitchell's favorite among the many "special" vehicles he and the other leading designers liked to drive.

As you might expect, things weren't always quite so "ethically pristine" in Design at that time. It was quite possible for senior designers and other key executives (in Mitchell's good graces) to have major restorations performed on their collector cars. Whether working on an old Auburn "boat-tail Speedster" or a prewar German "Horch" cabriolet, the Design shops at the time were as good as today's restoration specialists, doing complete, frame-off mechanical and cosmetic refurbishments, resulting in what the classic car trade calls "Condition 1" cars.

Some of these GM-restored vehicles are still regularly seen in major concours d'elegance. To be fair, it must be added that audits performed years later led to the owners being billed laughably small sums for the work. (I was a minor miscreant: Opel Design custom painted the racing fairing on my Honda CB-750 four-cylinder motorcycle. Luckily, I had left GM for BMW by the time the auditors showed up.) To say that Design's behavior rankled the more orderly elements in the company would be a crass understatement.

The "Empire" of finance, accounting, law and order, "the way a sound company is run" . . . all these sensitivities were assaulted on a daily basis. It had to stop. The Empire struck back! Mitchell was retired with full honors in 1977 and replaced by Irv Rybicki, a fine, upstanding, seasoned design executive of modest demeanor who spoke reassuringly of fiscal responsibility, teamwork, "design is just one link in the chain," and other homilies that went down like warm olive oil with the ascendant "professional managers."

No longer would the uneducated public think that the vice president of design was the CEO. No longer would GM produce flamboyant, impractical designs with crazy fins, menacing chrome grilles, and interiors out of a Buck Rogers movie. No more grinning, expensively tailored chief designers on the covers of magazines. No more "secret" or "no unauthorized entry" studios. Design was to be put in its place; the era of the prima donnas was over.

"These guys are just artists, for crissakes," GM execs declared. "They're no more important than the guys who design shampoo bottles at Procter & Gamble." Design was to become "part of the system." Design would no longer originate a product, the way it did with the original Buick Riviera, which was dreamed up by the designers as a premium Cadillac coupe. (Cadillac didn't want it, so it was shopped around until Buick wisely took it.)

From now on, products would be initiated by Product Planning (a department composed of recycled finance types); they would ferret out market segments and define exterior dimensions and interior roominess to the millimeter. Engineering suddenly had a lot more say in what went where, and Manufacturing weighed in massively on questions of ease of assembly and number of stamping dies per panel. Instead of being originators, as in the old days, the designers simply were told: "Here, we've decided what this car is going to be. How long the hood is. Where the windshield touches down. We've defined all the roominess criteria. By the way, for investment reasons, we're going to share doors across divisions. We've done all the hard work, so all we need from you is to wrap the whole thing, OK?"

As a result, the system created research-driven, focus-group-guided, customer-optimized transportation devices, hamstrung in countless ways, using a chassis too narrow here, wheels too small (but affordable!) there, and all sharing too much with the other brands. At the end of the "creative" process, the designers were now reduced to the equivalent of choosing the font for the list of ingredients on a tube of Crest. Yes, order, discipline, predictability, ease of manufacture, affordable investment, low cost, and a whole host of other desirable characteristics had been achieved now that the hegemony of Design prima donnas had been vanquished. But it came at a terrible price: gone were the style and flair that sparked such instant infatuation (dare we say lust?) in drivers, something that had been the hallmark of the design-driven era. Waste, arrogance, and hubris are never desirable characteristics, but the company rid itself of these at a terrible price. The ebullient, dynamic, seductive volcano of creation had been transformed into a quiet mountain with a gently smoking hole at the top, spewing forth mediocrity upon mediocrity. This shift to the predictable, so seductive to the bean counters, destroyed the company's ability to compete and conquer.

But not all wounds were self-inflicted.

After the first fuel crisis in 1973, the federal government wisely decided that America needed to conserve petroleum, the supply of which was firmly in the hands of OPEC (Organization of Petroleum Exporting Countries). Unwisely, the government, ever loath to withdraw a free lunch from the voting population, elected not to trust the market mechanism, which would have dictated a gradual, annual increase in federal fuel taxes. Instead, the burden was placed on the automotive industry, with draconian Corporate Average Fuel Economy (CAFE) targets that set a corporate sales-fleet average of 18 miles per gallon beginning with the 1978 model year, and established a schedule for attaining a fleet average of 27.5 miles per gallon by 1985.

These new fuel rules dealt a terrible blow to only the American companies; the Japanese, with their then-exclusively small-car portfolios, were already comfortably compliant with the new rules. In fact, they were left with enough leeway to start moving up in size and performance while GM, Ford, and Chrysler were forced to go down in size and performance over their entire product lines. A programmed, gradual rise in fuel taxation, along the European model, would have caused consumers to think of the future consequences of today's purchase and would have provided a natural incentive to move down a notch, opting for six cylinders instead of eight, midsize sedans instead of large. But this would have required bipartisan cooperation and political courage, both historically absent in Congress.

And so the Big Three had to spend massively and quickly to downsize and lighten the entire fleet. Chrysler and GM abandoned all rear-wheel-drive vehicles, while Ford managed to save one, offsetting the negative effect of massive forced production of highly unprofitable small cars. GM, in a colossal multibillion-dollar effort, transformed every one of its passenger cars from "framed" construction to weight-saving unitized, from rear-wheel drive to front-wheel drive, and from V8s to V6s and four cylinders (which meant changing all of the transmissions and drive systems that went with them). It overwhelmed the engineering and design resources of even the world's most powerful automobile company, not to mention the many suppliers of all-new manufacturing equipment and car components.

The size of the effort was staggering. Chrysler nearly went under and was saved only by Lee Iacocca and his successful effort to obtain federal loan guarantees. Ford struggled and struggled. GM plowed on and launched all-new vehicles in every size it offered. From the smallest Chevrolet to the largest (but now smaller) Cadillac, every part in every car was new! When that much change occurs in such a short time, the probability of error grows exponentially, and these hastily conceived cars were rife with problems, destroying, in two to three years, a reputation for industry-leading quality that had been built over decades.

My friend and former colleague Jack Hazen retired several years ago as my finance chief in Product Development. Jack lived through this CAFE era and, as it marked the turning point in GM's fortunes, it remained vividly burned in his memory. (Jack, it should be noted, was unusual among corporate finance types in that he possessed a keen sense for the product.) Here is his account:

> Prior to Pete Estes retiring, there were numerous "Product Deep Dives" with the chief engineers, general managers, tech staff, and a finance rep (I attended these meetings for Cadillac) from each division. The main goal was to establish the Product Program that would cover the 1982 to 1985 time period and allow us to meet the CAFE standards—which, for GM, required the biggest improvement due to our mix of large, luxury cars. The major discussion point was whether to convert all the large, large-luxury, and personal-luxury cars to transverse front-wheel drive (TFWD) or do RWD luxury versions of the current midsize RWD cars. Despite the fact that the engineering community at the divisions expressed considerable concern about their ability to do the conversion to transverse front-wheel drive by 1985 for all these cars, Pete Estes said we needed to do it to meet the CAFE standards. Additionally, since GM was in much better shape financially than Ford or Chrysler, who could not afford to do this, this dramatic move would end up really putting GM in an even stronger leadership position in North America. At the time, as I recall, we had about 44 percent market share in the U.S. Before he passed away, Pete had stated in an interview that the decision to convert everything to transverse front-wheel drive was a mistake.
>
> This, of course, ended up being one of the worst decisions

from a product leadership standpoint due to a couple of major factors:

- The infamous four-speed transverse front-wheel drive automatic transmission (THM440) to be used in these cars was only on paper at the time (1979) and would eventually go into production without proper validation and fail at very high rates, often two or three times during the first customer life with the car. This was the biggest problem, but there were some other product issues, too, as these cars were all new, and GM had little experience with the transverse front-wheel-drive layout. Relative to the QRD (quality, reliability, durability) problems GM had with all the new automatic transmissions in the 1980s, starting with the X-car, I asked Alex Mair (Group VP, GM Technical Staffs) later in the 1980s as to how GM could have gone from a company that was the automotive leader in automatic transmissions to having all these problems starting with the new automatics in the late '70s and early '80s. He said the biggest factor was that we had allowed a lot of the old automatic transmission engineers (with tribal knowledge) to retire in the mid-1970s when the first oil embargo happened.

  In this timeframe (1979), when this decision was made, the new transverse front-wheel-drive compact X-cars were just being introduced, and we were unaware of all the QRD issues that we would discover on this first iteration of transverse front-wheel drive (e.g., steering gear "morning sickness"—a quasilockup of the steering on cold mornings, air conditioning compressor issues, radiator failures, and on and on).

  The other major issue was the design of these vehicles, as they were so much smaller than the previous large/luxury cars that there was some consumer push back and, in the case of Cadillac, we lost a lot of customers to Lincoln. However, they actually sold quite well until the quality issues started to surface, and then customers fled in droves to the Lincoln Town Car. From a styling standpoint, the significant mistake was reducing the overall length of the DeVille/Fleetwood to 195 inches. Design had done a clay model that was about 200 inches long. It looked great! Engineering said we couldn't get the fuel economy/performance with this larger size, and so they literally chopped four inches off the rear of the car. We, of course, later added that back on in 1988–89. The large luxury cars were initially targeted for V6 engines no bigger than 3.1 liters.

At this time in the design, Pete Estes had retired and, as I recall, Irv Rybicki did not fight this decision or direction from the engineering community. Wayne Kady, who was the chief exterior designer for Cadillac, thought it was a terrible decision. I think if Pete Estes and/or Bill Mitchell had been there, things might have turned out different because the proportions did not look right. In all fairness, at the time, the feeling was that we should err on the side that "smaller" is better. Additionally, we were somewhat a victim of that first downsizing of our cars in the late '70s. While the Sales and Marketing guys were all concerned about the downsizing at the time, it was somewhat a nonevent, and GM gained share in the late '70s.

• The other major disaster was on the new TFWD personal luxury cars (i.e., Eldorado, Seville, Toronado, and Riviera). The various (LFWD) that we produced from 1979 to 1985 basically required two shifts and maximum overtime for the six years they were produced. We printed money with these cars, and the divisions fought about allocations of production volume for six years! With the new downsized TFWD versions, we could hardly keep one shift going. Again, a major drop in market share and profits.

Everyone had concerns that we had gone too far in downsizing these cars, and even though the divisions raised concerns, Jim McDonald said we were going forward. He did allow the program to be delayed one year in order to fit the Cadillac V8 in the Eldorado/Seville, which required widening all of them by three inches. Of course, as you know, we ended up redoing those three years after they came out to make them bigger and more stylish/better proportions, but it was almost too late.

One interesting point about this program: Design had actually proposed the Eldorado and Seville could share more panels. We had money for all specific panels, but Design felt that we could share deck lids, hoods, and front fenders on the two cars. I can't recall how much of this was driven by Irv, but given the challenges to come up with a dramatic design for the Seville, I can't imagine Mitchell supporting this. Irv was definitely more finance-oriented than the previous design leaders, but whether this in the end was the best overall business approach could be debated.

Look-alike cars haunted us during the 1980s and caused a question about GM's product design leadership that, I am sure, hurt us somewhat in market share but not anywhere near the magnitude that the quality issues did—mainly because our interiors were still pretty good compared to the competition at that time.

America's car buyers, blessed with better fuel economy, were disappointed with smaller cars and smaller engines, and even more disappointed by the constant trips to the dealerships to fix everything that went wrong. But what of Japanese and German competition? Surely they suffered too? Not at all—for decades, they had produced vehicles for the world markets, most or all with fuel prices at multiples of that in the United States, so their cars were already small, light, mostly front-wheel drive and four-cylinder. The antithesis of what the uniquely blessed American public wanted. What a gigantic gift to the imports: Detroit's own federal government was forcing the Big Three to be more like the imports, and fast! The Japanese and German companies, to comply with CAFE legislation, had to do exactly . . . nothing! No reengineering! No retooling! Just sanctimonious press releases (eagerly snapped up by a liberal anti–U.S. corporation media) emphasizing that superior Japanese wisdom and innate frugality plus marvelous technology and dedicated consumer focus had *already* achieved the CAFE mandates!

This marked America's introduction to the (alleged) superiority of Japanese quality. Millions of American buyers experienced trouble-free motoring for the first time in their Hondaoyotasuns. And many decided, then and there, that neither they, nor their children, nor the issue of their children, would ever buy an American car again.

So, here we have an exogenous event—the oil crisis— triggering politically expedient federal action (CAFE, "Make those rich corporations do it," applauded by an anti–U.S. business press), resulting in a buying public experiencing unaccustomed reliability and fuel economy (a lesser priority, but nice when you get it) in imports. And thus the myth of "Detroit dumb, imports smart" was born.

The ridiculous part about CAFE, other than causing devastating harm to the domestic manufacturers, is that, aside from populist politics, it did no good. First, if you reduce the cost of a commodity (improved miles per gallon means less cost per mile driven), people will tend to consume more of it. In general, America's car buyers buy the amount of fuel dollars they can afford per month. Double the mileage, and they won't pocket the difference or save the gas for Mother Nature's sake. Now, it's "Honey, I think we can afford the fuel consumption of that SUV we've always wanted!" Affordability drives more use, a basic law of economics. Mandating higher mileage at constant fuel prices simply encourages more miles driven and larger vehicles. This is a major factor in mainstream America's "escape" into trucks where, thanks to lower fuel economy standards, V8 performance and U.S.-style roominess were still available.

Meanwhile the Japanese, of course, were exploiting their "teacher's pet" position of CAFE compliance, constantly reminding an all-ears media how "socially responsible" they were while scheming to exploit their overachievement of CAFE mandates to move upmarket into the lucrative segments Detroit was being forced to abandon.

So, failure to address the *real* issue, fuel cost, created a chaotic situation which, in the end, cost the American manufacturing industry dearly. Sadly, it wasn't the only nail in the coffin.

At some point in the 1970s, when the geopolitical battle between the Western democracies and communism was raging, the U.S. State Department decided that special measures were called for to keep Japan in the U.S. orbit, to serve as a bulwark against China's expansionism in the Pacific. A healthy, prosperous Japan, interlinked economically with the United States, was the best guarantee for reliable, pro-Western stability in the area. Presumably at Japanese urging, it was determined that the best way to achieve this goal was for the United States to tacitly permit Japan to manipulate the yen to a le vel below that justified by the country's costs, wages, balance of payments, and general economic might. Administrations of both parties, while occasionally joining the chorus of protest against "blatant currency manipulation" by the Japanese, did precisely nothing to stop it.

Subsequently, under the most airtight protectionist umbrella ever witnessed in the era of alleged "free trade," the Japanese industrial machine cranked up and soon became a powerful force in cars, consumer electronics, watches, cameras—in short, just about anything that could be manufactured and exported.

The cost advantage handed to the Japanese carmakers by the artificially low yen was in the thousands of dollars per unit, estimated at as much as four thousand dollars. Add to that the much higher U.S. labor cost and health care obligation, not to mention the depreciation and amortization burden brought on by the massive retooling of the entire U.S. car industry, and it becomes abundantly clear why U.S. producers found it increasingly impossible to compete. When a major competitor has a systemic cost advantage of that magnitude, he can use it in various ways:

- Increase marketing spending

- Underprice his competitor

- Add more features, quality, and luxury to his product

- Increase profitability, enabling a faster product renewal cycle.

The Japanese did it all! Complaints from Detroit about the distortion of the dollar/yen relationship fell on deaf ears. Lee Iacocca, then CEO of Chrysler, tirelessly warned the media, the public, and Washington that serious damage was being done to U.S. industry. We had already lost the entire home electronics industry, as well as cameras, optical instruments, and much, much more. But politicians didn't want to listen, and administration officials professed it all to be for the common good, because Japanese cars were excellent and represented exceptional value. Why tamper with that? "You boys are crybabies. You've got to stop complaining and learn to compete! It's not the weak yen! You boys

gotta learn how to make better cars!" was the response Lee Iacocca and I received from one distinguished senator. Just *how* you
beat a competitor at making cars when he has a four-thousand-
dollar-per-unit cost advantage was not something the worthy man
cared to address.

Still, a partial "victory" was achieved in 1981 when U.S. and
Japanese trade negotiators reached a "voluntary restraint agreement" limiting import sales at least until the floundering U.S.
auto industry could get its retooled, more competitive, more fuel-
efficient models to market. The period of voluntary restraints
came during the sharp recession of the early and mid-1980s, when
prices were lowered due to depressed demand and steep incentives. Enter the recovery, the tide that floats all boats. Newly confident buyers snapped up vehicles with more equipment, more
options, and bigger engines. They bought more trucks and SUVs.
And all with no incentives.

Then someone at a Japanese car company did a study, using
U.S. Department of Labor statistics showing average U.S. car
transaction prices (the price at which the vehicle is sold) *before*
"Voluntary Restraints" (the deep recession) and *during* "Voluntary
Restraints" (the dynamic resurgence of demand).

The upshot: "Look at how the U.S. car companies unconscio-
nably raised prices during Voluntary Restraints! They were supposed to use this respite to gain competitiveness! Instead, they
gouged the American public by raising prices thousands of dollars!" No mention of the differing economic environments, no
mention of the rapid shift to trucks! The gullible (and pro-
import) media lapped it up, and broadcast after broadcast, editorial upon editorial pontificated on the obscene behavior of
Detroit's villainous Big Three. The propaganda, documented as it
was by the U.S. government's own statistics, became the accepted
truth: "Instead of becoming competitive, Detroit used the 'Voluntary Restraint' period to gouge the public." It's incorrect, but

that's the way history is written. It reveals key aspects of the rise of the Japanese: their incredible lobbying power in Washington (stronger even than our own, believe it or not), their "teacher's pet" stature with the fawning U.S. media, and their astuteness in regularly reinforcing the image of the Big Three as fossilized remnants of a failed industrial culture.

Needless to say, that propaganda assault precluded any further sympathy in Washington or elsewhere, and many elected officials went on the public record stating that the disappearance of the Big Three would not necessarily be a bad thing for America, as we would "still have an automobile industry" in the form of Japanese assembly plants (using high percentages of imported materials) in the southern United States. (As of this writing, the yen is finally strong, and the Japanese producers are all professing to being severely damaged. Let's see how well they play without the exchange rate advantage!)

And then there was health care. Long a cherished benefit of the United Automobile Workers, the quality of coverage went up with each three-year contract. Once again, the reader may well say, "Well, it affects every car company." Logical, but wrong. Japanese (and European) manufacturers have no, or minimal, employee health care costs because most car-producing nations have some form of universally available health care funded by general taxes on all businesses and individuals. While one may well, on ideological grounds, flail against "socialized medicine" and enumerate all its horrors of poorer care, old equipment, waiting times for operations, etc., it does have one undeniable advantage: the cost burden does not, in other countries, fall squarely on the shoulders of the manufacturing sector. It's evenly spread over all of society. Free from this cost, vehicles produced elsewhere enjoy yet another advantage.

The health care burden took a turn for the worse in 1990 when Bob Stempel, new chairman and CEO of GM, faced a strike threat from the UAW. Stempel, a brilliant technologist and genuinely all-around nice person, was new in his job, which is perhaps why GM was selected as the so-called "target" in that year's triannual contract round. This is the year when GM, and with it the entire U.S. auto industry (Ford and Chrysler were obliged to follow the pattern set by the UAW's "target company"), lost the family farm regarding health care. After negotiations lasting just forty-two hours, Stempel's GM acquiesced to just about every major union demand, including expansion of health care benefits (first dollar coverage, no co-pay) not only for active members, but for retirees as well. The results were to be catastrophic, especially for GM, with its enormous pool of current and future retirees.

Upon my return to GM in 2001, I repeatedly asked those who were present in 1990 just what the hell they were thinking at the time. The consistent reply, as near to the truth as I can get, is that a strike would have been more devastating to the company at the time and that most of the non–health care demands could be absorbed through productivity or future growth, or passed on to the consumer in price. In the case of health care, the most economically damaging concession of all, it turns out that, as so often in the past, GM's vast, IQ-packed corporate soothsaying departments, whose "scientific forecasting" techniques are about on par with astrology, had radically and fatally miscalculated. According to them, health care costs had peaked, and would rise less than inflation. Besides, they argued, GM's gains in volume and efficiency, hence profitability, would easily offset the cost of retiree health care. In fact, the opposite set in. Health care inflation was at between 10 percent and 13 percent all through the early and mid-1990s. GM was in a contractive phase from 1989 to 1991 as the country rode out yet another downturn. The ranks of active workers shrank much more rapidly than assumed, and the number of retirees expanded.

This contract round also saw the inception of the infamous "Jobs Bank," a system whereby workers could be laid off for reasons of productivity or economic duress, but had to be retained at close to full pay in a "labor pool." The UAW's ploy here was obvious: since the unneeded workers were being paid anyway, the temptation for the Big Three would be strong to place more manufacturing capacity in the United States as opposed to Mexico or Canada. "Why not? We're paying for the labor whether we use it or not!" Once again, GM's projections showed that granting the "Jobs Bank" was "sleeves out of our vest," since the company's ambitious growth plans showed all labor being utilized. Exactly the opposite happened, and the Jobs Bank, albeit to a lesser extent than health care, became yet another major boulder placed on the backs of America's Big Three as they continued their footrace against Japan's burden-free car companies. (The Jobs Bank was finally, mercifully, laid to rest in 2009.)

I am frequently asked if the UAW was a major factor in GM's misery in the 1980s and '90s. It's a tough call. I have always found the UAW to be led by honest, competent, and well-intentioned people. Skeptics of the UAW blame it for job-padding, hostile worker attitude, and a variety of other negatives, leading to dingy and dangerous plants. But over this period GM's plants became exemplary, and workforce relations could be described as good to excellent, especially in the late 1990s. After the historic contract of 1990, it became obvious that GM's belief in "reliable" analytical forecasts of vastly increased market share had led to excess plant capacity and overhiring to the tune of 40,000 UAW workers, many who were former Ford workers considered "surplus" when that company, strapped for cash, wisely reduced capacity and eliminated labor. (Ford had little choice: they didn't have GM's vast resources. And because they almost never had to dispose of any workers again, they became the darlings of the UAW.)

GM, on the other hand, had dealt itself a serious problem. In the first few years after the UAW contract of 1990, GM suffered no fewer than eighteen strikes, costing the company billions. Such was the price of confrontation.

It wasn't that the UAW leadership was recalcitrant or unco-operative; they had access to the same numbers as GM's leadership. They knew that the competitive pressures on GM and the "other Two" were mounting. They understood that GM's bet on increasing volumes had failed and that the sales practices employed to "move the iron" were further damaging GM's brands. The problem wasn't the leadership; it was the rank and file. Less well-informed, most of the members formed a sort of "working-class aristocracy," with average pay (including overtime) of over $100,000 per year. These were conservative, hardworking Americans with many years of service. They believed profoundly in the invincibility of the United States and its institutions. Sure, they'd heard "poor month" before, but they always got a better contract, better health care, a nice pension adjustment. And though the car companies always said these things would threaten their survival, the companies survived. The UAW rank and file, in their collective patriotism, would simply not acknowledge that a fifty-year stretch of onward, upward, more and better had run its course.

The UAW leadership knew the truth, but their freedom to act was severely constrained because they were elected by the membership. Stray too far from the majority sentiment and the UAW leader would find himself in an untenable position. Add to this the influence of lower-ranking demagogues who fought for greater standing in the union by branding the leadership as "soft" and "selling out to the company," failing to protect the union's hard-earned gains. In hindsight, it really did take Chapter 11 bankruptcy to convince the rank and file that GM, the unshakeable, invulnerable symbol of America's industrial dominance, had been milked to the point of collapse.

After the costly strikes in the post-1990 years, GM reluctantly

concluded that a policy of toughness, of confrontation, of cram-
ming a one-sided agenda down the throat of the UAW was not
going to work. It was a war of attrition with only one possible
conclusion—without production, GM would fail before the
UAW ran out of money.

A "fresh start' was called for, and GM delivered its architect in
the form of Gary Cowger, then managing director of Opel in
Germany. Gary was a longtime manufacturing executive and the
son of a union worker. Very intelligent, but also down-to-earth
and practical. He understood and respected the concerns, if not
the sense of entitlement, of the UAW's rank and file. As vice president for labor relations, Gary was soon to gain the trust of both
sides. Gary was a realist. His motto was "Face it. We can't break the
UAW. They're not going away. Let's all recognize that fact and
turn our attention to making the most of it." The resulting relationship was exemplary. Whether it was in terms of training, quality, or productivity, GM's plants became commendable, even
drawing favorable comments from visitors like Honda. On the
factory floor, the UAW and its membership became part of the
solution rather than part of the problem.

Some "Monday morning quarterbacks" will say that this was
all wrong—appeasement in lieu of all-out warfare and nuclear
solutions. It's easy in retrospect to say "woulda, coulda, shoulda,"
and it's an attractive fiction to say the U.S. industry failed "to
take on" the UAW. But why, in the face of a battle you know
you are going to lose because the adversary can outlast you, would
a management embark on such a short-term, self-destructive
course? Better, then, to play along, keep the peace, and meanwhile
figure out how to reduce manufacturing costs as a whole, offer
more buyouts, and work more advantageous additions into new
contracts. Ultimately, this long-term strategy was overwhelmed
by the financial meltdown of 2008: more than $100 billion in
"legacy costs" (primarily health care) over the previous years had

simply left GM with insufficient cushion to weather a sharp downturn.

It's a tragedy with no heroes, but also no villains. The UAW leadership probably moved as fast as they politically could. GM management used this close and trusting relationship to educate, to let people know what we needed and why. But the momentum of the rank and file, their steadfast belief that "more" was a historic right, their conviction that "no way is GM ever going to go broke," meant that the bleeding couldn't be stopped.

Health care costs grew and grew, accelerated, as always, by America's unique "contingent fee" legal system, whereby the penniless victim can see justice done by hiring a lawyer who is willing to help "for free" in exchange for a percentage of a possible settlement. Noble intent, but that's not how it turned out. In a classic example of the law of unintended consequences at work, "medical malpractice" (along with "personal injury" in general) became an ever more powerful branch of the legal profession, with active solicitation—in fact, aggressive searches—for possible new "victims" who could be lucratively "assisted." Trial lawyers like to point out that all this is untrue, that only a small portion of America's health care bill is accounted for by settlements, but, while technically true, that misses the point. A vast multiple of the actual settlement cost is devoted to the constant defense of suits, the defensive posture the medical profession has had to adopt, the outrageously high insurance premiums even a small family practitioner is forced to pay, the needless duplicative diagnostic testing used to confirm and reconfirm the initial diagnoses, the presence of third-party witnesses in examining rooms to testify to the doctor's innocence in later allegations of misconduct. These wasteful procedures and their attendant costs are all due to our (unique to America) "contingent fee" legal system, which results in our health care being the most expensive in the world while at the same time not necessarily the best.

Then there's the American media! With relatively rare exceptions, these men and women are well left of center, with over 70
percent of the profession cheerfully declaring themselves "liberal"
in surveys. Products of a higher education system that is itself riddled with professors who are anything but conservative, most journalism majors receive a massive dose of anti–free market, anti–big
business programming in college. I recall my own days at an esteemed institute of higher learning; even in business school, most
professors believed and taught that there must be "a better way"
than free-market capitalism. (Many people on the left, otherwise
perfectly smart, sincerely believe that the only reason socialism
failed miserably everywhere it's been tried is that the wrong people
were in charge.)

A compounding factor is that, unlike in Europe, where an
"economics correspondent" typically has a degree in economics,
the journalism student in the United States merely learns "journalism": how to write, how to interview, how to develop sources,
journalistic ethics . . . all good and legitimate skills when superimposed on some specific background in the area being covered. But
that's never the case here. And so we have people reasonably adept
at writing and interviewing not only reporting but actually opin-
ing and pontificating on corporate or financial matters of which
they have only the most superficial understanding. What can one
expect when reporters start on the society beat, move up to restaurant reviews, and follow that by a stint in crime reporting before
suddenly being assigned to business reporting? How can sensible,
accurate writing about such complex subjects possibly result?

Add to all of this the intense competitive pressure for scoops!
With speed of the essence, quality and accuracy are relegated to
the back of the bus. I have many good friends in the journalistic
community. "Listen, Bob, the *Wall Street Journal* just published this
negative piece on GM," one would typically call to say. "I know
it's wrong, but my editor is pushing the hell out of me and won-

dering where *my* negative piece is. I have to write something, and it'll be a rehash of the *Journal* piece. Just wanted to let you know I've got no choice." This is journalism? This is an institution we are supposed to revere and respect?

Nowhere has my faith in media integrity been destroyed more thoroughly than in the so-called "global warming" discussion. Resolutely parroting the now-discredited prophecies of Al Gore and his absurd movie, *An Inconvenient Truth*, hardly any of the so-called mainstream media ever gave fair coverage to the large and growing army of CO_2-caused AGW (anthropogenic, or human-caused, global warming) skeptics. Every network (Fox excepted) and every major newspaper gives endless coverage to disappearing glaciers (they've been melting for almost four hundred years), polar bears on ice floes (hello—they can swim! And far from being "endangered," the population is up sharply), rapidly rising ocean levels (they aren't), and higher ocean temperatures (they're actually lower).

It's all harmless, one could say, and how does this impact the automobile business anyway?

Once again, as happened so often in the past century, personal transportation, especially the automobile, has been singled out as the number one menace to the continuation of life on our planet. "Cars, Trucks Create 20 Percent of CO_2," the headlines continually blared. It's simply not true. Even Timothy Wirth, the global warming guru under Clinton and Gore, was once forced to admit, under my somewhat insubordinate questioning, that vehicles contribute far less than that amount to carbon dioxide levels.

The math works like this: according to accepted computer simulations, the Earth's natural "carbon sinks" can absorb only 98 percent of the CO_2 created in a given period. Two percent is "excess" CO_2 and allegedly the cause of global warming. Cars and trucks emit 0.4 percent of total global CO_2, and this is the source of the infamous "20 percent" lie. Mathematically, 0.4 percent is, of course, 20 percent of 2 percent, so if the reporting had been about 20 percent of *excess* global CO_2, I would not have objected. I spoke to journalists about this many times and all understood (having done their own research at my urging) that you could pour concrete down the engine bores of every car and truck on the planet and the reduction in CO_2 would be a rounding error. But all claimed that "editorial policy" was that AGW was real and that cars and trucks were the major cause. It was useless, they said, to fight it.

Meanwhile, things are getting increasingly tough for the "catastrophic global warming" gang, with renowned climatologists jumping off this limping, flat-tired bandwagon by the hundreds. The current state of the "movement" (religion, actually) is succinctly summarized by author Art Horn in his May 17, 2010, contribution to the *Washington Times* entitled "Wounded Warmists Attack: It's What Happens When Prophecy Fails":

> The global warming "science" community is feeling threatened by evidence and revealing emails—their funding, and therefore their careers, may be in peril. In reaction to this, they will mount an even more alarmist campaign to convince the world—and themselves—that humans cause global warming and that it must be stopped. As global temperature fails to rise in the future, we will be bombarded by increasingly shrill cries of global warming catastrophe. All will be considered proof of global warming. A more than willing media desperate for spectacular headlines will give them the front page.
>
> A creature or group that is damaged psychically will respond like a wounded animal. The ensuing attack will be more aggressive and prolonged—an attempt to convince their "enemies" that they are correct. . . .

Therein lies the problem for the American automobile industry, as well as for the rest of the country's manufacturing, commerce, and transportation industries.

I suppose I naïvely grew up believing that the media existed to provide new facts and information and, in the case of controversial subjects, to confine the publication's own opinions and bias to the editorial page. Not so with AGW, where 90 percent of the nation's media remain hell-bent on driving the societal change to "save our planet" from CO_2.

I find it interesting that, of all types of motor vehicles, sport-utility vehicles, or SUVs, were singled out as the epitome of automotive evil. Not 500-hp mid-engine sports cars costing $200,000 or more. Not large European twelve-cylinder sedans, which guzzled more than any SUV. No, the nexus of negativism centered on the workhorse of the American middle-class suburban family. The vehicle used to tow horse trailers, boats, snowmobiles; the vehicle that can carry five to eight adults in comfort over long distances and difficult terrain. I find it telling that vilification of the SUV often includes references to it being the vehicle of choice for the "well-dressed blonde suburban wife and her golden retriever." Can it be that the evil that must be banished resided not so much in the vehicle as in the affluent suburban lifestyle it represented?

This drumbeat forecasting imminent CO_2-caused global doom (despite almost twenty years of such predictions without a single one realized), coupled with the media-driven demonization of the SUV, again did disproportionate harm to U.S. producers who, between the three, commanded more than 90 percent of SUV sales. (Mind you, the Japanese and Germans, far from demonstrating the noble, even saintly motives generally ascribed to them by the media, were actively, but largely unsuccessfully, attempting to gain more access to this lucrative segment.) With the media-driven decline of the SUV, America's carmakers saw their profitability severely impaired, especially GM, which in the years between 2002 and 2010 accounted for half of all large SUV sales.

The body blow to the U.S. companies may or may not have been intentional. Many media practitioners carry an inherent bias against the domestic producers. They helped create the myth of Japanese infallibility and perpetuated it long past the time there was any semblance of truth to it. Given equal successes, it was "ho-hum" for the domestic company but enormous fanfare for the Japanese. For failures, the opposite applied. Massive early Toyota recalls (prior to the recent ones from 2009 on) were largely relegated to the back pages, but any recalls by one of the Detroit Three received front-and-center attention because they demonstrated once again the manifest ineptitude of America's car producers. During one major Toyota recall a few years ago, Micheline Maynard, journalist, Toyota fan, and author of 2003's *The End of Detroit: How the Big Three Lost Their Grip on the American Car Market*, breathlessly reported that the recall was *voluntary*. Hello! All recalls are voluntary. When NHTSA "suggests" a recall, you do it—voluntarily! Maynard added that correcting the problem had the huge advantage of putting Toyota in even closer touch with its customers.

Thomas Friedman, author, columnist, and noted person of the left, once suggested, in a scathing editorial, that the salvation of General Motors could be effected only if Toyota took over GM. What acute embarrassment both of these esteemed journalists must have felt when their shining idol, Toyota, the epitome of automotive, managerial, and technological excellence, suddenly developed major cracks in the marble pedestal, and the whole monument, lustrous from the constant polishing from countless glowing media testimonials, began to wobble and—HORRORS!—became *fallible*, just like any other automobile company.

Reeling from a tidal wave of unintended-acceleration reports, as well as Prius brake problems, one Toyota-worshipping journalist was forced to conclude that the company's image had "lost some luster" due to having been "beset by a series of recent misfortunes." Let me assure you: when one of America's Big Three has a quality problem requiring a major recall, the media do *not* describe it as beset by misfortune.

By no means am I suggesting that the media's reverse chauvinism (loving "foreign" more than "domestic") was the leading cause of GM's decline, but together with worker wages and benefits at unaffordable levels, crippling health care costs, and government regulation that caused seismic upheaval in manufacturing and engineering, it created an environment with no margin for error, where only the most astute leadership could prevail. As we have seen, and as the following will abundantly demonstrate, GM's leaders were not up to this admittedly monumental task.

A Failed "Culture of Excellence"

IN THE EARLY 1990S, A WELL-KNOWN AUTOMOTIVE ANALYST TOLD ME THE following: "I just can't understand it: When I talk to senior American car company executives and CEOs, I have the feeling that I am in the presence of superior intelligence. I get the feeling that these people are fully in command of their operation and deeply understand their business. Yet, they are losing. When I interview Japanese car company CEOs, I get the feeling, language problems aside, that they are not deeply knowledgeable, or highly intelligent, and yet they are winning! I don't get it." Well, I didn't "get it" at the time either, but I think I do now.

When the Japanese car companies began their push into the United States, they were young, vibrant, small, and extremely lean. Meanwhile, the Detroit Three were a good sixty to seventy years old. Their dealerships were third-generation owned, and often the facilities reflected that. Many manufacturing facilities had been world-class in the 1950s, with benchmark levels of efficiency, but had since been exceeded by the inevitable newer and better. The Japanese were not burdened by any legacy costs—pension, health care, or any of the other fixed obligations that burden a company that has existed for more than half a century. Effectively turbo-charged by a closed domestic market and a weak yen, it was easy for the Japanese to set up nonunion facilities in the southern states, using carefully handpicked workers, all young and all healthy. No pesky work rules, no pensions to worry about for at least thirty years, and very little in the way of health care costs, given the careful chronological selection process. They also got some lovely tax breaks for building new facilities.

Needless to say, even if they had been world-class in design and manufacturing (which they manifestly were not), the legacy-cost-burdened Detroit Three would have had a very hard time competing. Add to that the fact that the Japanese had a clean slate when it came to selecting dealers: get the best operators in the best locations, set up magnificent, modern facilities.

Faced with this environment, General Motors embarked on a series of initiatives to overcome both the perception and reality of the growing import threat. Some of these taxed the comprehension of rational minds at the time, such as the creation of Saturn, an all-new auto company, making a new kind of car with a new and more productive relationship with the UAW. Another was a mind-bogglingly bold move into China, with, of all brands, Buick. There was a series of alliances with various Japanese brands and—after GM was jilted in its quest for Jaguar—the purchase of the decidedly weird Swedish brand Saab. As we shall see, many of these initiatives were ill-advised and ultimately failed. Some were successful, but not enough.

As stated, the 1950s and '60s marked the decline of the "product guy" at GM and the ascendancy of "professional management," often individuals with a strong financial background. As one GM veteran said, "Some diversity is good, but the fact is, few engineering people progressed to operating jobs in the '80s and '90s." It's not that senior GM management disliked cars. It was more an atmosphere of "benign neglect," a generalized consensus that we were, after all, primarily in the business of making money, and cars were merely a transitory form of money: put a certain quantity in at the front end, transform it into vehicles, and sell them for more money at the other end. The company cared about "the other two ends"—minimizing cost and maximizing revenue—but assumed that customer desire for the product was a given. Responsibility for creation of the right product was delegated to lower levels in the organization, often to people with little understanding of quality design or great driving characteristics. I maintain that without a passionate focus on great products from the top of the company on down, the "low cost" part will be assured but the "high revenue" part won't happen, just as it didn't at GM for so many years.

Take the case of Cadillac: if never quite the "Standard of the World," it was without a doubt the standard of the United States, technologically advanced and featuring bold styling as part of a strong brand identity. Cadillac was synonymous with power and luxury, and the expression "It's the Cadillac of [name the product category]" found a justifiable place in the American lexicon.

In the early 1980s, a number of decisions were made that were inimical to the brand's heritage. A "product guy" (or gal) aware of what had gone before, with a genuine love for Cadillac cars and their owners, would never have pursued such a course. But, to the analytical bean counter, or volume-focused sales executive, such abstract concepts as "image," "heritage," and "tradition" were mere smoke screens propagated by the "artistic souls" who didn't respect spreadsheets, who didn't want to push for every possible sale.

One of the weirdest acts of mutually assured self-destruction occurred in the 1980s and 1990s: For some unfathomable reason, it was decided that Cadillac needed to greatly expand its sales volume and become the nation's number one luxury brand. This had always seemed oxymoronic to me: how can any product or service be simultaneously "aspirational and exclusive" while also "most popular in its class" and "near-ubiquitous"? "Best-selling Exclusive Brand" is a phrase akin to "World's Tallest Midget." It's a claim, but is it worthy of being made? At any rate, Ford's Lincoln brand and Cadillac became embroiled in a battle to near-death to remain "America's Number One Luxury Brand," using such weapons as massive deliveries to rental companies, which then ran screaming ads like "Lincoln Town Car: Only $24.95 per Day!" Overstuffing the rental companies, which don't keep cars long and sell them wholesale with low mileage, naturally resulted in a glut of Cadillacs and Lincolns in the used-car market. Prices, as will happen, dropped rapidly in response to excess supply, and the two luxury brands lost a key attribute: good resale value, or low depreciation. With so many low-priced "nearly new" Cadillacs and Lincolns on the market, it is small wonder that many working-class families started to buy them. With that trend came the loss of prestige, so that the more affluent, better-educated demographics began to shop elsewhere: Mercedes, BMW, Audi, Jaguar—brands that were more expensive, arguably of higher quality, and, most of all, in limited supply and therefore "exclusive."

The nadir came in the late 1990s when the much-followed (in the Detroit media) annual sales race between Cadillac and Lincoln for the dubious honor of "America's Number One Luxury Brand" ("World's Tallest Midget") ended with Cadillac the winner. The Lincoln folks, smelling a rat, did some digging and discovered that Cadillac had counted some sales that were never made. Cadillac had to apologize publicly and hand the crown to Lincoln, which, not knowing it was the kiss of death for a luxury brand, accepted it with joy.

Other things had a hand in destroying the once-great Cadillac brand—for instance, the misguided "4-6-8" engine that was to run on, depending on the situation, four, six, or all eight cylinders. This was to be a Cadillac exclusive, saving fuel when possible and delivering V8 power when required. Sadly, the electronics of the 1980s weren't up to the task. The engine, hastily introduced for God-knows-what marketing reason, never worked properly, became a constant source of inconvenience for owners, and achieved the dreaded status of late-night network comedy fodder.

Engines in general seemed to bring out the worst in Cadillac. One general manager insisted on Cadillac getting the V8 diesel destined for Oldsmobile. Diesels were in vogue; Mercedes had them on some models, and they were more fuel-efficient. Unfortunately, GM's diesel was converted from a gasoline engine, and countless car companies around the world had spent decades learning that the lightweight, low-pressure construction of a gasoline engine formed a rickety foundation for the much-higher compression loads of the diesel engine. Undeterred by the failures of others, GM converted a large gasoline V8 into a diesel engine, with exactly the results expected by the rest of the industry: GM's diesels failed expensively, often at very low mileages and requiring replacement with an equally flawed V8 diesel sibling. The resulting reputation disaster not only dealt another body blow to the "Standard of the World" (by now a laughably inappropriate designation for Cadillac) but actually soured the American public on the real fuel-economy benefits of diesel engines for two decades.

Should I mention the Cadillac Cimarron? It was, perhaps, the ultimate shaming of this once-proud brand. GM, eager to participate in the growing market for smaller luxury cars like the BMW 2002 and the later 3-Series, wanted a "small Cadillac." (This was in the late 1970s, when the American public, or at least the more educated portion thereof, ceased to blindly associate "bigger" with "better.") The idea was right, but the execution wasn't. Rather than design and engineer a vehicle of high style and appropriate import-matching chassis and engine technology, the company went "fast and dirty" on the assumption that the public wouldn't notice. A Chevrolet Cavalier was hastily "Cadillized" with a Cadillac grille and badges and an interior which, while plusher than its

Chevrolet donor, was still at least three grades too shabby to be taken seriously in a small luxury car. The Cimarron, too, flopped miserably and became the butt of late-night jokes, further degrading the tattered remnants of Cadillac's reputation.

Part of the problem with the Cimarron, as well as other Cadillacs of the era, was the front-wheel-drive layout used in all GM passenger cars except the Chevrolet Corvette, Pontiac Firebird, and Chevrolet Camaro. The key small-luxury-car competition, Germany's BMW and Mercedes brands, were rear-wheel drive, and that layout, for better or worse, was held to be superior in that category by the car magazines and the more knowledgeable buyers.

The man who locked GM into "all front-wheel drive" is the same one who launched the ill-fated Saturn brand and the push to automate virtually everything: Roger B. Smith, GM chairman and CEO from 1981 to 1990. We'll touch on those two well-intentioned catastrophes later, but first a little anecdote: While chairman of Ford of Europe, I ran into Smith in a hotel lobby during a major European auto show. After chatting amicably, he asked me if it was true that Ford of Europe's new midsize car, the Sierra, was going to be rear-wheel drive. I told him it was, and that we were very comfortable with the decision. It saved us hundreds of millions of dollars, and a positive reception was ensured because rear-wheel drive was already the layout of choice for the German prestige brands.

At this, Roger Smith's already florid face turned a radiant crimson. In a voice that can only be described as squeaky, he angrily pointed out my colossal mistake. I was, he said, just like the forces of tradition in GM, but he wasn't going to buy it. Everything GM was doing for the future was going to be front-wheel drive. Everything! No exceptions. Well, maybe the Corvette, but other than that, everything! He urged me to change the direction of the Ford Sierra to something more in conformance with his vision of automotive goodness, until I finally had to remind him that neither I nor Ford of Europe were subject to his orders. He gave up and ended the conversation with, "The whole world is going to front-wheel drive. Everybody! The whole industry! You'll be all alone, and the Sierra will be a flop!" Well, the whole world didn't, and the Sierra wasn't, achieving high volumes, market share, and profitability during its extraordinary ten-plus-year life. But Roger's behavior was disturbingly typical of the GM hubris: if we're doing it, we do it all the way. We know what's best, no matter what others are doing. I saw a lot more of that when I returned to GM in 2001.

This encounter was also a manifestation of another culture problem at GM: an exaggerated respect for higher authority, with the acceptance of everything uttered by the CEO and other senior leaders as infallible gospel. Again, this was still in evidence on my return in 2001; by that point, blind obedience to unwise corporate directions had done near-incalculable damage.

Roger Smith was also the initiator of the Saturn brand, essentially an autonomous automobile company within the GM fold. It was to be "different." This meant a uniquely tailored UAW agreement ensuring more worker participation and a strong union-management partnership. The retail organization was to be different, too. Selected from the best of GM's vast army of retail outlets, Saturn dealers were awarded large territories to inhibit internecine warfare, were specially trained, and had to agree to abide by the new brand's guiding principles, which mandated a high level of customer focus, no discounting, no haggling over price, no dishonest practices taking advantage of any customer. This was the best part of the whole Saturn project, and, despite some heroically mediocre cars, there were at one time vast legions of happy Saturn owners, many of whom (somewhat disturbingly) built their lifestyles around their cars. The annual "Saturn Homecoming" festival in Spring Hill, Tennessee, represented the high-light of many social calendars.

Less enlightened was the car itself. In an understandable drive to be "different" (even if not better), management decided that Saturn vehicles would be built with a so-called space frame construction. This involved a sort of welded-together armature of structural panels roughly in the shape of the car, onto which would be bonded composite panels. Thus, Saturns were essentially made of nonstructural plastic glued to a metal armature.

In theory, this solution promised freedom from rust, the absence of parking-lot dings and dents, and easier, cheaper style changes—just switch out the small plastic panels without touching the underlying armature. In practice, however, the plastic panels were finicky. They took longer to produce than conventional stamped steel, and grew and shrank when the temperature changed, requiring the cars to have wide, unappealing gaps around the doors, hood, and trunk for clearance. An effort was made to market the plastic panels, with ads depicting shopping carts bouncing harmlessly off of Saturn doors, but not enough customers placed "plastic" over "steel" in their preference ranking. The engine of the first Saturn was an oddity, too. All-aluminum, it was to be cast to "near net shape," with a revolutionary "lost-foam" process. The resulting engine was . . . OK! No better, arguably no worse than other GM engines. Just different.

And herein lay the big mistake in the creation of Saturn: in order to preserve its sanctity, it was given its own engineering, manufacturing, legal staff, and so on. This massive structure was to be supported by the sale of just one compact car: the Saturn S1 four-door sedan, which resembled a mini-Oldsmobile, was neither ugly nor beautiful, and offered average performance and fuel economy.

Initially, sales were brisk, but not everyone wants a compact, and it became clear that Saturn needed a broader product line with, perhaps, a midsize car and a small sport-utility vehicle. But management let Saturn wither on what had been a relatively promising vine; its pleas for the R&D budget to create more products were met with "Well, you guys wanted your own car company and your own budget, and you got it. If you don't have the money, earn it!" It's no secret that the other divisions—especially Oldsmobile, Pontiac, and Chevrolet—were resentful of Saturn and its early "favorite child" status. On a less emotional plane, there was the powerful feeling that the $5 billion the corporation had spent on Saturn would have enabled many badly needed new-product programs for GM's existing car divisions. But telling Saturn to "get profitable" with just one car was analogous to telling your ten-year-old son that you'll continue feeding him only if he gets a good job and starts paying rent.

Saturn finally did get a second car, a midsize unit wisely derived from the highly successful GM Europe Opel Vectra. Unfortunately, the Vectra was designed around conventional, all-steel construction. Saturn, for reasons of "brand character," insisted on a total reengineering to create another plastic-paneled "space frame" car. So, $900 million was spent (can you say wasted?) in converting the Opel Vectra from conventional construction to the Saturn brand model. Still, the Saturn L Series looked like the Opel Vectra, except for a truly unfortunate increase in front overhang (due to the severity of U.S. crash regulations), giving the car a "Snoopy-face" look.

Plastic panels couldn't help the fact that customers didn't like the car. It was a resounding flop. Rick Wagoner once told me that the decision to redo the Vectra as a plastic-paneled Saturn had been hugely controversial, but that in the end the company had no choice but to go along with Saturn. And that's where I say, "What? *Had* to go along? Says who?" This additional billion down the drain would never have happened if there had been a single senior person at the corporation with any sort of instinct for the product. Such a person, long-derided as "unnecessary to the scientific-management structure of GM," would have said, "Folks, the car is terminally ugly. It will not sell at a hundred thousand units a year. And there is no need for a 'conversion to plastic.' Save the money, duplicate the tooling of the Vectra, minimize investment, and accept lower volumes."

Saturn's need for a small sport-utility vehicle was finally answered with the Vue, a plastic-on-space-frame again, with the attendant ugly body gaps. The usual customer-visible thrifting had taken place as well: there was not a piece of brightwork on the vehicle. In fact, even the Saturn name was simply de-bossed into the plastic bumper to save the cost of a badge. One might well wonder about a brand that values its own symbol so little that it considers branding the name into plastic ample and appropriate identification. But there was more good stuff under the hood: not sharing GM's excellent and reliable automatic transmissions, the vehicle was blessed (cursed) with GM's very own continuously variable transmission (CVT). These are great in theory and do save fuel. But they must be adequately dimensioned for the size and weight of the vehicle. Due to chassis space limitations, the Vue's wasn't. The CVTs failed regularly and repeatedly, and the company had to sell only manual transmissions until a conventional automatic could be installed. Add to this the buzzy character of the engine, the cheap soundproofing, the spartan plastic interior, and it becomes testimony to the Saturn retailers that GM sold as many as we did.

Still, it was another blow to the credibility of America's Different Kind of Car Company. It turned out to be different, alright, but not in a good way. True, the years post-2005 finally saw a flood of outstanding products for Saturn: the Sky roadster, the Aura sedan (voted North American Car of the Year in 2007), the large Outlook crossover, the brand-new all-metal Vue—all of these vehicles were world-class in design, execution, and quality. But the reputation damage and the irrelevance of Saturn to most Americans (the brand, like all GM brands, was drastically under-advertised) conspired to bring about the end of the Saturn experiment in 2009. It had never made a profit and had consumed well in excess of $10 billion in capital. Plastic, clearly, had not helped.

At roughly the same time as the gestation of Saturn, GM adopted a policy of gaining the upper hand through manufacturing cost reduction, primarily by automating assembly and metal stamping processes wherever possible, almost regardless of the cost. The scheme was to overwhelm the U.S. (and Japanese) competition with unprecedented capital expenditures that financially constrained Ford and Chrysler couldn't match. The vision was for workerless plants, operating in the dark, three shifts daily, reproducing parts and subassemblies at ultralow labor cost and with high repeatability and, thus, quality.

It didn't turn out that way. The robotics were far from perfect, and most people recall the embarrassment of GM's paint-shop robots playfully painting each other. Most disappointing of all was the reality that, after all this, labor costs actually went up. Sure, the so-called direct labor (people actually making parts or assemblies on the line) went down, and that's what all the measurements focused on. But indirect labor—the highly skilled, specially trained repair and maintenance crews—expanded exponentially with the overautomation. The result was a huge rise in GM's manufacturing cost: the combination of paying for the displaced labor and more hours for the costly indirect labor, coupled with the depreciation and amortization of all that new equipment, made GM the high-cost producer, showing once again that having too much money can result in amazing folly.

Meanwhile, Ford and Chrysler, the poorer cousins, focused on the Japanese model: don't create new plants unless necessary, automate only where absolutely needed for quality or worker fatigue, seek the optimum blend of humans and machines. It worked, just as decades later it's working for GM as well as it ever worked for Toyota.

The misunderstood "drive for excellence" bore some really strange fruit. A favorite of mine came from a senior executive in the advertising agency that served Cadillac back in the 1950s and '60s. At the time, Jim Roche was head of the division. It was time to design the annual Cadillac Christmas card, and Mr. Roche instructed the agency to find something "heartland"—down-home American, an original work from a good artist. One painting found Mr. Roche's favor: a snowy scene with a small boy pulling a sled upon which was tied a Christmas tree. The lad's destination was a modest cabin on a hill, with a winding road leading up to it.

Mr. Roche loved it—but wait! Where was the relevance to Cadillac? Roche ordered the small boy-with-sled away, to be replaced by a Cadillac sedan, with the trussed tree tied to the roof. The artist was able to render the Cadillac accurately and duly pasted it over the boy-with-sled. The deadline for printing was approaching, and the modified card was again presented to Jim Roche. He discovered a new flaw: the humble cabin on top of the hill was no longer a suitable destination. Why would an achiever live in a dump like that? The agency was told to make the dwelling more appropriate for a Cadillac family, so the watercolor artist once again went to work and rendered a substantial residence which required a major expansion of the hill it sat on. After that cut-and-paste, all was expected to go well. There was one more modification to the house as a second garage was added. Mr. Roche felt that a single-car garage looked out of place next to a home of that size. Portions of the original painting were starting to get a bit thick, but it looked like smooth sailing from here on in. At the final Cadillac Annual Christmas Card Review, all were silent until Roche, staring at the now-crusty watercolor, asked in his usual soft mono-tone, "Are those tires approved by Engineering?" "How's that, Mr. Roche?" came the response. "The tire tracks in the snow. They're very pronounced. Is that an approved snow tire?" Mr. Roche was righteously indignant over this blatant lack of due diligence and ordered *one each* of the "approved" snow tires shipped to the artist in New England. He or she had the artistic freedom to decide *which* snow tire pattern would be immortalized in the Official Cadillac Christmas Card. After that modification, it was finally ap-proved, sent to the printer, and mailed out.

Can anyone begin to fathom what that card cost—the mate-rial and intellectual resources that were squandered in its tortured path to perfection? Does anyone really believe anyone checked the tire tread imprints in the snow? Was the card with the large house, the multicar garage, the expanded hill, and the Cadillac sedan more appropriate and artistically meritorious than the orig-inal boy-with-sled?

In a normal culture, that card would have been given to an executive of Roche's station, who would have looked it over, checked the text (easy in those days; "Merry Christmas" was still a politically correct wish), and said, "Sure, looks good, get 'em printed." But not in the "Culture of Excellence," where manage-ment had to improve on every detail, no matter how trivial.

The unfortunate thing is that Jim Roche so embodied the charisma-challenged, nitpicking, detail-focused perfectionist that he later became GM chairman and CEO.

I remember another telling event in the late 1960s, while I served at Opel. We had just completed the Dudenhofen Proving Ground, east of Frankfurt, the first modern, totally capable prov-ing ground in Europe. There was much fanfare and media activity, during which we emphasized the huge acreage and the "thirty miles of test roads." We soon received a telex from the Office of the Chairman: "Why were we claiming thirty miles of roads? The original capital appropriation request, over two years earlier, had listed twenty miles of paved roads. Mr. Roche wants the discrepancy explained." I drafted a quick reply for my boss, the CEO of Opel, explaining that there had already been about ten miles of forestry roads before we began construction, so, "best foot forward," we included them in the press release. My boss signed off, and I confidently believed we had heard the last of it.

Wrong. The next telex read, as I recall, "Mr. Roche seeks assurance that no roads not covered by the appropriation request were built. Please submit plans, maps, and aerial photographs, marking, in detail, paved roads covered in the appropriation, unpaved roads or features covered in the appropriation, and preexisting forestry roads not covered in the appropriation." I put it all together, airmailed it in, and never heard another word. Another example of the grindingly negative, detail-focused, customer-distant "culture of excellence" at work.

Meanwhile, on the product side (where it really mattered), Opel was handed one cost-cutting mandate after another. No "culture of excellence" here, as Opel's cars were systematically stripped of quality in the name of thrift. The tipping point came in the late 1960s, when Opel was ordered to stop "metal finishing" car bodies prior to paint. Metal finishing and wet sanding after coats of primer gave the painted bodies a smooth, glossy finish, hiding minor imperfections in the metal such as rough welds or minor dents. (Nowadays, this is irrelevant: sheet metal comes out of the presses with such perfection that no wet sanding of the metal is necessary. Back then, it decidedly was.)

It had been decided in the United States that the public would "accept" (not "like," but "accept") all kinds of scratches, lumps, dirt, and grinder marks "reading" through the final paint, and so the same "substantial labor saving" was prescribed for Opel. After trying it and hearing dealer reactions (not to mention customer outrage), Opel quickly went back to full metal finish—it was impossible to do otherwise. So, when it came to the customer and the product, GM's "culture of excellence" was absent.

Another more harmless anecdote came from my good friend, the late David E. Davis Jr., dean of automotive writers, lecturer, author, pioneering writer at *Car and Driver*, and founder of *Automobile* magazine. A sought-after speaker highly knowledgeable about our industry, David accepted a gig as speaker to a large group of GM executives. The speech appeared to go well, and the applause felt genuine. David went home pleased and thought no more about it until he received the following letter:

Dear David:

You asked for feedback on your remarks at our recent conference. The data is just now available.

The rating scale was zero to ten with ten being "best." The five non-GM speakers had scores ranging from zero to ten. Yours ranged from three to ten. The five "outside speakers'" average scores ranged from 5.25 to 8.25.

Your average was 7.35.

Two speakers had higher scores than yours. Your standard deviation from the mean was 1.719 and ranked second among the variances, showing that most people had a similar opinion about your remarks.

I personally enjoyed your remarks very much. Your refreshing candor, coupled with your broad understanding of people, product, and the market, gave us exactly what we asked you for—"widened competitive awareness."

Thank you for your participation.

Signed:

Outside Speaker Effective Analysis Group

An "outside speaker effective analysis group"? Implausible, yes, but I am not making this up. This was the result of too much money and too many overly educated, almost academically oriented people focusing their ray guns of unbridled excellence on targets of complete irrelevance.

A few years before jumping the GM ship and going to BMW in 1971, I was asked to go to Detroit to explain Opel's proposed midsize car (then Ascona, later Vectra, roughly analogous to the Chevrolet Malibu in the United States). Mr. Roche was *not* going to approve the appropriation request because he did not believe any of the analysis demonstrating the market opportunity for the car.

I flew to Detroit, reported to Mr. Roche's secretary, and was asked to wait in his vast hotel-lobby-like outer office. For days I arrived at 8:00 AM and left at 5:00 PM, watching the great man stride past me with nary a nod of the head, waiting for hours as a dog would wait for his master, only to have him emerge and depart his office with again no acknowledgment of my humble self. It was clear that I was being punished as the father of the midsize European car proposal.

Finally, the big day came. I was almost in disbelief as I entered Roche's inner sanctum and actually saw him leafing through Opel's proposal. After a few minutes, in his usual soporific monotone, he said, "I don't believe any of this. Take this presentation to the head of my personal special analysis group. He'll take it apart and do his own analysis, and I'll believe that one." So I sought out this man—let's call him Jack Brown: young, well-groomed, handsome, and superbly tailored. The conversation went something like this: "Hi. I'm Jack Brown, and I'm really busy. What's the problem? Oh, he didn't believe the numbers. OK, how many charts do you have? Is this the market growth line? Will it hurt you if I pull it down a quarter of an inch? OK, that one's done.

Now, is this midsize segment growth? Tell you what, I'll increase this one to compensate for taking the total market down." (He sketched in a slightly larger "midsize" pie slice.)

And so we zipped through twenty-odd charts, graphs, and tables in twenty minutes. "Take the whole thing to George over there," Brown told me. "Tell him to put it on Roche's special slides with the orange borders. That's the sign that my group did the analysis. I hope you're not in a hurry; best if we wait a week so he'll think I actually did something. He'll approve it, don't worry. Glad to help. Gotta go now." And with that, he disappeared into the mist of the upper floors of the GM Building, and I never saw him again. Needless to say, the Ascona midsize car program was approved. The "culture of excellence" at work once more. The car, by the way, became a resounding success.

Is it any wonder that a headhunter had little trouble persuading me to accept the position of BMW executive VP for global sales and marketing at five times my GM pay? My father, a career banker and admirer of GM's financial power, was shocked and dismayed by this seemingly foolhardy career move. I had told him I was frustrated with the arrogance and stupidity of the GM system. I remember my father saying, "Let me get this straight: my thirty-eight-year-old, midlevel son, with only nine years' experience, has come to the conclusion that the world's largest, most successful, most powerful, and best-managed car company does not meet his standards?"

"Yes," I answered, meekly. "That about sums it up." Pa was not pleased.

(Of course, BMW was a different kind of shock. I went from a group of well-intentioned, scrupulously honest yet inept GM folks into a nest of fast-moving, high-performance Germans, many of whom practiced self-enrichment at a level of corruption unthinkable in a U.S. corporation at the time. See my first book, *Guts*.)

GM was anything but quiet between my departure and my eventual return. Massive, wrenching reorganizations were accomplished, sometimes with severe consequences to effectiveness. Right or wrong, popular or not, GM had to shrink, shedding activities and people. As retired finance executive Jack Hazen recalls:

> During the Jim McDonald/Roger Smith era, two major policy/organizational changes had a significant impact on our ability to lead in product in the future and hampered decision making. The first was the major reorganizational change in 1984, which divided up Fisher Body and GMAD (General Motors Assembly Division), turned the divisions [brands] into marketing divisions only, and established two new Car Groups that didn't make much sense to anyone. The organizational gridlock that happened in engineering and other staffs took us twenty years to straighten out, and we never recovered from dividing up the body and chassis engineering expertise.
>
> The second was the decision to build new assembly plants and automate both the assembly plants and stamping plants, which burdened GM with huge capital expenditures, excess capacity as our market share declined, and many labor problems.

I dealt with this organizational monstrosity firsthand in the early 1990s. By now, Bob Stempel was in charge of one of the two huge new groups. I was president of Chrysler at the time, and our transmission people were attempting to respond to a "request for quote" on a manual truck transmission that Chrysler was engineering and tooling for GM. My people came to me in frustration. While GM continued to ask for quotes and specs on the transmission, nobody on that side felt empowered to actually commit to an order. The situation was becoming pressing, because we needed to know what production quantity to tool up for:

Dodge trucks only? Low investment, high unit cost. GM plus Dodge? Much higher volume, more investment, lower piece cost. My transmission specialists had gone from GM Powertrain Planning to Light Truck Planning, from there to Powertrain Purchasing, then GMC Marketing, Chevrolet Truck Marketing, and on and on, with each expressing a favorable opinion but declining an actual commitment. I volunteered to call Bob Stempel, whom I knew from his European assignment, and did so. After I described the dilemma to him, we both decided it would be beneficial to get everybody into one conference room at the same time and stay there until we had a decision. Fair enough.

Ten days later, I showed up with my transmission specialist at the old General Motors Building on West Grand Boulevard and was sent to a long, elegant conference room with antique-looking wall sconces and no windows. The room was soon teeming with well-dressed GM executives, all brandishing shiny binders and handing out business cards to each other. I still remember how bizarre that felt: people in the same company, working on the same issues, who recognized one another's names only from various memos and papers, and had never met.

Eventually, Bob Stempel came in and sat at the head of the long table with me at his left elbow. He greeted the Chrysler supplicants with the "we all know why we're here" speech and emphasized the need for a decision. There followed a procession of GM planners, each approaching Stempel and showing him the data in "their" book, each taking care to hold the cover in such a way that I could not possibly peek in. Book after book was viewed by Stempel, with the owner rewarded with grunts and nods of approval.

After an hour, Stempel turned to me and said, "Bob, I know I promised you a decision coming out of this meeting. I'm afraid I can't deliver. There are some delicate aspects here that require more discussion among ourselves. But I promise you a decision in forty-eight hours. And I intend to keep my commitment." My Chrysler colleague and I left and congratulated each other in the elevator. Forty-eight hours was a victory!

"See, when you have a problem like that, come and see me," I boasted. "I don't mind calling the top guys, and that's the way to get action out of a place like GM."

Three weeks later, we had no decision, and Bob Stempel wasn't returning my calls. (We ultimately did sell GM the "D-Spec" manual transmission.)

At about this time, during my tenure as president of Chrysler, I liked to invite one supplier each week to a private lunch in our lavish, Iacocca-instigated Italian-style dining room. The meetings were usually frank, no-holds-barred, because I was anxious to improve the notoriously rocky OEM-supplier relationship and, for Chrysler anyway, transform it into more of a partnership working for mutual success. I usually asked, "Which auto company do you prefer to supply, and why?" The depressingly familiar answers were nearly always Toyota and Honda, but Ford and especially Chrysler were improving rapidly. GM was always the pathetic caboose in the rankings.

Then, one day, a supplier of bearings surprised me by answering, "My favorite customer is GM!" Whoa! "Why on earth is that?" I inquired. The supplier replied, "Because they're so monumentally screwed up that we can sell them the identical bearing in seven different boxes, with seven different part numbers, and seven wildly different prices. Their purchasing groups are only dimly aware of one another's existence. It's a bit hard to keep it all straight, but boy, is it lucrative!"

Well, there you have exactly the *wrong* way to be the favorite customer of a major supplier. Much of the overspending and overorganization was later tackled once Jack Smith became president in 1992. He reduced bloated senior executive ranks, closed plants, shifted the manufacturing and supplier "footprint" out of the high-cost United States and into (then) lower cost Canada and Mexico. Given GM's enormous size, organizational complexity, the vigorous defense waged by its time-honored fiefdoms, and its many powerful and influential believers in the status quo, the task accomplished by Jack Smith, Rick Wagoner, and their team should not be lightly dismissed. It was, as they say, hard slogging.

And some initiatives were brilliant: the early foray into China in the early 1990s, well before the potential of the country became obvious, was a masterstroke of long-range planning and acceptance of intelligent economic risk. Opting for Buick as the initial brand seemed odd to most outside observers: why place a huge bet on a traditional, U.S.-size, near-luxury car in a country where most of the population rides bicycles? But it actually made perfect sense; most of the production of the early years was absorbed by government officials at the central, provincial, city, and rural levels, and by corporate executives. In China, Buick was a revered brand; people still remembered the pre-Communist era, when most Western business leaders and traders, as well as the last emperor and Republic of China founder Sun Yat-sen, were driven in Buicks. I must shamefully admit that, from a distance at Chrysler Corporation, I was a vocal skeptic of GM's China move. I viewed it as a naïve and foolhardy bet, made with the wrong brand.

In retrospect, I was wrong. GM, in partnership with SAIC (Shanghai Automotive Industries Corporation), has become a profitable powerhouse in China. As manufacturing capacity increased, other brands (Chevrolet, Cadillac, and Wuling) have joined Buick in consistent double-digit rates of annual growth. Buick sales in China handily eclipse those of the brand in the United States, and it would not be an exaggeration to say that the enormous success of Buick in China has enabled its rebirth in America. China is the world's largest car market, and GM's share is growing. In a modern application of Alfred P. Sloan's dictum "A car for every purse and purpose," GM in China has a well-executed brand strategy, with Wuling fulfilling basic rural transportation needs, Chevrolet positioned for a growing middle class, Buick targeting officials and the affluent (it should be noted that, as of this writing, the average age of Buick owners in China is twenty-eight!), and Cadillac, gaining ground slowly but steadily, competing with the European luxury makes.

A far sorrier tale is that of Saab. This was a "marriage on the rebound" if ever there was one. Irked, feeling diminished, and worried over rival Ford's successful acquisitions of Land Rover/Range Rover, Jaguar, and Aston-Martin (organized into what was called "PAG," or "Premium Automotive Group"), GM decided that they, too, needed a premium European brand, and set out to buy one. Naturally, in this particular dance hall, all of the pretty girls (BMW, Mercedes, Audi, Ferrari) were taken. But what of the lonely, somewhat undernourished wallflower over there, the one called Saab? Thus commenced a journey into misfortune.

Saab had never been a strong or powerful company. An offshoot of Saab aircraft after World War II, the company built small, unusually shaped cars, initially with two-stroke engines (which trailed blue smoke and went "ring-ding-ding" when the driver lifted foot from throttle) but later with the European Ford V4—a lumpy and charmless engine, but the only one that, presumably, would fit in the Saab 96 engine compartment.

The very weirdness of the cars endeared them to those in academia and other intellectuals. Saab ownership was like a badge of nonconformity, of daring individualism. Some of my professors explained their Saab devotion by repeating the fable that the company's cars were superior because "it's the only vehicle in the world designed by aircraft engineers." (Having flown various U.S. military jets in the 1950s and '60s and experiencing their less-than-stellar reliability firsthand, I'm not sure how impressive—albeit fictitious—a claim that really was.)

Saab, always hovering at around 100,000 units per year, never could survive without a partner, and thus later, larger and more conventional Saabs shared their basic architecture with a midsize Fiat. Financial breakeven still eluded poor Saab. If you add up all the professors of sociology and political science, all the leftish intellectuals who admired the failed Swedish experiment in 90 percent tax rates and womb-to-tomb welfare, all the well-to-do who for some reason eschewed Mercedes, BMW, and Audi, you still couldn't get to 150,000 sales. But GM bought in anyway, first at 50 percent and then 100! Saab would henceforth use two sizes of GM Europe's Opel architectures and share systems such as heating and air-conditioning; the resulting better cars and lower cost would make Saab successful at last. (Frankly, I would have steered clear of this charming loser, and I later advocated sale or wind-down every chance I got.)

Every effort to expand the appeal of Saab by making it more "mainstream" and less "quirky" ended in failure. Mainstream buyers simply didn't consider Saab (or had never heard of it and thought it was spelled "sob") while the intellectual fringe that adored "the unusual" was deeply resentful of what they considered a sellout to mass taste. They didn't buy, either. The media were also very harsh on the "mainstream" cars, writing scathing pieces on the absence of the old Saab charm and decrying its "normalcy." ("Saab Story," as the reader can well imagine, was often too tempting a headline to pass up.)

But GM's worst failing was not in the purchase of Saab, but in the failure to do what is normally done in the acquisition of a smaller competitor: consolidate. Saab continued to operate largely autonomously, with all functions, including design, engineering, and purchasing, soldiering on as though they were still independent. The last Saab 9-3 was supposed to share most major systems with the well-engineered (but stylistically challenged) Opel Vectra. But, in a spirit of "we know better," almost everything was changed, including the entire wiring and electrical system, as well as the engineering-intensive heating and air-conditioning unit. Since Saab sourced these and others to new suppliers, the economies of scale were lost, and the car became needlessly expensive. The fact that the specific Saab electrical system turned out to be heavily failure-prone didn't help. This type of "brand character" can only be called wasteful stupidity. As I frequently (and irritatingly, I'm sure) said, "As if a Saab owner is going to crawl under the instrument panel and declare, 'What a rip-off! These are the same wires as in my neighbor's Opel Vectra!'" Systems like electrical, air-conditioning, and window lifts are customer transparent: if they function well and are dead reliable, they can and should be shared across similar-size cars, as they are between Toyota and Lexus. (The state of affairs I found at Saab when I joined GM in 2001 will be described in a later chapter.)

Other so-called "alliances" or minority ownership stakes in mostly Japanese auto companies were part of a broad "alliance strategy," the results of which were mixed at best. Isuzu was a decent source of Chevrolet medium trucks and provided the diesel know-how for what was to become the renowned GM "Duramax" engine. Suzuki, where GM ownership peaked at 21 percent, was at least highly profitable, but the synergies dreamed of for shared small-car engines and platforms never came about; GM and Suzuki both clung stubbornly to their own "solutions." The European venture with Fiat, in which GM ownership was to rise to 20 percent, provided some synergies in purchasing and one semishared platform between the Fiat Uno and the Opel Astra. Best of all, GM gained access to Fiat's excellent passenger car diesels (some European markets are over 60 percent diesel), an area GM had neglected due to investment and engineering "thrifting." But in the early years of the new century, GM was cash-poor and wanted out of the then-moribund Fiat. The latter played its cards well: it cost GM $2 billion for the divorce.

The strangest alliance was with Fuji Heavy Industries, or

Subaru. Born of the correct belief that Subaru was the master of low-cost, all-wheel-drive passenger cars, the planners forgot or ignored the fact that Subaru's platforms and its flat-four longitudinal engines and transmissions were completely incompatible with anything anywhere in the GM lineup. Nor was Subaru at all interested in adopting GM's chassis and engine technology, although they did try a Subaru version of Opel's small minivan, the Zafira. (It was overpriced, did not offer Subaru's trademark all-wheel drive, and was, in all ways, a sharp departure from what Subaru's domestic customers expected of the brand.)

Meanwhile, back in the USA, the pressure was on to find some way to share a platform with Fuji, thereby demonstrating to the world the frequently doubted value of the "alliance strategy." A modern crossover was to be developed, shared between Pontiac and Subaru. After months of fruitless haggling over features, prices, and sales volumes, it became abundantly clear that the aspirations of Pontiac, a low-priced brand, were incompatible with the upmarket ambition of Subaru. The program was shelved, mercifully, only to resurface later with Saab as Subaru's partner. That one bit the dust as well, as the vehicle was deemed insufficiently Saab-like and too investment-intensive. Still, the pressure to "make use of the Subaru alliance" existed, resulting in one of my less good ideas: creating a small Saab, the 9-2, off the Subaru Impreza station wagon, the rear two-thirds of which bore a remarkable resemblance to the large Saab 9-5 wagon. With all-new Saab-identity sheet metal, it would be credible, right? Wrong! It was hated even before testing by the media, who called it a "SAABaru," and we managed to offend both the quirky-addicted Saab loyalists as well as the hardcore Subaru fans. Sales were dismal; the 9-2 required heavy discounting, and arguably damaged both brands.

We ultimately had an amicable divorce (the Fuji-Heavy/Subaru executives were a very likeable and capable bunch), and

Subaru is now, as the Japanese like to say, "under the motherly wing of Toyota."

And thus—with a whimper, not a bang—ended the experiment with alliances with Japanese manufacturers. One exception was NUMMI, or "New United Motorcar Manufacturing Company," the Fremont, California, joint venture with Toyota. Born in 1984 under the then-leadership of Roger Smith, NUMMI was GM's first serious dip into the waters of then-superior Japanese manufacturing culture. GM's best and brightest were cycled into and out of NUMMI in the expectation that the lessons of lean production and worker participation would quickly spread throughout the vastness of GM's manufacturing operations. It did, but not quickly. The ex-NUMMI "missionaries" were often treated as representatives of an alien culture, and the phrase "let me tell you how that was done at NUMMI" was guaranteed to cause 90 percent of minds to snap tightly shut.

The first jointly produced vehicle was essentially a Toyota Corolla with a Chevrolet clone dubbed "Prizm." The Corolla sold well, as always, while the Prizm had a hard time: it overlapped GM's own Cavalier, offering roughly the same size and performance. And here I offer a curiosity I have observed several times at various stages of my career: The NUMMI-Corolla performed with the usual bravura in the *Consumer Reports* rankings, based on voluntary assessments by owners. The Chevrolet Prizm ranked way lower. Yet these cars were engineered identically, had the same features and specifications, and were built in the same plant, on the same final assembly line, by the same workers. Where did the "quality and reliability" difference come from? I observed the same phenomenon in the late 1980s when Chrysler had a NUMMI-like venture with Mitsubishi in Bloomington, Illinois. It was called "Diamond Star," and it produced a small sports coupe for both Mitsubishi and Chrysler (Plymouth Laser, Eagle Talon, and Mitsubishi Eclipse). Again, same engineering, same parts, same factory, same workers, and yet in *Consumer Reports* and other surveys, the Mitsubishi product scored far better. What's going on here?

My theory is that the "self-reporting" by owners brings with it an inherent bias: owners of Japanese cars truly believe they have made a superior purchase. They are part of the "smart buyers" club. Then why did the windshield wiper fall off? "Oh, well, that's just a minor error; someone didn't tighten a bolt. I'm not going to besmirch the reputation of [insert Japanese brand here] by reporting this minor little incident." The owners of domestic cars feel no such overwhelming obligation to the maintenance of their brand's image; it probably wasn't that great to start with. They feel no need to retroactively justify the wisdom of their purchase, so everything gets reported. A theory? Sure. Maybe wrong? Quite possibly. But it will have to do until someone offers a better one.

GM's relationship with Toyota was unusual. It appeared to be a case of mutual admiration. Toyota admired GM's huge size and global reach, while GM, finally aware of the competitive threat, wanted to glean the secret of Toyota's enviable quality record and manufacturing prowess. Regular meetings were held between the two management groups; areas for legal collaboration (such as hydrogen fuel cells) were explored, but to no avail. In retrospect, I believe Toyota played us. We were sincerely interested in a good relationship; Toyota, on the other hand, was always tight-lipped, except to tell GM repeatedly what a fine company we were, how much they admired us, and how they harbored the modest dream of being a really big car company . . . not as big as GM, mind you—they would never be that presumptuous. But still, you know, *big*. Meanwhile, they were on a maximum growth plan to become "Number One" in the world, an ambition that was to be attained briefly, but which wrought serious harm in terms of quality and their much-polished reputation.

The NUMMI relationship was ultimately to give birth to two

generations of small crossovers, sharing common parts but with styling differences: the Pontiac Vibe and the Toyota Matrix. I hope Toyota made a little money on theirs; we lost a bundle on ours. Have you been paying attention? Test question: which one of the "twins" performed better in quality surveys, Matrix or Vibe?

At the end of the 1990s, through a combination of unfortunate government regulation, an antiquated non-product-driven culture, a union incapable of agreeing to anything but "more," U.S. geopolitical and trade policies that favored foreign producers, and an increasingly hostile American media that loved picking on the big, dumb guy, GM's U.S. market share and profitability proved increasingly elusive. Worse, what profitability there was came mostly (at times more than 100 percent) from our then-wholly-owned financial company, GMAC (General Motors Acceptance Corporation). This gave rise to the oft-repeated phrase "General Motors is a finance company that also produces cars and trucks." The basic vulnerability of the company was obvious to all, and Jack Smith and Rick Wagoner were determined to solve these monumental problems.

Among many initiatives of the mid-1990s was the ill-advised foray into what is called "brand management." Let's back up: Every U.S. auto company has, at some point, been influenced at the board level by the CEO of a consumer products company (Paul Sticht of RJR-Nabisco at Chrysler, Joe Culman of Phillip Morris at Ford, and, during this time, John Smale of Procter & Gamble at GM). What all of these experienced CEOs had in common was a deep belief, based on decades of experience with detergents and toothpastes, that "brand management" was the only effective way to run a multibrand operation. In its most basic form, it means putting some smart, young marketing person in charge of Crest toothpaste. If she wants a new flavor or package design, she asks the chemists or the package designers to whip up a batch of, say, ten thousand tubes to try in a test market like

Skokie, Illinois. When the product is ready, the brand manager sees to it that it's distributed there and appropriately advertised locally. If it takes off, it might be rolled out nationally. If it flops . . . well, the experiment didn't cost that much.

Without question, the brand management approach works in the world of soap, toothpaste, and cleaning supplies. The error lies in transposing it to cars, which every one of the former consumer products CEOs tried to do. Here's where it goes awry: a brand manager in the car business can't do a small test batch. Changing the design or engineering of a car consumes hundreds of millions of dollars and three years. And the federal government doesn't care whether it's a test batch or not; every car model, regardless of production volume, must be fully certified from an emissions and safety standpoint. Unlike a Crest toothpaste tube, these cars, assuming a negative test outcome, will hang around as worthless orphans for years.

I advanced all of these arguments in 1990, when RJR-Nabisco's CEO convinced Lee Iacocca to go "brand management" at Chrysler. The late Jerry York, a later ally of Kirk Kerkorian bearing a reputation for near-infallible business instincts, inherited the Dodge brand. But what to do? Dodge already had a full lineup of cars and trucks, and they were selling well. Yet Iacocca demanded that "brand management" result in some new, segment-creating products. Jerry had little room to maneuver. Something had to be done, yet anything significant would require sums of engineering expense and capital that nobody would approve.

The solution, finally, was to have an outside body builder (in this case, ASC, using its Mexican facility) design, engineer, and build a convertible version of Dodge's small Shadow sedan. It was not a happy program: Even after countless fixes, the cars filled with water in downpours, and the squeaks and rattles demanded high radio volume to drown them out. It was a financial and technical flop. Jerry's second "brand innovation" was something the market had forgotten to ask for: a convertible pickup truck! And so, again using an outside shop, we proudly announced the world's first, and only, pickup truck with a folding cloth top! It was a resounding failure; almost none were sold. "Brand management" at Chrysler was soon abandoned.

But car companies rarely look at one another's failed experiments, just as every left-wing politician believes that the only reason socialism has always failed is because he or she wasn't in charge.

John Smale, non-executive chairman of GM, strongly encouraged a move to brand management, but with a twist: going beyond Chrysler, the GM system decreed that every *model* be a "brand." Thus, unlike Chrysler (where, at least, Dodge, Jeep, and Chrysler were legitimate brands), Chevrolet was itself a collection: Impala, Malibu, Cavalier, Camaro, Corvette, Lumina, and the plethora of truck nameplates . . . all of them "brands." And this across all of GM North America! With Chevrolet, Pontiac, Buick, Oldsmobile, and Cadillac, GM encompassed over ninety distinct "brands." Each had a brand manager to whom reported a brand product manager and a brand marketing manager. But there was also a need for coordination by category, so the passenger car brand managers were, in turn, supervised by a Chevrolet passenger car manager; this was repeated in the other GM divisions (couldn't call them "brands" anymore, even though that's what they were!), and trucks.

Smale found the ideal executive to run this organizational quagmire: Ron Zarrella, recruited from pharmaceutical and optical company Bausch & Lomb. Ron was an intelligent and affable executive who, it later turned out, had lied about having an MBA. He brought in dozens of bright, young marketing people to man these hundreds of new positions and create individualized advertising for each and every car line. Breaking the overall ad budget down into ninety-plus separate budgets resulted in so little expenditure per car line that almost every "brand" wound up below the awareness threshold level. Many, if not most, of the stalwart newcomers came from such complex industries as beer and soft drinks. Most didn't have the remotest clue about the car business. Many came from New York City and barely drove. The industry press didn't fully believe the brand management hype, and GM was hard-pressed to defend it, especially after one ex–consumer product whiz announced publicly that there was really no difference between marketing "baby wipes and Cadillacs." The same skills were involved, he claimed.

Across town at Chrysler, where I was now president, automotive reporters frequently asked me what I thought of GM's brand management. I couldn't help but be totally honest, just as I had been years before when I derided GM's new, much-touted composite-bodied minivans (the ones with the long noses that begat the nickname "dust buster"). I had asserted that Chrysler had little to fear from these "plastic pachyderms," forecasting dismal failure. I'd been right. And so, I probably enjoyed a certain level of credibility with the media when I heaped renewed scorn on this latest scheme, this latest "breakthrough" in the automobile business. Once again, I forecast dismal failure and once again I was right. (My forecasting skills could not have been regarded with favor over in the General Motors Building.)

But it was even worse than I thought. Each of these brand managers, with the attendant "product" and "marketing" people below them, then had to *do something*. Given the industry reality of shared platforms and drivetrains, how could they engender some new, wonderfully unique product for their brands? Sorting it all out became a near-insurmountable task for Product Planning, the group that translates Marketing's wants into an actionable product description to guide the designers and engineers.

To establish a degree of order and consistency, a "check the box" set of visual requirements was ultimately established for each "make" (Chevrolet, Buick, etc.), and each of the "brands" (Cavalier, Malibu, etc.) within that make that would share them. The focus, then, was not on design excellence but, rather, on the presence of certain "brand characteristics." Thus, every Chevrolet was to have a huge, chrome "whisker" across the front end. (The idiotic fallacy behind this was that the Chevrolet truck buyers loved the appearance of their vehicles, including the wide chrome band. So, the reasoning went, if we make the cars look more like the trucks, people will start loving the cars, too. Didn't work.)

All Pontiacs were to have plastic body cladding, lumpy and unappealing as it might have been. A further Pontiac "brand characteristic" was headrests that were like padded rectangular picture frames, with nylon mesh forming the inside. All Chevrolets, and only Chevrolets, were to have five-spoke wheels . . . no other GM make could. I wonder if anyone let the competitors know, as five-spoke alloy wheels are a fairly general configuration. The cruelest visual fate was reserved for Saturn. The brand management rocket scientists had divined that Saturn buyers were not "car" people; they cared more about friendly, gentle dealers and good service. These buyers received the label "postmodern," in that they cared only about the transportation value of the car, and not, presumably, its appearance. Thus, it was solemnly decreed that the proper brand characteristic of Saturn would be . . . no character! Total blandness was to rule, and this article of faith explains a number of Saturn sedans, as well as the first-generation Vue small SUV, that had no front-end identification and no grille, but simply a sort of gaping air intake. Since "postmodern" buyers presumably didn't like useless adornment of any kind, there was no chrome brightwork on the cars, resulting in an overall impression of depressing cheapness, much like a person wearing an ill-fitting burlap suit.

Personnel-heavy, bureaucratic, detail-focused, wasteful, unworkable, and absolutely guaranteed to produce lousy results, "brand management" was one of the first things I wanted to see destroyed when I returned to GM.

The imposition of brand management was the final straw, the element that was to doom GM's North American cars to a no-win level of mediocrity. GM's European and Latin American operations, unburdened by the MBA-driven bureaucracy of the home base, fared much better overall. And the North American truck group, single-mindedly focused on creating a better pickup than Ford or Dodge (and that same culture is evident among the "truck guys" in the other two companies), largely ignored the politically correct marketing dictums and just forged ahead, producing one smash-hit sport-utility and full-size pickup after another. Their success and profitability, in an era of economic expansion and low fuel cost, largely masked the disastrous state of the passenger-car side of the business. An overfocus on trucks was a dangerous thing. Sensitive to economic cycles and fuel prices, the truck market suddenly collapsed in 2008 before most of the new and competitive passenger cars had rolled out, triggering GM's ultimate financial distress.

By the turn of the century, GM had become a sort of bad joke. It was widely credited (by those who cared) for its excellent trucks, but reputations of car companies are based much more on their passenger cars. And GM's, while not awful, were well below expectations and the repetitive "wait till next year hype" always propagated by GM. The car magazines rarely had a kind word for GM in their evaluations, and the damning-with-faint-praise was picked up by the mainstream media, which generally lacks the expertise to tell a good car from a not-so-good one.

Even post-takeover by Daimler, Chrysler brought forth one more hit: the boldly styled Chrysler 300. The car was a home run, with pundits concluding that poor GM really was the only company that just didn't get it at all. Into this climate of false pity (liberally spiced with ridicule), GM proudly launched the Pontiac

Aztek, a minivan-based vehicle designed for a niche somewhere in the U.S. market. Since it was often displayed with a large tent deployed from the back end, one can only assume it was created for people who go camping regularly or who otherwise have no permanent dwelling. It was atrociously ugly, with featureless, flat body panels offset in front by what appeared to be one lower and one upper grille opening. I remember staring at it in disbelief the first time I saw it: I could not imagine that a group of professional automobile designers and executives had green-lighted this Quasimodo of crossovers.

The Aztek became the butt of jokes, just like Ford's ill-fated Edsel four decades earlier. It was an all-too-easily-grasped shorthand icon of GM's ineptness, a metaphor for a disoriented company. But, as I was to learn, even worse was waiting in the wings, baking to golden-brown perfection in GM's design and engineering functions. Aztek would be a reputational low point for GM, and the true magnitude of the situation was not lost on Jack Smith or Rick Wagoner.

Ground Zero

MEANWHILE, HAVING BEEN "ENCOURAGED" TO RETIRE FROM THE NEWLY
created DaimlerChrysler at the very young age of sixty-six, I, as
previously mentioned, accepted a position as CEO of Exide Corporation, the world's largest producer of lead-acid batteries, and a
company with many automotive customers. Soon the events described in chapter 1 unfolded . . . the overtures from John Devine,
the meetings with Rick Wagoner, and finally the job offer. And
thus was sealed my return to GM after an absence of close to thirty
years. An acceptable compensation proposal was soon agreed upon,
and I was to report to work on September 1, 2001.

My first company event was before my start date, at the August
board meeting, where members review prototypes of the forthcoming product pipeline, in both metal (for soon-to-launch vehicles) and foam (a very realistic, full-size plastic model virtually
indistinguishable from a real vehicle). The products I saw, whether
small, midsize, sport-utility, or large-car, were obviously doomed
to failure. But at this initial introduction, I kept my candor in
check, preferring to use descriptors like "unusual" and "certainly

different." I could see from this sampling of the future portfolio that the situation was, indeed, in urgent need of correction.

My next encounter with the GM of 2001 was in Monterey, California, at the famed annual Pebble Beach Concours d'Elegance, which each year features a few hundred of the world's finest historic and classic vehicles. It was August 18, 2001, and GM had chosen the venue to introduce the soon-to-be-launched Cadillac CTS to a group of leading international automotive journalists. My return to GM already announced, I was there to help pitch it. This was not without difficulty. The car was modern and unusual in its design, with flat planes converging in sharp, origami-like creases. It was well-proportioned, well-engineered, and dynamically on par with premium German sedans of the same class. The design was certainly polarizing and found great favor with some buyers. What the car lacked was any charm or warmth in the form of tasteful chrome accents to offset the unfamiliarity of the "stealth-fighter" sheet metal. The interior, the element that can make or break the sale if the potential customer is attracted to the exterior, can only be described as a failed experiment in attracting the computer generation. Someone had apparently decided that the young, upwardly mobile like computers, so why not make the instrument panel look like one? Not like the workstation, mind you, but the ugly, upright rectangular lump that's under the desk or in the cabinet. Most didn't know what this leaning tower of black plastic in the center stack of the instrument panel was supposed to represent, and hardly anybody liked it. The rest of the interior was deliberately sparse, though made of high-grade materials. (Many designers at the time were in love with the spartan, decorless design of Bang & Olufsen stereo equipment, an arcane aesthetic not shared by enough people to really work.)

In short, we had a very expensive interior that looked cheap. Clearly, not something to shoot for. I got a lot of practice that

Saturday doing something that would be required of me for the next few years: finding ways to point out the excellence of a vehicle while dismissing the weak points as a matter of taste, all without destroying my credibility with the media. They knew I knew the difference!

The evening after the Pebble Beach Concours, Wayne Cherry, vice president of GM Design, invited me to his ground-floor suite at the Pebble Beach Lodge. Sitting at a table on the elegant patio, Wayne produced some thick binders. These, he announced, contained photographs of all the projects Design was currently working on.

It was a horror show.

The photos Wayne showed me confirmed the worst suspicions I'd harbored since seeing the board meeting prototypes. But these were worse, some in earlier stages of development, but all noncompetitive. For each picture, Wayne would ask me what I thought. As diplomatically as possible, at least initially, I tried to keep my words from being hurtful, with phrases like, "Umm, that has some nice elements, but it's really misproportioned." Wayne quickly set me at ease: "I don't like any of these, either. Most of them are really awful." I did find this strange, since Wayne was, at least in title, the head of GM Design and, as such, responsible for the aesthetics, inside and out, of the company's vehicles. Yet, proposal after proposal, Wayne would ask, "How do you like this one?" and I'd say, "Jeez, Wayne, it's god-awful," and Wayne would say, "You're right. I hate it, too." After about ten of these, I said, "Wait a second, Wayne! These are your vehicles. It's your design team that did them. How can you trash them?"

"Well," Wayne replied, "in a normal company, you'd be right. But this is GM, and we have VLEs." Vehicle line executives, modeled after Toyota "shusas," are very powerful senior executives, usually engineers, who act as program managers for individual vehicle programs as they progress through the gestation process from sketch all the way to production. GM had refined the VLE system and had, as was so frequently the case, gone the extra mile in conducting elaborate psychological testing to make sure these men and women were up to the responsibility. But the VLEs, mostly men with two excellent women, were by and large a fine and experienced group and dedicated to accomplishing their mission.

Where the GM system departed from similar program manager schemes at other automobile companies is that the VLEs were given responsibility for design. Sure, the designers belonged to Wayne Cherry, but the decisions, the aesthetic judgment, the green-lighting of a proposal were all under the purview of the VLE. Wayne could criticize, argue, and harangue, but mostly the VLEs didn't listen. They had other priorities: In the VLE's list of objectives, attainment of which would be crucial to his or her future compensation, the words "world's most appealing sedan in the segment" were nowhere to be found. Instead, quantified objectives covered cost (good!), investment, quality, warranty cost, assembly hours per vehicle, percentage of parts reused from the prior vehicle (believed to be the secret to Toyota's success), and, important to note, time to program execution. Saddled with a reputation for endlessly delayed major programs, GM's senior management had really focused on speed of execution. The media also placed major emphasis on the number of months needed from sketch to production and breathlessly reported every new Toyota pronouncement regarding ever-shorter programs. It became a sort of litmus test for how good a company was: if you were over three years, you were slow; if you could point to twenty-seven months, that earned kudos. When Toyota announced that they would soon be at a year to eighteen months, it was further proof that the world's smartest automobile company would soon run away from everybody. (Of course, they never got there and, in fact, had to add months back due to poor execution and deteriorating quality statistics.)

So this was the environment in which our VLEs operated. Speed, speed, speed. Things had to be right the first time; going back for a redo would blow the timing. Typically, design research involves testing a future proposal against known competitors in a so-called "product clinic" involving hundreds of selected respondents. I suspected that GM hadn't actually researched any of the vehicles I was seeing, or at least that the methodology was wrong. Neither turned out to be the case: these lackluster designs had all gone through product clinics, and they had all failed. But a complete redo would have been too time consuming, so it became a matter of "Can we quickly fix the part they hated the most without blowing the timing?"

Cherry, mindful of the damage these aesthetically challenged dogs would do to his reputation, protested and didn't sign the VLEs' "contracts"—documents blessed by the head of every major function stating agreement with the vehicle program as constituted and promising support to make it happen on time. Theoretically, if a function as important as Design refused to sign a contract, the program was not to proceed. But Wayne was known by this point as the lone critic and eternal pain in the butt, the guy who was never pleased, so why listen to him? "I'll just blow my timing and, besides, Wayne's guys signed off."

And so, a marginalized Wayne Cherry saw program after program proceed to production despite his specific dissent. At this point, the hard-charging reader will say, "Why did he put up with a situation like that? Why didn't he complain to senior management, even lay his job on the line?" The answer is that designers are artists, and artists, by and large, are gentle souls and have little or no taste for harmony-destroying conflict.

This is why we were staring at binders full of pictures of full-size clay models that were pathetically inadequate in terms of triggering any "buy me" lust in the viewer. I now knew what I was facing. First, I was going to have to get Design back in charge of vehicle aesthetics, and let Design run design. We had, as I recall, fourteen VLEs. There is not any car company anywhere in the whole wide world that has fourteen senior people capable of making sound aesthetic judgments on vehicle design. Most companies, if they're lucky, have two or three. If the CEO or the president is one of them, it makes things much easier. Some companies have none, or none for a while, and that explains the oft-observed sudden loss of style by some companies who had previously done well in that area.

I knew also that I was going to have to wrest control of Design away from the VLEs (who were all to report to me), and I thought I was going to have to keelhaul product research. I also realized that many of the programs were too far down the execution pipeline to stop. They'd appear two or even three years after my arrival, and inevitably I would be held responsible for them.

I briefly wondered whether, perhaps, signing on with GM had been a bad idea. As my first day approached, I began to ponder what I had seen and heard, both officially and anecdotally, about GM and its core North American operation thus far. I hoped I could make a difference.

"Here's What We're Going to Do First"

THINGS STARTED AUSPICIOUSLY ON MY FIRST DAY OF WORK, SEPTEMBER 1, 2001. I was handed what by all accounts was the best administrative support team in the company: Betty Gonko, administrative assistant, and Mark Walkuski, long-term professional chauffeur. It's hard for an outsider to slip comfortably into his or her slot in a new company; it's doubly hard when that company is of the size and complexity, and possessed of the cultural history, of GM. My "office" knew who to call, where to go, what to take seriously (almost everything at first, but I soon encouraged them to reduce that to about 20 percent), and what the so-called time architecture would mean to my evenings and weekends. Their efforts removed 80 percent of the reentry stress and permitted me to focus on what had to be done.

After being led downstairs to be photographed for my magnetic all-door-opening ID tag, I reported in to Rick Wagoner. In his usual calm and gentlemanly fashion, he encouraged me to go through the overly ambitious product portfolio and cancel whatever I thought wrong or useless, and, if it was too late for erasure, perhaps inject modifications that would perfume the pig sufficiently to achieve at least a modicum of market success. (I was to be only partially successful at both, but I'll get to that later.)

I soon attended the first series of meetings of the NASB (North American Strategy Board) as well as the even more exalted ASB (Automotive Strategy Board), the most senior operating committee in the company, attended by the heads of all functions, direct reporting staffs, and geographic regions. Both of these meetings, which occurred monthly, lasted hours, if not a full day. Many three-ring binders were prepared, but most presentations had been distributed electronically in advance. Myriad subjects were addressed, from market performance by region to financial results, just as in any senior-level corporate meeting. But huge amounts of time were also devoted to far less important issues not of legitimate concern to such a senior convocation, like discussions of parts reuse or cost per stamping die. I remember one hours-long, heated argument over which of a list of future senior leaders were more "functionally oriented" than "general management" in their abilities. "Both" was not an acceptable answer. Small wonder I became infamous for pulling out my BlackBerry and working on my "Brick-Breaker" scores during these meetings.

Another ritualistic time suck was the annual creation and cross-checking of the so-called PMP (Performance Management Process). Whole mornings would be devoted to "aligning goals" among the meeting participants to ensure that each of the dozens of individual objectives were consistent across functions and geographies. This was called "box balancing" the PMPs, the "box" being where a functional leader's objective intersected, or overlapped, with that of a "geographic" leader. After one interminable, mind-numbing "global PMP box balancing" session, Rick Wagoner asked if everyone on the Automotive Strategy Board now agreed with their own and everyone else's objectives in the PMP. Seeing heads nod assent, Rick pronounced the coming year as good as in the bag. "All we have to do now is work to achieve

those objectives," he said. "I know you can do it. So, we're going
to have a very successful year."

Say what? I submit that the whole idea of annual "management by objective" (the generic form of PMP) schemes is hopelessly flawed, an exercise in abject futility, possessing not a smidgen
of customer value. My reasons for this categorically negative assessment are twofold. First, the "objectives" are all based on a series
of dubious projections on market size, economic activity, competitor actions—none of which ever come true, resulting in a
PMP document that is, for all intents and purposes, worthless
when finally published and never seriously referred to for "guidance" again. The "value" is only to the small army of human resources personnel who keep track of the whole mess.

My second reason for disdaining PMPs is this: a senior executive who needs a quantified list of objectives to know what he or
she should be working on should not be a senior executive in the
first place.

Because Soviet-trained fighter pilots were taught an elaborate
sequence of carefully choreographed and endlessly practiced ma-
neuvers to use when entering a combat situation, the Arab MiG
and Sukhoi pilots were easy pickings for the Israeli Air Force,
which, like its U.S. counterpart, relied on situational assessment,
intuition, and flexibility in a fast-evolving air combat situation.
The U.S. Marine Corps adage is "No battle plan survives the first
two minutes after initial engagement with the enemy." This lesson
was lost on GM.

The North American meetings were little better. Presided
over by Ron Zarrella, the previously mentioned brand management guru who had lied about having an MBA, they were equally
devoid of pragmatic, customer-oriented focus. Zarrella was soon
to depart, returning as CEO to the more comfortable and lucrative world of Bausch & Lomb.

After one particularly dreary meeting, I asked Ron how he,

as an outsider, could possibly deal with the clerks-running-the-business environment. His candid reply: "You fight it at first; then you see you can't change it, so you go with the flow." He was half right! I finally gave up on the administrative thicket but managed, ultimately, to change product development for the (much) better.

A little gem that came up in the North American Strategy Board meeting is the following, which I saved—a "mission statement" of yet another high-minded, high-IQ group:

> Creating an enterprise strategy and knowledge development resource to support decision-making of functional and operational organizations attempting to achieve enterprise objectives.

Come again? Zarrella quickly penned a note to me explaining that this was Vince Barabba's initiative. Barabba was GM North America's resident intellectual, an author and consultant who was very helpful in the needless intellectualization of a pretty simple business. The initiative "should be cut in half," the note concluded.

No kidding! But nobody cut it in half, and Ron was president of GM North America. He was the one to do it, but I presume he feared that "they" (Rick Wagoner and Jack Smith) loved Barabba too much to let it happen. Complete elimination is what ultimately took place—but not soon enough.

A salient feature of these top-level meetings was the notable absence of any focus on the thing that matters most: the company's products. When they were on the agenda, it was always in a highly abstract form: a description of category, size, investment level, cost and profit targets, and other legitimate financial measures. And the discussions were invariably devoid of visuals. No photographs, no design renderings, nothing that would convey any emotional content or any compelling reasons why this particular vehicle would win against the competition. In one endless Automotive Strategy Board meeting, we were faced with an on-screen five-by-five matrix (or maybe even six-by-six) which, in its twenty-five (or thirty-six) cells, listed every known corporate priority. These ranged from "increase market share," "reduce assembly hours per vehicle," and "speed time to market" to "achieve diversity targets" and "reduce LTI (senior executive) count." Buried somewhere in the middle of this grand mosaic was a little cell, no bigger than the others, which read "achieve product excellence."

I managed, barely, to contain myself. (Remember, I was new!) There, on the screen, was the core of the GM problem: "product excellence" was merely one of twenty-five (or thirty-six) things the company should work on. As I later told Rick Wagoner, that matrix should have been in the shape of a giant sunflower, with a huge "PRODUCT EXCELLENCE" in the giant circular field, with all the other initiatives, helpful as they were to the achievement of the big one, forming the pretty little yellow petals around the periphery.

Meanwhile, over in the Product Development staff meetings, things were better only by a degree. My predecessor, Tom Davis, was still in office, helping with my transition into the company. Tom was a seasoned engineer, a GM lifer who had presided over the fantastic transformation of GM from an also-ran in the truck business into a near-dominant player. It is a testament to the excellence of the Detroit truck teams that, perhaps due to decades of benign neglect by top management, they knew their competition (there were only three players), knew their customers, understood the business and its demands, and always had a burning drive to set the bar higher with the next full-size truck or SUV. And this is why, despite repeated efforts, the vaunted Japanese could never put more than a minor dent in the Detroit Three when it came to the big stuff. The media would always gleefully announce that "Detroit's last bastion, the full-size truck" was about to fall now that Toyota had launched the new Tundra, or Nissan the Titan, but show me the owner of any American full-size truck or SUV who is just dying for a Japanese offering.

Tom was a good executive and administrator, and his meetings reflected this. It was all very procedural and process-focused. Are the engineering releases on time? Why are we behind on that prototype build? Has program X passed such and such a "gate"? Why is it late? What's the plan for recovery of the lost time?

It was all tactical—work that had to be done, of course—but in the company's most senior product meeting, where was the strategy? What kinds of cars do we want to make, and why? Why are we failing? What needs to happen to turn this around? How do we raise our game? Meetings under Davis were more akin to the cleaning and maintenance of a complex machine that, on the car side, was producing the wrong products. The quality gurus preach "doing it right the first time and every time." And that was what the GM product development process was doing. But what never got said by the "Total Quality Excellence" consultants of the 1980s and '90s was that one must, above all, do the *right* thing right the first time. Perfect mediocrity, as GM had shown, was doomed to fail.

Tom, his health failing, soon retired. He left with some trepidation: having read my first book, *Guts*, he had grave worries that this "opinionated swashbuckler" (a title long ago bestowed on me by the head of human resources at Ford) would dismantle or seriously modify the carefully crafted, predictable, reliable, and seemingly risk-free process that was turning out one terminally dull passenger car and crossover after another.

Actually, Tom's fears were well-founded, but I like to think of what I subsequently did as "creative destruction." Soon, I became immersed in GM's brands and their future products. I was scheduled for lengthy meetings with the brand teams led by very smart young men and women, all equipped with big brains and sterling academic credentials. Significantly, I was not allowed to look at the products until I had been subjected to seemingly endless presentations on the quintessential character of, say, Buick or Saturn. This involved staring at large boards on which were proudly displayed the "brand pyramid," a huge triangle broken into fields containing profound (but painfully obvious) information on the customer and why he or she would buy this brand. All of this was invariably accompanied by a wall of photography showing unbelievably good-looking people of all genders and races who would form the typical customer base of, say, the forthcoming Buick Regal. Other pictures would follow—homes, furniture, watches, sunglasses, pens, pots and pans, and (almost without fail) a golden retriever or two, all indicative of the mood, or soul, of the brand.

It was unmitigated hogwash; almost any of the boards, including the human models and the pots, pans, dogs, and tropical fish, could have been assigned to any of the brands. And, far from being peopled by upscale urban sophisticates, our passenger car owner base was comprised largely of corporate or rental fleets and the less educated, less affluent, less photogenic Americans whose main reason for buying GM was what the "new buyers studies" lump into the category of "price/deal." In other words, we offered such large incentives that the Pontiac buyer could justify his purchase to his sneering, import-owning friends on the basis of fiscal responsibility.

To make matters worse, these "brand pyramids" were rarely, if ever, put together by the actual marketing people for that make. Instead, they were farmed out to advertising agencies, those vast repositories of "brand knowledge."

After the agony of feigning interest in the brand presentation, I hoped relief would come when the curtain finally lifted on the cars themselves. But relief soon turned to abject horror. The upcoming Saturn lineup was so ugly, inside the vehicles and out, that even the designer's mother would buy Japanese. None of the Saturns had any charm or ornamentation to delight the eye. Without grilles, none had any "facial" character, usually a key attribute in brand identification. Cars are like people that way.

When I remarked, "These vehicles seem somewhat devoid of character," I saw the marketing team beam with pleasure. This, I realized, is exactly what they had wanted! This is what they wanted to offer their carefully researched "postmodern" buyer, the person who (allegedly) didn't care about character, proportion, or design, but wanted a bland, anonymous appliance. Checking the brand boards, I saw that Saturn featured everything from store-brand detergents to functional, drab Birkenstocks. The Saturn Ion was an all-plastic marvel, as was the upcoming Vue. Both were too late in the process to stop. Both required loss-generating pricing and incentives to move them in the market. Some interior and exterior upgrades (including a front grille and some attractive chrome ornamentation) ultimately helped the Vue later in its life, but both vehicles showed that not even the "postmodern" buyer was willing to drive an amorphous blob.

We then had a lively discussion about Buick. Here, the "experts" had decided that the brand's focus would cater to the needs of the elderly. Toward this end, a system called "Quiet Servant" was conjured up. To my amazement, I was shown an interior mock-up featuring no instrument panel and no visible controls whatsoever. It was to be the world's first car operated entirely by voice command. Speed, gas level, and other relevant information were projected on the windshield.

"Folks," I said, "this is nuts!"

"No, no!" they insisted. They had shown a video to older people, where the fictitious driver merely said "headlights" or "left turn signal" or "radio" and the car instantly delivered. And, at the end of the video, 75 percent had expressed a strong preference for this miraculous system. But I'd learned to be skeptical of research in which subjects are shown an ideal, simplified version of a new technology where everything just works. Real life never quite lives up to the fantasy. Still, I agreed to drive a prototype.

I will never forget that drive through downtown Milford, Michigan, and the engineer sitting next to me probably won't forget it either. At his urging, I asked for "more cold air." "No, no!" he said. "You have to scroll verbally! First say 'climate control.' When the car says 'climate control,' you say 'blower.' When the car repeats 'blower,' you say 'up one.' Same with temperature." Of course, it wasn't that easy, and a comedy of errors ensued. I did the best I could, trying to remember the sequence. So fixated did I become with the marvels of voice input technology that I casually cruised through two red lights, nearly causing an accident each time. Quiet Servant should have been called Quiet Assassin!

The new system officially died the next morning. I announced it to the Buick team in person. One earnest young woman almost broke out in tears, seeing the whole purpose of the last two years of her life float away. But, to my surprise, it was a hugely popular decision, and many congratulated me on having the courage to eradicate what had been a festering sore in product development. It was going to cost a fortune to develop and nobody knew how to make it work. Flushed with success, I pressed on, terminating more bad designs and bad projects, but never enough.

GM's real illness resided, contrary to the foregoing, not in Engineering or the brands, misdirected as they were, but in Design, or, as it was formerly called, Styling. And it was here that I would focus my attention.

Even before officially joining the company, I knew Design was dysfunctional, but from the inside I could now see why. Normally, in an automobile company, and at GM during the golden age of the 1950s and '60s, the design department reports at a fairly high level and works with engineering, manufacturing, and marketing to design beautiful vehicles that, of necessity, can also be engineered, built, and sold at a profit. This was too simple for the brand-focused GM of the 1990s. One or several of the high-IQ group decided that "great design" could be subjected to a rigorous, multistep process, just like anything else.

The GM creative process began with APEX. (I was never sure what this acronym meant, but assume it was "Advanced Products Experimentation.") APEX resided in its own building. The employees were "conceptual designers"—that is, they could imagine things but couldn't actually draw them. Furniture consisted of orange beanbag chairs. Facial hair was rampant, dress was casual, and so was the work routine. The designers' purpose was to brainstorm, to conjure up that next big hit product that nobody had yet imagined. Free-ranging creativity was the order of the day, and, while I'm absolutely positive that there was no pot smoking going on, if the reader will imagine that there *was*, it sort of completes the mental picture. The output from APEX included jewels like "Why don't we do a flying car?" This actually received some attention, as well as a deluge of less extreme ideas which, when rendered on paper, would be researched with the public. The "big idea" was that perhaps out of hundreds of APEX ideas researched, four or five would advance to the next stage. I couldn't find any.

After APEX, projects moved to an immense studio that looked like a Hollywood set. Crammed with brand-significant "lifestyle" objects, including, weirdly, a yellow Ducati motorcycle, this major investment in "stuff"—screens, computers, scale models, theatre-seating furniture—all had a function I never quite grasped, nor did I particularly want to.

The next step in the convoluted process was the brand studio, the first place where actual, recognizable work was done. Under the leadership of Anne Asensio, a gifted French designer hired from Renault, "Brand" actually produced so-called theme models for upcoming vehicles of each brand. Once Anne's studios had produced a full-size model deemed acceptable and in keeping with "brand design cues" as handed over from Marketing and Design's own "Brand Central" (the Hollywood set) studio, it would be handed off to Jerry Palmer's "production" studios. It was here that the traditional design work, as we know it from other automobile companies, was actually done.

But, there were major problems. First, Palmer had limited freedom in creation, as he was basically handed a "theme" from the brand studios. Second, there was now time pressure from the vehicle line executives, who urged speed to compensate for the inevitable slippage in the upstream labyrinthine process. So Palmer, responsible for delivering finished designs acceptable to the VLEs on time, became adept at very quickly "productionizing" (further diluting) already boring and badly conceived "themes."

Wayne Cherry, vice president of design and Jerry's boss, vetoed many of Palmer's slapdash cars, only to be overridden by the all-powerful VLEs, who had the final say on vehicle aesthetics. Having nondesigners pass judgment on design is a bit like sending a sports bar full of beer drinkers to a wine tasting; besides, the VLEs were all in hot pursuit of one of their prime goals, one on which much of their PMP-determined success would depend: timing!

After killing off some of the more misbegotten future products (like a seven-seat Saturn Vue that looked like someone had grafted half of a camper body onto a normal Vue), I began to wonder what kind of consumer research the company conducted on future designs. I suspected it was lousy, and used poor methodology, and I said so openly.

Stung by the criticism, GM's design research folks came to see me and took me through the methodology used in the so-called Product Clinics, where future design proposals, in the form of very realistic (but unbranded) mock-ups, were tested against the current models offered by the competition. The goal in clinics of this type is to ensure that your new model scores a clear-cut, unequivocal win over the competitors currently in the marketplace. The win obviously must be by a substantial margin because by the time the new car comes out, the competitors will have upgraded as well. To my surprise, I found GM's research methodology to be excellent, much like that used to great success by Chrysler, and in some ways even superior. "Then how the hell do you explain all these ugly cars cleared for production?" I asked. Dave Mazur, the head of GM's research (now with Nissan) and his number two, Andy Norton, who now heads the group, assured me that every single new model had performed exactly as predicted by the clinics: they had all failed!

Shocked, I demanded to see the clinic results but was told that this was prohibited: only the pertinent VLE had access to the aesthetic performance of his or her vehicle. This well-intentioned rule was meant to prevent meddlesome intervention by third parties, like senior management. It also assumed that the VLEs would have a profound interest in ensuring that their design was a clinic winner—why wouldn't they be the proper custodians of the results?

Logical, but wrong: the pressure on meeting design-release dates was so intense that there was no time for redo. Jerry Palmer would address glaring concerns that could be handled with little or no slippage, declare the design fixed, and release it into the waiting hands of body engineering and manufacturing.

Now why, you may well ask, would a vehicle line executive knowingly accept a design he or she knew could not win in the market? The answer is simple: declaring the design unacceptable meant immediate admission of program timing failure, with swift criticism, probable loss of bonus, and other acts of retribution an inevitable result. Remember: the VLEs were *responsible for the design*. They approved it, so if it failed, they would have to be asked why they ever let it get that far. Pretending the design was OK and rationalizing the research results ("What do those people know about design anyway?") would defer evidence of failure by at least another two years! By then, who knows? He or she might have been promoted or might be in a different job altogether. Yes, better to defer the bad news, hide the problem in the time-honored GM fashion. I call it Pooping Pooch Syndrome: when a dog leaves a nasty pile in the house, he or she generally selects a spot where it won't be found for hours, maybe days. Why be swatted with a rolled-up newspaper first thing in the morning when there's a good chance of delaying it to late in the day or even to-morrow? This explains a lot of steaming piles found "later" in a lot of large organizations.

I ordered that all clinic results be shown to me, and that hence-forth the results be given reasonable distribution to those with a need to know, including Rick Wagoner. But I took that first pile of accumulated reports home over the weekend and realized, to my chagrin, that every GM car to be launched in the first three years after my arrival would be greeted with only the mildest of applause at best. (Predictably, in 2004, the media embarked on a "Lutz has failed" theme, noting that I had been in office for three years now and the vehicles were still found wanting.)

Some cars could be partially solved by delaying them—in one case, against the bitter resistance of the VLE. Buick's midsize sedan, the Regal, was to have been the lucky recipient of "Quiet Ser-vant." The brand-cue-driven design of that car was so horrendous and so overly directed by people with no sense of automotive art that the senior designer assigned to the project became physically and emotionally ill over having to execute a ridiculously propor-tioned, check-the-brand-cues monstrosity which he knew would fail. He needed a leave of absence. I saw the car and ordered it redone, which meant accepting a roughly nine-month delay. Using much of what was already locked in place, we executed an accept-able, tasteful car that didn't set any hearts on fire but that at least wasn't an embarrassment. It was the first-generation LaCrosse.

The Cadillac STS was another disaster in the making. With a steep windshield and a very flat roof, it exuded all the charm of a brick. I asked why the roof was so wide and flat, and the VLE explained that it was so we could reuse the sunroof from the prior model. (Remember: VLEs had "parts reuse" targets in those pesky PMPs!) I commented that it seemed silly to ruin the appearance of the vehicle just to save a sunroof and suggested that if reuse were the goal, they should take the one from the smaller CTS instead.

All saw the obvious "brilliance" of this proposal (which was also less expensive), and the roof shape, windshield angle, and tumble-home (the angle at which the car narrows toward the top, important for proportion and the look of stability) were now all available for correction, albeit with about a one-year delay. The VLE, mindful of his timing goals, was not amused and had the finance people churn out reams of data quantifying all the revenue lost by the delay. When this disagreement reached Rick Wagoner, he, to his everlasting credit, said, "I'm tired of seeing financial analyses telling us it's better to do a lousy car earlier rather than a good one later. We are going to delay this program, and get it right!" It was one of many times that Rick's support, at a critical juncture, facilitated the changing of the product-creation culture.

To illustrate my point on the state of design and research at GM on my arrival, here are summaries from some of the clinics and subsequent actions in the period just before I rejoined. These notes were supplied by a person close to these product programs at the time. Read and believe, if you can. It's all true!

1. Research for the original Cadillac SRX indicated that consumers disliked the angular, wagonlike exterior styling. A key designer, however, believed strongly that the car tested poorly due solely to its high level of design reach. He argued that they would like it in two years when it hit the market,

and that current consumers could not predict this future state. The marketing division made a strong plea to stop and redesign the vehicle. In the end, the decision was made to move forward in spite of the weak research results, in the belief that future consumers would be more accepting of its angular lines. Unfortunately, as predicted, consumers did not warm up to the design once it reached production, and it did not sell well.

2. The original Buick LaCrosse was tested in what was thought to be its final design form in September 2000. Despite poor ratings from consumers, however, virtually nothing changed in the design until [Lutz] came to GM in 2001. The car was also disliked by many people internally, and even the designers directly involved were upset at the results from rigidly applying brand character cues to an old architecture that lacked styling enablers, to the point of causing extreme stress and health problems for one of the designers. Similar to other programs at the time, it was on its way to being produced, even though it had tested so poorly, due to timing pressures and a general disdain for consumer input. I believe that [Lutz' team] redesigned the car as much as possible; however, the team was still somewhat tied up by timing, architectural constraints (old W car), and capital. More research was conducted on the redesign in June of 2002, and there was significant improvement . . . enough to make it a reasonably strong entry, but not a home run.

3. The Saturn Ion Sedan was tested in January 2000, and was less appealing than the car it was supposed to replace. Some modifications were made as a result of this clinic, but clearly not enough to create a strong design. Further changes to the design were necessary; however, this was resisted by the pro-

gram team and marketing, who were more concerned with program timing than creating a winning design.

4. The 2003 Pontiac Grand Prix was taken to a clinic in November 1999, and, like the Saturn Ion, was much less appealing than the prior-generation Grand Prix. The debate over this design was intense, with the frustrated VLE saying that he should "take a baseball bat to the research and forecasting group" in front of the NASB, and no one disagreed. Perhaps he should have taken his bat to the clay model as the car never sold well, and was primarily sold as a fleet car by year two of its life.

5. The Chevrolet Malibu was tested at a clinic in February 2000. This was the last-generation Malibu before the current model. What we saw in the clinic results was just mediocrity. It wasn't terrible, but clearly, it wasn't great. I think everyone internally had a more positive memory of this one because it was better than much of our other vehicle work at the time. Compared with our current standard, however, this program would never have made it. . . .

In the case of the Chevrolet Malibu, I asked the vehicle line executive if, perhaps, we should consider a redesign, since the car appeared to me (prior to viewing the research results) to be seriously wanting in both interior and exterior appeal. "Are you kidding?" he replied, "That car has done better in research than any other car in the last few years!" I found it hard to believe, but the clinic results showed it to be true. It was the best of those that failed, the valedictorian of the reform school graduating class.

And then there was "Bucky Beaver," a name bandied about by some of my new colleagues who had seen the all-new, aesthetically challenged Pontiac Grand Prix. The unfortunate moniker stemmed from the grille, which, with its sharply pointed twin ports, looked for all the world like the incisors of some demented, giant rodent. It left me fairly stunned; how could something that bad, the brunt of internal disparagement, be allowed to progress through failed research to ultimate design approval for production? I suggested the grille be changed, the opening widened, the sharp-toothed graphic removed, but due to the dictates of timing again, only minor changes in graphics were possible. "Bucky Beaver," bereft of his two front teeth, now looked more like a very large car with a very small grille. It was better, certainly, but the car, despite some undeniable attributes—for some reason, it was widely touted as the only car that could swallow a nine-foot kayak—never did well in the market. The number of kayak owners had been overestimated.

At this point, sensing that I was decidedly not dealing with the creative, vibrant GM I had known in the 1960s, I decided to take pen to paper and issue a few polite proclamations. Following is an excerpt from a note I penned to Rick Wagoner under the assumption that he had small inkling of the extent of the problem:

Dear Rick:

Attached is a memo that I've sent to my direct reports and some of my "process leader" colleagues.

Overall, I admire what the company has done over the last few years to create order and relative simplicity out of what used to be an unmanageable, chaotic "federation." It's working well, ensures discipline, and it works predictably.

However, the product creation system, as a whole, is too "democratic," gets too many inputs from too many cooks, and has to abide by too many questionable (but well-intended) "criteria" or maxims.

I already mentioned the weak position of Design, so I won't repeat myself here. My greatest concern is the near-robotic nature of the Product Planning (Portfolio Planning) process, an area I have discussed with Larry Burns. The so-called "needs" and "emerging segments" analysis system, I think put in by Vince Barabba, may also have "brought order" and I believe it brings a certain rational aspect that is necessary. But it is far too "user segment" focused and not enough "fashion trends" oriented. In other words, the system will identify "large sport-utility," but it won't identify "the Hummer H1 and the Schwarzenegger mystique may be telling us that there could be a market for a more producible derivative." The system will identify increasing interest in T-car-sized monovans, but it won't come up with "growing interest in funky, retro-styled, high-cube sedans á la PT Cruiser." And it could find "high-package, high-performance small car," but won't find "BMW Mini." The trouble is, we're analyzing segment, and sub-segment and sub-sub-segment growth without understanding what taste trends are causing those segments to grow in the first place. In the U.S., the PT Cruiser, through design, is *making* the segment.

I went on:

As I told Larry (basically, "I don't like all aspects of the system, but I *do* like *you*"), the process has the advantage of being just that: a repeatable and predictable way of generating data that is useful *as one input*. But it can't, by itself, drive the portfolio, or we'll proliferate ourselves to death with more and more 50,000-unit/year "needs fulfillers" and less and less 300,000-unit/year home runs.

I'm thinking of ways to improve this and to find a parallel

creative process, but I'm not there yet. In other words, I'm describing a problem without yet proposing a solution. Suggestions are welcome!

I also promulgated a set of what I called "strongly held beliefs." I didn't want to call them "rules" because that would imply a claim to absolute correctness, which is way more than I want to claim for my opinions, generally. So, the list is really a compendium of accumulated experience in four automobile companies, plus a strong jigger of medicine for what I thought ailed GM. Addressees were all my direct reports.

Strongly Held Beliefs

1. **The best corporate culture is the one that produces, over time, the best results for shareholders.** Happy, contented employees, and an environment where nobody argues or disagrees, and everyone compromises because the other person has goals, is usually not the culture that produces great shareholder value. A performance-driven culture is often a difficult place to work, and it certainly isn't "democratic." Democracy and excessive consensus-building slow the process and result in lowest-common-denominator decisions. As Larry Bossidy, former CEO of Allied Signal, so aptly said, "Tension and conflict are necessary ingredients of a successful organization."

2. **Product portfolio creation is partly disciplined planning, but partly spontaneous, inspired, all-new thinking.** A good planning process can be an excellent baseline tool, a means of generating solid data. But it cannot robotically create a good future portfolio. It will generate bunts, singles, walks, and the occasional double. But triples and home runs

come from people who say, "Hey, I've got an idea!! Listen to this!" Needs-segment analysis can find a "small monovan" niche. It can't find a PT Cruiser, or a new Mini, or an H2!

3. **There are no significant, unfilled "Consumer Needs" in the U.S. car and truck market (except in the commercial arena).** What there *are* are "consumer turn-ons" that research alone won't find.

4. **The VLEs must be the tough gatekeepers on program cost, content, and investment levels.** After (and maybe before) contract, requests for "priceable" content (it never works out that way, anyway) or "volume-improving" content can no longer be honored without offset. The VLE needs a program contingency, to be reserved for last-minute fixes or enhancements (and maybe I need one, too). But the VLEs must evolve into often-unpopular "benevolent dictators" when it comes to protecting their cost position. It must be *inviolable*. Programs that miss their cost targets cannot be tolerated.

5. **Much of today's content is useless in terms of triggering purchase decisions.** Most customers want a vehicle of new, fresh, exciting appearance, with a rich, value-transmitting interior. They want a great powertrain, superb dynamics, and, obviously, safety and quality. The thought that huge advances in voice recognition or display technology or embroidered floor mats will somehow override other deficiencies (or, worse yet, "averageness") is wrong. What focus groups say they would "really like in their next car" is not reliable because they are, when questioned, not actually paying for it. ("Talking cars" and all-digital instrument panels received high "want" ratings in their day.) The vehicles that are succeeding today (Honda, Toyota, Audi, VW)

are *not* highly contented, or if they are, they charge for the option packs. A "base" Camry is *really* base!

6. **Design's role needs to be greater.** Design is being "corporate-criteriaed" to death. By the time the myriad research-driven "best-in-class" package, the carryover architecture, the manufacturing wants, the non-stone chip rocker placement, the carryover sunroof module, and on and on are loaded in, and the whole thing is given to Design with the words, "Here, wrap this for us," the ship sailing toward that dreaded destination, "Lackluster," has already left the dock.

7. **Complexity-reduction is a noble goal, but it is *not* an overriding corporate goal.** Standardizing options for the sake of simplifying the BOM, engineering, and releasing effort, pricing, dealer stocks, etc. is very worthwhile. But it can be counterproductive if it reduces vehicle margins; i.e., the net revenue loss is greater than the demonstrated savings in the enabling disciplines. A good rule of thumb is that, in the case of an option with a significant cost, where the freestanding "take" is less than 70–75 percent, the incorporation as standard will cost money. If "priced for," then a large proportion of customers are being asked to pay for something they don't really want. If it's "eaten" and not priced, we are reducing margins without enhancing value to those who don't care for the option. My experience is that options running at 25–40 percent should *remain* options (perhaps grouped into packages), options running at over 75 percent should be incorporated as standard. The area between 40–75 percent requires judgment in each individual case, and a good dialog between affected parties.

8. **We all need to question things that inhibit our drive for exceptional "turn-on" products.** Edicts and criteria do

some good; they create consistency and order, and they help someone achieve a goal that he or she feels is important. But many of our criteria are *internally focused* and prevent us from doing high-appeal, exciting, dramatically new products. A salesman cannot say to the customer, "It takes a bit of getting used to, I admit, but did you know that it satisfies one hundred percent of GM's internal criteria?" We don't want anarchy, but we do need more of a "Who says?" attitude. The focus has to be on the customer.

9. **It's better to have Manufacturing lose ground in the Harbour Report, building high net-margin vehicles with many more hours, than being best in the world building low-hour vehicles that we take a loss on.** We need to recognize that everything is a trade-off, that we can't maximize the performance of any one function to the detriment of overall profit maximization. The same goes for every discipline: A gorgeous vehicle that disappoints in quality will fail. A car incorporating every conceivable new safety technology makes no contribution to safety if it becomes unaffordable to the customer or we can't afford to build it. A vehicle with a single-minded focus on "absence of things-gone-wrong" will fail miserably if it is dull, unexciting, a dog to drive, and ugly. Even if it's the best ever found by J. D. Power!

10. **Remember the Bob Lutz motto: "Often wrong, but seldom in doubt."** None of us is infallible, and we all make errors. Remember baseball, where a batting average of .400 is unheard of! But pushing and arguing for what you believe to be the right course (while recognizing you just might be wrong, therefore, still willing to listen) is the key to moving forward. Errors of commission are less damaging

to us than errors of omission. In our business, taking *no* risk
is to accept the certainty of long-term failure. (Even Aztek,
in this sense, is noble!)

This memo, with distribution to only my sixteen direct reports, circulated through the GM system, top to bottom, propa-
gating at near light speed. Soon, the media had it and reprinted it
in its entirety. I was actually glad for the visibility it received, for it
put all on notice that a new wind was blowing in GM product
development.

Most of the talented engineers and designers at GM saw this as
a long-awaited freedom manifesto, and that's how it was intended.
In a large company, the real talent often lies among those with
specialized skills but no MBA, doomed to toil in relative obscurity
while their more managerially trained colleagues get the promo-
tions. It's hard to get real leadership intent down to "the troops," yet
it is vital if they are to be fully motivated. This memo did it, and I
received many messages of thanks and encouragement, some even
from hourly employees. A minority was less than thrilled; they
were deeply invested in the status quo. Some e-mailed Rick Wagoner, complaining that Lutz's swashbuckling, antiprocess religion
views were risking the destruction of the carefully crafted, reliable,
and utterly predictable GM product development machine, where
everyone did their job (sort of), was tolerant of everyone else (part
of the big problem), and produced a seemingly endless stream of
cars which, though bravely carrying names like "Achieva," could
well have been badged "Mediocra."

I also encouraged the employees of Product Development
to develop a healthy sense of anarchy, to question process that led
nowhere and edicts or requirements that made little sense but
were treated with the reverence normally reserved for scripture. I
created stickers bearing the words "Sez Who?" and handed them
out by the hundreds. I wanted to see some cracks in the rigid

foundation, cracks big enough to insert the necessary sticks of dy-namite. My two initial targets were Design and the whole "brand management" system, the latter being beyond my organizational responsibility.

We started with Design, but even before undertaking any or-ganizational changes, I ordered up an additional concept car for the upcoming North American International Auto Show in De-troit, slated for early January 2002, just four short months away. It was to be an attention-getter, an unexpected statement from "moribund" GM, a demonstration of practical design excellence in a novel format. It would become the rear-wheel-drive Pontiac Solstice two-seat roadster, using as many major components from the GM "parts bin" as possible.

The effect on the Design group was electrifying: they were being granted the freedom to create the world's most desirable, affordable sports roadster, with no list of hundreds of "require-ments" to hog-tie them. So powerful was the emotional appeal that Wayne Cherry, the disenfranchised head of design, saw it as a way to reestablish his now-questionable legacy, and became per-sonally involved. He started a competition among all of GM's thirteen far-flung design studios; the ensuing tidal wave of newly liberated creativity was gratifying.

The design that captured the imagination of all was one from a young designer at GM's advanced studio in California, Franz von Holzhausen. The sketch was compact, muscular, loaded with pent-up energy. (Interestingly, when the car appeared at the De-troit show to tremendous acclaim, I was asked by European jour-nalists who the designer was. When I gave the name, the Germans said, "Ach, no wonder," as if to say, "We knew it! Way too good to be American." They were crestfallen when I pointed out that Franz was third-generation U.S.-born. Trust me, chauvinism and provincialism are alive and well in the automotive media.)

We set about transforming the sketch into full-size clay, and it was then that I sensed the first inkling of the creative power and drive to succeed, to overwhelm, to be the best, that had lain dormant in the quiet halls of Product Development. Fostered by years of frustration and repression, the energy was about to burst forth and result in a stream of new products that would amaze the experts and the public alike with their beauty, craftsmanship, and driving characteristics.

The surprise came in the form of an advance concepts group led by Mark Reuss, serving as president of GM North America as of this writing. Mark, captivated by the idea of Solstice, decided that, rather than an engineless design study, the little two-seater would be a fully functional, drivable car. With only four months left before the January 2002 Detroit show, it was a near-impossible task. But the fact that it was accomplished, with a real, stamped metal body, a fully functional interior, and a four-cylinder, rear-wheel-drive powertrain which, at the time, didn't exist in the GM inventory, was a stunning demonstration of a capability in the company that the media and analysts would continue to deny. It was thrilling to be able to reveal the little car personally at the Detroit show, where it was voted "Best Concept." It served to put the outside world, and me, on notice that great things could be expected. Media acclaim was huge and justified.

But transformations in mentality and focus are not created overnight by one single car, no matter how strong a signal for change it sent out. An early setback came in the form of the GMC XUV, one of the proposals I had initially wanted to kill. This was a curious beast. Riding on the chassis of GM's midsize SUVs (Trailblazer and Envoy), this proposal, on the longer wheelbase, was the unfortunate child of one of GM's intellectual edicts: 40 percent of all future products were to be "innovative," an all-new vehicle type, not a GM version of something someone else had already successfully launched. But, while the thought and desire were laudable, it was the pernicious GM philosophy of setting numerical targets for everything that caused trouble. Instead of a free-flowing system where creativity came naturally, GM had a rigid, highly analytical planning structure that struggled to meet the "40 percent rule." Consequently, some really unfortunate projects consumed resources because they helped meet the goal.

The XUV, in short, was plain weird. With the overall profile of an SUV, it possessed a movable center partition that could be placed vertically behind the front seats. With the rear two rows of seats removed, it possessed a load floor, not unlike that of a midsize pickup. But what about the roof? That was the "big idea," a 1960s Studebaker station wagon redux: on top of what would normally be the roof was mounted a large cassette (making the vehicle look strangely high and pinheaded) containing a mess of connected slats not unlike the front of an old rolltop desk. At the touch of a button, the roof over the rear two-thirds of the vehicle would slide open, enabling the owner to transport trees as well as grandfather clocks in a vertical position.

My instincts said, "This thing is salesproof," and I suggested cancellation. It was then that the vehicle line executive set his analytical machine in motion. I was invited to a meeting presided over by a young woman of enviable intellect. In one hour and with countless PowerPoint slides, she showed me overwhelming numerical evidence that this vehicle, the unique XUV, would be good for *at least* 90,000 units per year, maybe even 110,000! The resulting profitability would be huge! And these 90,000 units were necessary to "fill" the second assembly plant, which, if I insisted on cancellation, would be gravely underutilized! The unabsorbed fixed cost would then have to be allocated over the existing midsize Chevrolet and GMC SUVs, thereby damaging *their* financial performance.

Although still skeptical, my "newness" to GM's vast analytical prowess thoroughly intimidated me. After all, with all this intellect and all this crunching of numbers, all this examination of "owner profiles" and "user segments," how could I, intellectually no match for the assembled brilliance, override them? I said, "Well, OK, let's leave it in the program."

Two years later, after endless hand-to-hand combat with sensor reliability, motor sequencing, lubrication, durability, water leaks, redesigns, and cost overruns, the XUV was proudly unleashed on a motoring public that didn't have the foggiest clue what they would ever use the thing for. Besides, it was ugly and expensive. Sales struggled, and after a grand total of 13,000 units were produced and forced into an unwilling market, production was stopped and the loss written off. It was a bitter lesson for me, but it taught me to adopt an attitude of total disdain for what the legions of high-grade-point-average MBAs in the "volume" planning group came up with. While my gut was sometimes wrong, a ten-minute look at a product and its pricing normally delivered a more accurate estimate than one delivered by "the system."

So, the situation I faced in the first few weeks was this:

- A disenfranchised Design group incapable of establishing an aesthetic direction, as they had no control over the final design.

- Input from Marketing ("Brand Management") that was perhaps appropriate for a soft drink or cosmetics company, but wide of the mark for automobiles.

- A Planning group obsessed with "needs segments," thinking that vehicles fulfilled certain identifiable consumer "needs." (As I pointed out frequently, the only real vehicular "need" that most customers have is easily fulfilled by a two-year-old used car; everything else is psychology and "wants.") These various segments all have complex but ever-so-important-sounding designations, like "Macro 34."

- An Engineering group that, over the decades, had established a stifling thicket of criteria: where the wheels had to be placed relative to fenders, how the windshield should slope to permit easy viewing of overhead traffic lights, how ashtrays were to open and close—all well-intentioned, and all inhibiting the freedom of design to create beautiful cars. (Prior to my arrival, GM had purchased a Chrysler 300M, the most spectacular of the successful "LH" cars. In the center of the Styling Dome, having been asked by senior management why GM couldn't come up with a car this beautiful, Design displayed the 300M adorned with more than ninety Post-it notes, identifying the areas where Chrysler had violated GM criteria.)

- A vehicle line executive system which, while orderly and predictable, was obsessed with meeting internal goals like cost, weight, hours of assembly time, parts reuse percentages, and, especially, timing. "Success in the marketplace" and "best new vehicle in its class" were targets pursued solely by the full-size truck and SUV VLE and the near-maniacal VLE in charge of Corvettes. And the other VLEs routinely rejected valuable input from the market research group.

- A generalized tolerance of sloppy execution. Body gaps (the width of the space between adjacent body panels) were large and uneven. Upholstery was lumpy and crooked. Plastic parts were cheap, poorly grained, and shiny. Switches and controls looked and sounded like plastic toys. Paints lacked sparkle and luster. No wonder that import owners, renting a GM car on a business trip, routinely found themselves reinforced in the resolution never, ever to consider a GM car. (Again, things were much better in full-size trucks and SUVs, and more than a few owners of high-end German cars owned a Tahoe or Yukon full-size SUV.)

• A senior management team, at least in the United States, that was seemingly oblivious to these problems. "We have smart people, carefully hired engineers, skilled planners, a history of great designers . . . we set budgets, quantify targets; what could possibly go wrong?"

• A regionalized patchwork of product development organizations and manufacturing groups around the GM world. This resulted in needless local duplication of essentially similar products in each of GM's main regions. While there was some sharing of engines and transmissions, there was little or none in platforms, brakes, suspensions, air-conditioning, seats, body structures—all the elements in a car that consume engineering investment and which can easily be done once, globally, with local adaptations. Even testing methods and protocols were different from region to region. GM, I realized, wasn't the world's largest car company—it was a holding company aggregating the sales numbers and financial results of four regional car companies operating quasi-autonomously.

So, it would be a daunting task, one that would require much more than the three years of my initial contract. Without much analysis or making of to-do lists, I tackled them pretty much all at once. Luckily I was soon joined by an ever-larger force of motivated people who saw, in my presence and priorities, liberation from the shackles of mediocrity.

Tackling the 800-Pound Gorilla

DESIGN CAME FIRST. I KNEW THAT THE TEA-LEAF-READING APEX GANG, brainstorming useless ideas from the comfort of their orange beanbag chairs, had to go. So did the massive "Brand Central" studio, with its mix of artifacts from all walks of human life and multimedia displays. The "brand development studios" that came next in the sequence held no real value either since their efforts were routinely trashed and redesigned by the production studios under Jerry Palmer—the only studios that were creating any added value in the sense that their designs would actually be produced. The trouble was, they were the wrong designs, the focus on pleasing the VLEs and meeting their timing.

I just wanted a good, old-fashioned design organization, one where individual studios, under studio chief designers, worked on individual vehicles from inception to production with no hand-offs. But what to do about the people? Jerry Palmer, although a fine designer, was locked in perpetual battle with his boss, the venerable Wayne Cherry. We couldn't afford that, and Palmer was about to retire.

Human Resources, acting on behalf of Rick Wagoner, advised me that my first priority was to replace Wayne Cherry. The view, apparently, was that he was nearly sixty-five (true) and no longer capable of overseeing great design (false). As in so many instances, the problem was seen in the person rather than in the institutional obstacles to the person's performance. When responsibility for selection of the production design went from the vice president of design to the VLEs, the former became powerless and doomed to failure. Still, I dutifully conducted a search and interviewed a selection of the world's most renowned and successful automotive designers from the United States, Europe, and Asia. I couldn't find one with better artistic skills than Wayne Cherry; I had to stop searching and get on with fixing the place. I asked for, and was granted, a one-year extension for Cherry.

It was to be a year of redemption for him. Freed once more to decide what would go into production and auto shows, his crowning achievement was the incredible Cadillac 16 show car (another "runner," by the way, with a 1,000-horsepower V16 engine under its long hood, acclaimed universally as the finest expression of an ultraluxury sedan in modern times).

Within weeks, the dreaded APEX was gone, as was Brand Central and the "brand development" studios. Every studio now worked on real projects, supported by some small, unfettered advanced studios in California, the UK, and Warren, Michigan.

The vehicle line executives grudgingly accepted their loss. Emotionally, they felt slighted; rationally, they couldn't argue that their stewardship of design had produced any notable successes.

In the new organization, Design would create a winning proposal, one that was declared feasible for production by Manufacturing and Engineering. The operative word was "winning." No car or truck was to proceed to approval for production unless and until it had scored a resounding victory in the design clinic, where the full-size mock-up, unbranded, was arrayed against the best of its natural competitors, also stripped of brand identification, and assessed by impartial observers. The proposed GM car or truck had to win on exterior appeal as well as interior appeal, and it had to win by a substantial margin. After all, the competitors might well be replaced by an improved product by the time ours came out.

This produced some interesting tensions. Frequently our winning design (and they pretty much all won their clinics after we placed the focus back on styling) would be subject to some detailed criticism for poor visibility or lack of shoulder room compared to the competitors. This almost always triggered cries of "We've got to fix that. They want more room. They want more visibility." In the bad old days, that got fixed: a more upright, boxy car with a stiff windshield. Problem solved, but nobody bought it. I had to keep pointing out, "Hey, guys, we won the clinic by a wide margin! They know it's less roomy, they know it's harder to see the overhead traffic lights. Yet they still want that car because of the way it looks. So, let's be happy and quit screwing around, or we'll mess it up again." A seemingly simple lesson, but one that bore endless repetition: even the smartest of the left-brain thinkers had trouble with the concept of trade-offs. In the automotive game, as in other parts of life, appearance counts. If the public loves a car, its other deficiencies are quickly rationalized away.

Only when the vehicle design was an uncontested clinic winner was it turned over to the VLE for execution. That was their job, and they did it, for the most part, well.

It proved to be a good move to keep Wayne Cherry that extra year. He provided stability and motivation during the tough transition back to normal automotive design activity. He would be replaced, once we completed researching the best the outside world had to offer, by our very much homegrown Ed Welburn, the first African American ever hired into GM's lily-white Design staff in the early 1970s. Upon his elevation, he became the first-ever African American vice president of design, and just the sixth man to lead GM Design in its long history. It was to be my finest personnel decision: Welburn, with his style, taste, coaching and mentoring abilities, has taken GM Design back to a level exceeding the halcyon days of the 1950s and '60s.

As stated, when he started, Welburn inherited a department trying to change an entire culture, not to mention a stable of product shortcomings. Above all, there were the interiors: dark gray plastic wastelands. Some Pontiac instrument panels had all the appeal of molten lava that had spilled through the sunroof and cooled. GM's interiors were the worst in the business. When I complained, I was told, "On the contrary! We have fewer problems with our interiors than any other car company, according to J. D. Power." Ah, once again, the analytical left-brainers coming up with the wrong answer. Our "freedom from defects" merely meant that our speedometers worked and the knobs didn't fall off. Of course, many potential customers never experienced the "defect-free" part because the depressingly shoddy appearance of the car's insides kept them from making the purchase.

Interiors had, over the years, gotten short shrift. They were not only an afterthought; they were the last happy hunting ground for the stressed VLE trying to make his cost target after absorbing dozens of overruns from suppliers. So, the part of the car that, next to the exterior, is the most important, the one in which the customer spends 100 percent of her driving time, was cheapened to a level that could only be termed hopelessly uncompetitive.

We established, within Design, an Interiors Group, initially led by the hard-driving, no-nonsense Anne Asensio, who had been freed up when "brand development" was cancelled. Equal in rank to the head of exterior design (up till then, designers assigned to interiors thought they were being punished and sent back to the minor leagues), even the formidable Ms. Asensio had trouble with the added cost she was proposing. The solution was simple: we established category-relevant targets based on competitive cars. We

laboriously cost-estimated interiors of Audi and Lexus (for Cadillac and Buick) and Toyota and Honda (for Chevrolet) and set those
costs as "allowable targets." Thus, interiors had their own, more
realistic targets, and were freed from the grasp of the cost reduc-
ers. It was another painful takeaway from the VLEs, but a necessary one.

Product Planning was another area mired in a morass of data,
attempting to find a quantitative, reliable, repeatable way to come
up with hit products. As with everything else at GM, the approach
had sterling intellectual credentials, but in a world driven by whim,
fashion, and fluctuating fuel prices, it just didn't work. Product
planners in the car companies I have known tend to be much like
finance people: everything must be based on numbers, whether
historical or projected. As the numbers get played out in elaborate
tableaus of predicted volumes and profits (minus, of course, the
volume and profits of other, vaguely similar GM cars displaced by
the projected new one), numerical precision tends to be confused
with accuracy. It always amazed me to witness a room full of highly
educated, intelligent executives looking at Product Planning's
future sales projections, broken down by retail and fleet, with the
list of substituted existing GM models calculated down to the
single unit five years from now. I frequently punctured that bal-
loon by asking, "Are you quite sure that, in 2012, we'll lose 581
Cadillac Escalades due to this program? Are you quite sure that
582, or even 585, wouldn't be a better number?" I'm not sure the
irony in my voice ever penetrated the impassable closed-loop walls
of Planning's quantitative fortress, because years later the same
type of data would still be presented. The only difference was that,
in the later years, it tended to be greeted with more of the scorn
and derision it deserved.

The error in the traditional Product Planning methodology is
that it crowds out art, creativity, and spontaneous invention. It as-
sumes that automotive consumers are highly rational people who

will perform analyses and elaborate feature comparisons before making their purchase. As we well know, they don't. The customer buys brands, and some are cool, and some aren't. The customer is highly design-sensitive, and some cars are attractive, and some aren't. When I was first taken through GM's hugely complicated "needs segments" model, I said, "OK, your model can find categories of vehicles, but can it identify fashion trends and segments? Would it, for instance, have identified the (highly successful) Chrysler PT Cruiser?"

"Of course we can nail that 'needs segment'! It's Macro 389, small multiplace monospace!" would be the response. I argued that identifying a segment for what is essentially a small minivan was *not* the equivalent of coming up with the highly fashion-oriented, retro-styled PT Cruiser. One was defined by its physical characteristics, the other by the space it occupies emotionally. Endless repetition of this theme did not make much of a dent in the Planning group's mentality, and this overly analytical approach to the future portfolio is not exclusive to GM. At Chrysler, the group of executives who essentially ran the whole show had developed such disdain for Planning that I, at one point, had to address the Chrysler Planning group en masse and explain that I didn't dislike them; I just disliked what they *did*.

As at Chrysler, we learned at GM to use the Product Planning group to do what they were good at: run numbers and conduct analyses of alternatives, with the results sometimes accepted, sometimes not. Some of the future cars were the product of the Planning group, while others were born of the inspiration of the Design group (the natural repository of creativity in an automobile company).

I began pushing some products through to production that were not blessed by Planning, or were not born of their "needs segments" model. One was the Pontiac Solstice, fresh from its triumphal tour of auto shows. Where would one find a "rational

Harley Earl in the famous 1938 Buick Y-Job, the world's first concept car.
(COURTESY OF MICHAEL LAMM, LAMM-MORADA, INC.)

The 1937 Buick fastback sedan with a well-executed art deco design.

The 1940 Cadillac convertible. This is another example of a sleek design theme with superb attention to chrome décor.

The hugely successful 1955 Buick.

(COURTESY OF GENERAL MOTORS LLC. USED WITH PERMISSION, GM MEDIA ARCHIVE)

The 1955 Coupe de Ville: the apotheosis of the Harley Earl era.

(COURTESY OF GENERAL MOTORS, LLC. USED WITH PERMISSION, GM MEDIA ARCHIVE)

The first iteration of the Chevrolet Corvette, America's most successful sports car.

The 1959 Chevrolet: the height of the fin era.

(COURTESY OF GENERAL MOTORS LLC. USED WITH PERMISSION, GM MEDIA ARCHIVE)

The 1965 Pontiac GTO. Early GTOs are prized collector cars because of their elegance, power, and affordability.

(COURTESY OF GENERAL MOTORS LLC. USED WITH PERMISSION, GM MEDIA ARCHIVE)

The 1969 Chevrolet Camaro is still considered an iconic design of impeccable proportions.

Bill Mitchell, the vice president of GM Design from 1958 to 1977, whose work drove the company's market dominance.

Jim Roche, the CEO of GM from 1967 to 1971. Even the smallest details never escaped his attention.

**The ill-fated Pontiac Aztek, produced in 2000,
shows how far GM's designs had fallen.**

(COURTESY OF GENERAL MOTORS LLC. USED WITH PERMISSION, GM MEDIA ARCHIVE)

**The Aztek represented a low point in GM's planning and execution process,
and its unbridled homeliness became the stuff of comedians' jokes.**

(COURTESY OF GENERAL MOTORS LLC. USED WITH PERMISSION, GM MEDIA ARCHIVE)

The 2005 GMC Envoy XUV.

(COURTESY OF GENERAL MOTORS LLC. USED WITH PERMISSION, GM MEDIA ARCHIVE)

The 2003 Chevrolet Silverado pickup, showing an excessive hood-to-fender gap.

The 2007 Silverado showed much-improved quality.

The interior of a prior generation vs. current Cadillac interior. A complex and disorganized design is replaced with a graceful and elegant approach.

(COURTESY OF GENERAL MOTORS LLC. USED WITH PERMISSION, GM MEDIA ARCHIVE)

The 2007 Chevrolet Malibu displays a tighter fit between the adjacent parts.

(COURTESY OF GENERAL MOTORS LLC. USED WITH PERMISSION, GM MEDIA ARCHIVE)

GM's product development hit its stride in 2007, winning double honors: both the North American Car and Truck of the Year awards for the Saturn Aura and Chevy Silverado.

(COURTESY OF GENERAL MOTORS LLC. USED WITH PERMISSION, GM MEDIA ARCHIVE)

The Chevy Malibu, crowned the 2008 North American Car of the Year.

(COURTESY OF GENERAL MOTORS LLC. USED WITH PERMISSION, GM MEDIA ARCHIVE)

The 2008 Cadillac CTS, the *Motor Trend* Car of the Year.

(COURTESY OF GENERAL MOTORS LLC. USED WITH PERMISSION, GM MEDIA ARCHIVE)

The revolutionary Chevrolet Volt, an extended-range electric vehicle, which entered production in November 2010.

(COURTESY OF GENERAL MOTORS LLC. USED WITH PERMISSION, GM MEDIA ARCHIVE)

need" for a small, high-styled two-seat sports car with almost no luggage capacity? Another was the Chevrolet HHR, a somewhat boxy, funky five-seater with strong 1950s overtones. The thought behind it was "Why let Chrysler have it all with the PT Cruiser?" Why, indeed, since vehicles of that type typically command a higher price than the mundane compact sedans on which they were based, while the cost to manufacture was only slightly higher.

I asked Design to start a full-size HHR model, and this caused considerable consternation. In the hands of Bryan Nesbitt, who had designed the PT Cruiser before coming to GM, the full-size clay was termed "out of process." Not fully understanding the term, I discovered that "the process" called for six more months of analysis before the decision would be made regarding possible derivatives of the Cobalt compact architecture. It was too early to settle on one! I wanted to know why. "Because there might be other, better, alternatives."

I countered, "Like what? You have a sedan and a coupe. You can't do a pickup. What on earth could you possibly come up with other than this high-cube, cool retro model?" Well, there was no answer that made any sense, and it was clear that the HHR idea was the only viable option, but the point was, it was in violation of "process." In this particular case, and in many others, slavish adherence to a predetermined, rigidly followed sequence of events merely slowed precious time to market. Over time, and especially in the case of the Pontiac Solstice, "process" and its application became more flexible.

A digression: What I call the "process religion" stems from the 1980s and 1990s "Total Quality Excellence" consultants, who descended upon corporate America like a swarm of rapacious locusts. It was generally argued that Japanese manufacturing superiority was due to a rigid adherence to "standardized work" in the assembly and machining plants. Every worker, no matter which shift or plant, was to perform a given operation in a rigid, unvarying way. No experiments by the worker were permitted, no using both hands to feed the line faster if that wasn't what the "process" called for. In this way, variability was taken out of the factory environment and reliability, predictability, and quality was put in. So far, so good, and a valuable lesson for the West. But then the concepts of "process" and "standardized work" were expanded beyond manufacturing. If it's good for the factories, some reasoned, why wouldn't it be good for every other part of the company, even the creative ones?

Here is where the profound intellectual error was made: the rest of the company *isn't* a factory. Almost nothing is done repeatedly, exactly the same way, a thousand times per day. Whether it's Design (the least amenable to standardized work), Sales, Marketing, Purchasing, Engineering . . . new situations, vendor products, competitive actions, legal changes, and software upgrades occur daily and weekly. The attempt to reduce these activities, which require flexibility, adaptability, initiative, and "Hey, let's try this shortcut" thinking, to a "process" merely results in an unthinking, robotic organization where everyone is on autopilot. The best part is that if you follow process and the result stinks, you're safe: you did what you were told. A lot of money was misspent in the last couple of decades of the last century on process apostles.

At any rate, my healthy disdain for an orderly but failing planning process came to be accepted by the planners, and we achieved a satisfactory and often humor-filled mutual tolerance between the unfettered idea guys (me and the growing number of right-brained creative people now enjoying greater autonomy and flexibility) and the mechanistically data-focused planning activity. Neither liked the way the other operated; both recognized the value of what the other was doing.

One curious cultural characteristic I encountered at GM was an exaggerated respect for authority. It is bred into the system. Senior people are seen as being in possession of some superior wisdom, to be revered if not downright feared. The reality is that the company's most senior executives are just people who happened to get promoted and who daily face the insecurity of wondering if they are doing the right thing. The good leader deals with that insecurity by putting forth his or her ideas, then letting subordinates dissect and critique them. At Chrysler, we often had chaotic meetings, where some of my direct reports engaged in behavior that an outsider would have termed insubordinate bordering on mutinous. But that's when we had the clearest communication and surfaced ideas and opinions devoid of the buffering wads of tissue paper designed to avoid hurting someone's feelings.

At GM meetings, I often found that not a lot got said. Other than "the presenter" (often hardly listened to, because everyone had seen all the material in advance), no voices were heard. In fact, for the most senior meetings, GM invented a crazy system wherein not only the subject presentation was seen in advance, but questions and comments based on the presentation were also distributed. By the time the meeting actually occurred, everyone had read the presentations as well as the usually sycophantic comments (intellectual tours de force, many of them, designed to display the depth of thinking and profound knowledge of the commentator), and only "questions" were dealt with. The answers had also been created in advance, appeared on the big screen, and it came down to asking the original questioner if the written answer satisfied his or her curiosity. It always did.

What was lacking in all this organizational, almost ritualistic perfection was the spontaneous, productive, healthy, sometimes angry discussion that ensues in a less structured format. It was as if the system had been set up for the sole purpose of promoting "smoothness" and lack of discord. An admirable societal goal, perhaps (though I doubt it), but hardly the sign of a high-performance organization.

In my area, Product Development, I could set the tone. I chaired my early meetings—with my staff and the dozen or so vehicle line executives—with my usual blend of outrageous statements, deliberate exaggerations, mild sarcasm, and funny stories. This has usually proven effective for me: people see through it, realize it's a bit of an act, feel more at ease, and begin to relax and contribute.

Not so in some of my first meetings with the Product Development folks. As I delivered my usual soliloquies, I saw nothing but heads bent over the table, pens scribbling furiously on notepads!

"What are you people doing?!" I asked.

"Well," they told me, "you're talking, and we want to remember what you're saying, so we're taking it all down."

"Look, people," I replied, "I tend to have a lot of ideas and strong views, which are not necessarily correct. But I want you all to know what I think and believe about a lot of subjects. I know I'm full of crap a lot of the time, but that comes with the territory. Your job is to provide me with honest feedback. I don't know everything, especially not in this company. I guarantee I will never be angry or hold a grudge if you argue intelligently with me. You can even, with impunity, tell me that I'm full of crap, but you will need to preface it with the phrase, 'With all due respect, sir, you are full of crap!'" That brought forth the first genuine laughter, but the group was still wary.

A few weeks later, during one intense meeting, a stocky, powerfully built VLE and successful amateur race driver named

Tom Wallace looked first at me and then at the group, took a deep breath, and said, "OK, here goes, I'm gonna try it. . . . 'With all due respect, sir, you are full of crap!'" There was the slightest moment of tense silence, and then I congratulated him on being the first to test me. We all laughed; the meetings got progressively better after that. (By the way, Tom wasn't right in his opinion on the subject, but it didn't matter.)

All in all, the vehicle line executive system was a good one. It resembled the successful "Platform Team Leader" structure then in place at Chrysler. But it was flawed in that it gave the VLEs authority over critically important areas for which they were not qualified, such as Design. And, as mentioned previously, their ocus was on a set of dozens of carefully quantified goals. These were pursued with great zeal and energy, for a "perfect" all-green scorecard at the end of a program could mean substantial additional compensation for the successful VLE.

One VLE came to see me in "one-on-one" time and brought his scorecard. He made sure I understood that he had met or beaten every single target; it was solid green, with no yellows or reds. He deserved, in his opinion, a big juicy chunk of that special VLE compensation fund. "How's it selling?" I asked. "Well, really not that well; the press on it was lousy, and the public is unenthused. But, I can't be held accountable for that. I was handed my numerical goals, which were signed off by everybody, and if I make them all, that's success!"

Once again, the tyranny of process over results! I was speechless and realized that I had to teach the VLEs that they would be held accountable for the success of the vehicle, and I didn't give a damn if they had some "yellows" and "reds" sprinkled around their report cards.

It went down hard. A few weeks later, I met with one VLE, Dave, to review his clay mock-up in Design. It was nicely shaped but, without any ornamentation, it looked depressingly cheap. "It needs some chrome, Dave, especially around the DLO." (DLO means daylight openings, or side glass. Expensive cars almost always have the DLO framed in chrome.) Dave said, "I know it needs it, and I'd love to put it on, but I can't afford the cost or I'll miss my objective."

Me: Does the car need it?

Dave: Yes, it does, but—

Me: Would it do better in the market with the chrome?

Dave: Yeah, sure, but who's going to protect me at report card time? I'll have a red on cost!

Me: Dave, you'll get a gigantic red on the whole goddamn program if it doesn't sell in high numbers. And if it does well, you're a certified hero, and nobody is going to question a minor cost overrun.

Dave: I sure hope you know what you're doing, Bobby!

The car was the current Impala, a relatively low investment re-skin of the truly homely predecessor. Although not an exciting car, the Impala, with its tasteful shape and well-applied ornamentation, has been one of America's secret best sellers since 2004, regularly turning in volumes of between 250,000 and 300,000 per year. It is a frequent winner of the title "America's best car for corporate fleets," where it's a roomy, fuel-efficient, and attractive mainstay. It has delivered extraordinary profitability for a moderately priced full-size sedan. Nobody ever talked about the chrome-induced cost overrun. And Dave retired a few years ago as a respected and successful VLE.

But the VLEs were not the sole defenders of mediocrity. Manufacturing, Engineering, and Purchasing also played their roles. Again, all of them strove earnestly to meet predetermined and process-driven goals; nobody was goofing off or dropping the ball. Everyone worked hard to feed the internal demands of GM, fulfillment of which would lead to praise and compensation.

Take GM's exterior body paint, which I had criticized from the outset as dull, almost grainy. None of our cars in 2001 had paint that exuded vibrancy or stood out in a parking lot. My complaints drew a sharp reply from Manufacturing: "You're totally wrong. We have the best paint in the entire industry. In J. D. Power, we have the lowest number of paint defects per car of any company, Toyota included!" Once again, the usual confusion: a restaurant that advertises "the lowest incidence of food poisoning of any restaurant in the state" does not necessarily serve the best food. (In fact, it almost certainly doesn't.) And "absence of complaints" does not equal excellence.

Throughout my career, I have always been surprised by how often people mistake customer satisfaction for an absence of complaints. Ford of Europe, in the early 1980s, wanted to kill the popular Escort convertible because, like most convertibles, it received a high number of complaints for wind noise, top-flapping, water leaks, and so on. Taking the convertible out of the lineup would have improved the average Escort quality score to the target level even though no single Escort had actually improved! This was supreme idiocy: the Escort convertible had the highest level of owner satisfaction of any Ford of Europe product. Kill the car the owners like best to meet your numerical "things gone wrong" target? It didn't make sense to me, and I told the crestfallen "Escort Quality Improvement Team" to find some real improvements.

The GM paint was another spectacular example: by reducing the sheen of the paint, minor defects such as an embedded dust mote or a minor "run" on a vertical surface were much less apparent to the customer. Of course, the customer experienced no joy or pride in her car's paint; it was just "OK."

My nagging finally induced Gary Cowger, soon to be presi-

dent of GM North America and an executive of impeccable manufacturing background, to investigate further. Some months later,
I was invited to a joint Engineering/Manufacturing paint team
meeting. The team's conclusion: I was right. In scientific measurements of paint brilliance, image clarity, and reflectivity, we were the
industry's worst performer. (But . . . low complaints!) The team
presented an upgrade plan, involving both paint type and application methods; the stated goal was to beat everyone in paint excellence without giving up too much in "things gone wrong." In less
than two years, we got there; even our competitors, who conduct
the same type of cross-make benchmarking we had performed,
asked our people, "What the hell happened?" From rock bottom
to parity with Lexus. The change was noticeable by all; any car
looks better with a superb paint job. The average buyer may not
be able to say *why* it looks better, but it just does.

This was but another example of GM knowing how to do it right,
rallying to the challenge, and getting the job done. The obstacle
had been, as always, pursuing a subgoal that was easy to game instead of putting the real objective above all.

There's an old, presumably apocryphal tale about body integrity, good body sealing, and absence of unsightly gaps around the
hood, trunk, and doors. It goes like this: To test for the car's air-
tightness, Toyota engineers would leave a cat in the car in the evening. The next morning, if the cat was active and chipper, there
was obviously too much air entering the car somewhere. But if
the cat was limp, listless, or near dead, this indicated a tightly built
car. Hearing of this cat test, a GM assembly plant also placed a
feline in a just-assembled car, shut all the vents and doors, and
awaited the morning. But, when the engineers came back to
check the next day, the cat was gone!

The obvious exaggeration can't hide the fact that GM's body

fits in North America (we knew how to do them in Asia, Europe, and Latin America) were deplorable. The precision of sheet metal, like paint, is another element of so-called perceptual quality. Most people will tend to prefer a car on which everything fits perfectly, even though they can't articulate *why* it looks good. GM's standard for body gaps was five millimeters, with a variation of up to two. In practice, this means a trunk lid could have a three-millimeter gap on one side, a seven-millimeter gap on the other, and be declared "acceptable." The German cars routinely show four- or five-millimeter gaps, but with little or no variation; same goes for most Japanese brands. In the United States, Ford had begun to master well-assembled sheet metal.

I complained and complained and started carrying a gap gauge with me, making a show of using it whenever reviewing one of our production cars, loudly proclaiming the bad results and wondering, rhetorically, when somebody was going to fix this. It turned out that I had an ally: GM retiree Alex Mair, a car enthusiast and former GM chief engineer, would spend his free time going from dealer lot to dealer lot measuring the gaps on, say, twenty Cadillac DeVilles and then, down the street, doing the same on twenty Acuras. The results would be painstakingly recorded in Alex's jiggly handwriting: he would calculate the average of each brand's gaps, as well as the size of the plus-minus range. The news was never good for GM, and I doubt that Alex got much positive feedback for his trouble except from me. (I hadn't been on the distribution list initially because he felt it was more of an issue for manufacturing than product development. He was right, but the fact is that I cared *deeply*.) So, "Alex Mair's gap analyses" became a weapon of choice, and my incessant barrage increasingly got attention.

Several weeks later, a large meeting was held out at Milford Proving Ground, north of Ann Arbor, Michigan. Dozens of new GM cars were lined up, as well as many new competitive cars from

Japan, Korea, and Germany. Senior executives from Product De-velopment, Design, Quality, and Manufacturing trooped from car to car with a young, dissatisfied, disruptive executive rattling off the bad news. His name was Mano Mavroleon and his criticism of the status quo was so strident that he was seen as "disloyal." ("If he likes other people's cars so much better than ours, why doesn't he go work for them?") It's true that Mavroleon could have been more sensitive to the feelings of those who weren't addressing the problems, but he was essentially focused on the same things I was. But, when a vice chairman is critical, it's wisdom. When a junior person does it, it's insubordination. (How I ever survived that phase of my career is still a mystery.)

After sheet metal analysis of at least twenty cars, with plenty of editorial comment from me, a curious thing happened: a truly gigantic man, at least six-foot-five and 240 pounds of muscle, placed himself squarely in front of me. He leaned his rough-hewn face down into mine, grabbed me by the lapels of my suit, and raised me up on my toes. (At six-foot-two-and-a-half, I'm no midget, but this guy was in another league.)

Making sure that every word would register on me and his audience, the giant said, "OK, I think I've heard about as much of this shit as I want to. YOU are now going to take ME to the car that you think is best, and we're going to focus on that one."

Shrugging my nice suit back onto my shoulders (my antago-nist was wearing a Harley-Davidson leather jacket, with much embroidery and many patches), I walked over to the best car, sheet-metal-wise, of the bunch. It was a Hyundai Sonata, 2002 vintage.

Joe Spielman, for that was this intimidating figure's name, pro-ceeded to march me around the Sonata. His finger would point to a hood corner: "You want sharp 'bird beaks' like that?" Yes. Next, the doors: "You want flushness and gaps and parallelism like this?" Yes. "You want moldings to align like these here?" Yes. "You want . . . you want." Yes, yes. "OK, I got the goddamn picture. Guys?" he said, calling his subordinates. "See this car? That's our new standard for sheet metal. I want you all to remember what you're seeing. Measure it out and take pictures."

Turning back to me, Spielman said, "This is what you want, and if you give me just a couple of months, this is exactly what you're gonna get."

I was a bit doubtful: an encouraging performance, but I had seen those before. Still, it was Joe Spielman, and he was in charge of "Metal Fab," the division responsible for sheet metal. And Spielman was known far outside GM as a manufacturing executive who actually got things done. Before I joined GM, several people knowledgeable about GM had told me, "Remember the name Joe Spielman. If you ever need something done, he's your guy." Now we were going to place Joe Spielman in a culture where excellence is not only encouraged, it's expected.

Sure enough, the ultrapatriotic, Harley-riding, Corvette-collecting Joe Spielman made good on his promise. He greatly improved the build of existing cars, but the vehicles in the pipeline would be engineered, and their metal stampings tooled, for world-class perfection.

Over time, Alex Mair, to his astonishment and delight, would report that twenty randomly selected Chevrolet Malibus had, on average, much better, tighter sheet metal fits than twenty Honda Accords. Our cars became so close to perfection that Mair stopped his dealer visits and turned his attention to other aspects of retirement, presumably equally rewarding.

In the later years, before Spielman retired, I asked him how the miracle was performed and with so little apparent investment. His answer was another eye-opener: "It didn't cost much. We had to upgrade some hemmers [presses that create the folded edge of the outer sheet metal panel over the inner one] for a crisper hem flange, but mostly it was just explaining to the supervisors and operators that this is what we want. Turns out, they knew how to do it, and actually wondered why we had never asked for that kind of precision before. They were enthusiastic!"

So, once again, the company had people with both the talent and the desire, but it never put them to use. Sometimes, the media would ask me when GM would start producing "decent" cars, like the Japanese. I frequently challenged them to do the Alex Mair Test: "Go to dealerships and see for yourself. Take a new Chevrolet Malibu and go down the street to a BMW dealer. Place the Malibu next to the Beemer, look each over carefully, and then tell me which one is assembled to a higher standard." To my knowledge, nobody ever did it. It probably didn't fit the generally accepted "truth" that GM's cars were sloppily stamped and assembled.

Meanwhile, over in Interiors, the redoubtable Anne Asensio was fighting a battle with all the "best practices" folks from all the functional areas. "Best practices," those ways to do things that were written down in some digitized scripture, usually involved specifying methods and materials that were lowest cost and involved the least amount of assembly time. This meant using nameplates like "Chevrolet" or "Equinox" cast all in one piece to reduce mounting time (and avoid spelling mistakes), or using the "hider" design technique (beloved by thriftier manufacturing organizations) on the instrument panel. Instead of adjacent plastic pieces being sharply squared off to minimize any gap between them, the "hider" technique calls for making everything with big radii at the corners, more or less the shape of an old TV screen. That way, if adjacent panels don't quite line up, it's much harder for the customer to tell. It's analogous to mounting pictures in elliptical frames: hard to tell if they're crooked! Or designing a watch with really fat pointers so that it's tough to see if it's a few minutes off.

"Hiders" are nothing more than a cheap trick to reduce complaints about poor fits by making everything so nonlinear that the customer can't quite figure out if it was supposed to be that way or not. Needless to say, many other auto companies eschewed the practice and created instrument panels that looked like the work of a skilled cabinetmaker. I wanted that!

There was resistance: It would cost more (true). It was more difficult to assemble (not if the build of the car is sufficiently precise). Customers wouldn't notice the difference (they hated GM interiors for *some* reason). Anne and her team fought bravely, but once beyond the design stage, the new instrument panel would be engineered, and the materials specified. "There must be some mistake here," the responsible engineer would say. "We've never specified sharp corners like this before, or half-millimeter gaps. I'll just change this all to the way we've always done it!" And so, low-gloss would change back to high-gloss, fine graining (the leatherlike imprinting of plastic parts) would change back to coarse, tolerances would revert from "tight" back to the old standard. As Anne chased these practices through the system, adopting a "seek and destroy" mind-set, she ultimately wound up at the suppliers. And here it started all over: "GM has never asked for anything like this before. There must be some mistake. We'll just change the specification back to what they've always accepted."

At Anne's request, we called all the suppliers of interior parts to a large meeting. I addressed them personally and told them what we wanted. If there was any doubt, or if they were getting "mixed signals" from our own engineers and purchasing people, they were to contact Anne or even me directly.

My friend, fellow Marine aviator and vice president of engineering Jim Queen (more on him later), was a powerful ally: he appointed a senior executive as the person responsible for interior perceptual quality. Jim called him "the knothole"—everything had to pass through him until the new standard was fully understood and accepted.

The beleaguered, brave Anne Asensio was viewed by many as the mad Frenchwoman who was disturbing the carefully nurtured culture of poorest-fit, lowest-quality material that would reliably hold together. It was like a clothing store selling tailored burlap bags that fulfill all the functions demanded of clothing.

To reach the people who actually performed the work, we initiated Friday afternoon Perceptual Quality Program Review, or PQPR, meetings. Vehicles at every step of the pipeline would be analyzed for crooked seams, clunky knobs and switches, gaps between adjacent parts, too much or too little gloss . . . anything a customer would see, feel, hear, or touch.

Key competitive vehicles, usually Audi, VW, or Lexus, were routinely present in the room. For four or five solid years, I "taught" those classes personally. Was that the best use of a vice chairman's time? Most organizational theorists would probably say no. I just couldn't find anybody else to do it, at the outset. Later, as the culture changed and the participants from Design, Interior Engineering, Purchasing, and Manufacturing all became infused with the vision of making GM interiors the envy of the automotive world, it became self-sustaining. By that point, I knew the culture, as far as interior and exterior precision were concerned, had reached the point of no return. Bad executions were simply no longer going to get through the system. So focused on excellence did these teams become that, as a proud observer at the later PQPR meetings, I would sometimes find myself thinking, "Wow! I didn't even notice that, and I doubt many customers would!" But I always kept that reaction to myself.

The "perceptual quality" problem was, after a few painful years, solved for good.

Meanwhile, Vietnam veteran, F4H Phantom pilot, and U.S. Marine captain Jim Queen, a man of medium stature but towering presence, created a team to clean out many decades' worth of antiquated "engineering requirements"—methods adopted by

GM after something went wrong. In the 1920s and '30s, for instance, there was a problem with tires blowing out against rocks in the wilds of Alaska. Solution: create a test at the GM Proving Ground so severe that this could never happen again. It's called the "curb test," whereby the car is driven over a four-inch steel-edged curb at normal speed. The tires and wheels must survive the brutal impact. Good! But to achieve that performance, tires must be fat and pillowy and the steel or aluminum wheels small: exactly the opposite of today's style trend to larger wheels with tires of much-reduced height. So, no eighteen-inch (or, heaven forbid, nineteen-inch) rims for us. I asked about competitors who routinely sold cool-looking wheel and tire combinations in the U.S. market and was told, "Oh, they all fail the test! In fact, [German competitor with a great reputation] actually suffers front suspension failure!" So, we had ugly wheels because of a problem we experienced seventy years ago!

The position of the wheels relative to the side of the car bothered me, too. Cars look dynamic and stable when the outside tire face is flush to the body, a look many competitors, notably Audi and BMW, pursued consistently. Our wheels tended to be "tucked" under the car, with a lot of sheet metal clearance to the outside of the fender. It made the vehicles, seen from front or back, appear overbodied, unstable, even unsafe.

One reason: less damage to the paint when driving on gravel roads. This might have been a major issue in the 1930s, but today it's easily solved by applying a rubberlike primer to the lower portions of the body. It's called anti–stone chip primer, it's universally used, and it's not rocket science.

The second reason was the tire clearance standard. Our tires and wheels had to be sized and located in such a way that, under full-lock, with the largest tire and wheel available, and under full suspension travel (as in going over a large pothole, at speed, with the steering maxed to one side—an unlikely combination of events, when you think about it), there was to be no tire contact with any sharp, unfriendly metal. Fair enough. "But please tell me how BMW and Audi do it and, closer to home, Chrysler?" "Oh, well, they use a different type of flange to join the front fender to the wheelhouse. There is no unfriendly contact." "Is there anything preventing us from using the same type of flange?" "No." Problem solved. We got larger wheels and tires, and they moved outboard to greatly improve the visual proportions of the cars.

My favorite was the sliding ashtray. One day, comparing the interior of a Cadillac STS with a similarly sized and priced Acura, I touched the tray, which shot out of its recess as if from a gun. To return it, I nearly stressed my index and middle fingers to the point of discomfort overcoming the massive spring pressure. But on the Acura, a slight touch to the face of the tray sent it gliding slowly and silently to the open position. A gentle, effortless push returned it, just as silently, to its closed position. A senior interior trim engineer was watching me perform this comparison: "Did you see the difference?" I asked. "I sure did, Bob, and this is a proud moment for me!" Say what?! "Proud?" I exclaimed. "Proud of the fact that ours is almost impossible to use?" "No, sir, but ours is the only ash receiver in the industry that meets the requirements of GM standard 33909664780 [I am making this number up]. None of our competitors, not one, not even Mercedes, meets that standard!"

The standard, and you will have a hard time believing this, was that any movable opening in a GM interior must be fully functional after a night at minus 40°F. (Or Celsius, for that matter—they're the same at 40 below.)

So here's the logic: A guy goes to his car in North Dakota at 5:30 AM on a minus-40° morning. The doors, hopefully, are not frozen shut. The engine, mercifully, starts, assuming the battery is fairly new and in good condition. As the car coughs to life, the driver, shivering and waiting for the defroster to clear the windshield, decides he needs a cigarette. Imagine his surprise and shock, his utter disgust with the car, when the gliding ash tray won't glide! Once again, we engineered for an extreme situation, one likely to occur, oh, maybe once every five years, and alienated literally thousands of customers living in more normal climates on a daily basis. People could be forgiven for thinking GM doesn't "know how"! But, sadly, we *did* know how; we just wanted something "better."

There were hundreds, maybe thousands of these sacred do's and don'ts embedded in the engineering culture, and Captain Queen's special team, meeting day in and day out at 6:00 AM, systematically eradicated 90 percent of them. (The rest, I think, probably made sense, somehow.) The fact that this "death by a thousand small cuts," as Design liked to say, existed in the first place is, once again, testimony to a culture that was inwardly focused in pursuit of its own goals, with the customer left out of the equation (except for that chain-smoker in New Leipzig, North Dakota).

Learning to Go Global

(What Took So Long?)

FOR ABOUT TWENTY YEARS, A TOYOTA COROLLA HAS BEEN THE SAME, whether built and sold in Japan, China, Brazil, the United States, or Europe. The same is true for the Honda Accord, all Volkswagens, Audis, BMWs, and Mercedes. This wasn't so much a strategy as it was the natural consequence of a company with only one headquarters, and one engineering and design staff. There is no other way but for the "home office" to execute the product offerings for its far-flung regions, because the "regions" don't have their own capability.

But Ford and GM, having expanded overseas way before World War II, did have capable product "sources" around the globe. In GM's case, it stemmed from the acquisitions of Vauxhall in the UK in 1925, Opel in 1929, and Holden, in Australia, in 1931.

For decades, having these regional, semiautonomous car companies was an advantage: brands were still largely regional, they were close to their markets, the types of cars demanded by Europe versus the United States were light-years apart, and economies of scale were available at lower volumes.

But beginning in the 1980s, this began to change rapidly. Brands such as Audi, Nissan, and VW became recognized throughout the world. Federal fuel economy regulations were driving the size and mechanical layout of U.S. cars ever closer to the rest of the world. Tastes, thanks to the mass media as well as specialized car publications, were converging. (It's interesting that, when GM conducts consumer clinics to test a potential new design, there is little divergence in results between China, Brazil, Chicago, or Frankfurt. Every culture, it seems, responds to the same aesthetic signals when it comes to cars.) Economies of scale ran away from the regional model. As competitive pressures and government regulations increased, so did the cost of designing and engineering an all-new vehicle. What used to require $200 million of engineering was now easily $700 million. Suddenly, GM's regions found it increasingly difficult to create a full portfolio of competitive products while remaining within some reasonable range of overall engineering expense.

A good example was the perceived need, in each region, for a small SUV. With independent budgets for engineering and capital, each region saw the need and the relatively small volume (it was an emerging segment). The combination of a huge engineering and capital outlay for a new and unique little four-by-four could not be financially justified by GM Latin America. Europe's volume was a bit higher, but it didn't "pencil," either. Nor did proposal after proposal in North America.

Toyota, with the hugely successful RAV4, faced no such problem: each sales region in the Toyota empire identified the need for the new small SUV niche: 20,000 here, 30,000 there, 50,000 for Europe, 80,000 for the United States, and so on. Add the numbers up in one program and suddenly the engineering bill makes sense. The potential component volumes get the favorable attention of world-class suppliers, unique regional "wants" are either incorporated or rejected, the program is approved and becomes a huge success, and is followed shortly by the Honda CR-V, a result of the same centrally guided process.

But GM was culturally locked in to the concept of regional autonomy. It was argued that skilled, relatively empowered executive teams in the four regions—Latin America, Europe, Asia-Pacific, and North America—responsible for their own resources and held accountable for financial and market success, would provide optimal results. It sounds true. It was true, twenty years ago, and aspects of it are true today, but all the advantages of regional autonomy simply got swamped by the increasing market demand for ever broader product lineups as well as the ballooning cost of developing an all-new vehicle. Product sharing among regions was a necessity, and if some of the benefits of regional, close-to-the-market decision making got lost, that had to be considered collateral damage.

The emotional distance between GM's regions was even larger than the thousands of miles of physical separation. An illustrative story: Circa 2000, about one year before I rejoined GM, *Car and Driver* published an overwhelmingly favorable road test on GM Australia's locally developed Holden Commodore SS, a V8-powered rear-wheel-drive sedan of about the size and layout of a BMW 5-Series. The subtitle of the article went something like, "The good news: it's the best GM car ever. The bad news: you can't buy it." I thought to myself at the time: "Why wouldn't GM do the relatively modest amount of engineering change to make the car legal for the United States, import it as a Pontiac or Buick, and finally give the American performance car enthusiast the product that nobody believed GM was capable of building anymore?"

So, I asked the question when I got my feet under the desk at GM. The reasons not to do this came pouring in, mostly revolving around the fact that it wasn't "our" car. It "belonged" to GM Asia-Pacific. GM Holden, when it found out about my interest, was very enthusiastic, but GM North America, as a whole, was not.

At one point, I was presented with a Pontiac Grand Prix which had been extensively modified, switched from front-wheel drive to rear-wheel drive and fitted with the ubiquitous small-block V8. "If this is really what you want, why deal with Asia-Pacific? We can do exactly the same thing, right here in North America!"

I wasn't buying. Changing a car that much really meant "all-new car," and at the anticipated modest sales volume, would never make business sense. I just kept insisting on a Holden-based idea, which had evolved into a coupe body style, to be marketed as a reborn Pontiac GTO.

Months passed in arguments over "transfer price" and "Who's going to pay for the engineering and the tooling for the U.S. headlights?" GM North America's view was "Why should we fund an Asia-Pacific project so they can sell in our market?" Asia-Pacific's view was "You're the customer and the beneficiary; why should we pay?" My somewhat naïvely utopian view was "Hello! This is all GM. These are wooden nickels we're pushing back and forth. Toyota wouldn't be having this stupid discussion, since they care about *corporate* profitability and don't suboptimize by region."

A trip to Australia by a number of us convinced the skeptics that the car was great to drive, unique among Big Three offerings, and potentially very profitable. The Australian dollar was, at the time, worth about fifty-seven U.S. cents. Unfortunately, during the unnecessarily long gestation period, it rose to eighty cents. That difference destroyed what was to be a very nice profit and caused final pricing of the GTO, initially targeted for around $25,000, to rise above $30,000, ensuring a lukewarm market acceptance.

It was during Australia's execution of the program that we found out just how different the regional GM "companies" were. Engineering standards were not the same. Measurement and targeted life of components bore little resemblance to those used in the United States. Testing standards were entirely different, requiring most durability testing to be painstakingly duplicated in the United States because we couldn't trust what Holden had done. It *was* as though we were dealing with a completely unrelated car company.

The car finally reached North America, looking less fresh with an additional two years of age on the design and a price tag which, at more than $30,000, was very much on the high side for a Pontiac. Nevertheless, fans of V8-powered American rear-wheel-drive cars loved them, and the reborn, short-lived, Australian-built Pontiac GTO is now a sought-after cult car.

But the GTO's value to GM transcended the disappointing sales numbers: it had gotten the two engineering groups together and had convinced many previous skeptics that maybe, just maybe, there were other parts of GM that also knew how to engineer outstanding automobiles.

I argued tirelessly for a global, centrally administered product development and capital investment budget. Fortunately, the waste involved in creating very similar but totally unique cars for Daewoo (now under partial ownership of GM), Opel in Europe, and Chevrolet in the United States was not lost on Rick Wagoner, so "global product development" began to appear on the agenda of the monthly Automotive Strategy Board meetings. It inevitably encountered fierce and, at times, emotional resistance. From a human standpoint, it was utterly logical: control over "the product" is the ultimate prize in the car business. The regional leaders had painstakingly climbed the complex career ladder to be finally appointed as a GM regional president. A whole, mostly autonomous auto company, with tens of billions in revenue, was there to be guided. What greater power trip than to stride into a design studio, followed by an entourage of loyal staff, and, after due contemplation, point to one of the clay models and state, "We'll do *that* one!"

It all came to a head when GM Asia-Pacific decided they needed a compact SUV and proposed creating an all-new, ground-up vehicle. I argued that we already had a successful architecture, fully engineered, in the Saturn Vue and Chevrolet Equinox. Using what we had, I argued, would save time, money, and scarce engineering resources. Further, if we made the Daewoo SUV stylistically and mechanically excellent, it could, in turn, become the long-desired compact SUV for GM Europe. And, finally, the styling and engineering done for Europe's Opel and Vauxhall could, in turn, become the next-generation Saturn Vue. My vision was to have a family of GM compact SUVs—Chevrolet Equinox, Saturn Vue, GMC Terrain, Daewoo Winstorm and Opel Antara—all different as necessary, all adapted to their markets, but all sharing common parts in those areas where differences provide no brand value: air conditioners, seat frames, braking systems, basic body structures, and more. Fierce arguments raged over this program, and Fritz Henderson, at that time the president of GM Asia-Pacific (later, CEO of GM after the firing of Rick Wagoner), quite naturally led his region's charge for its very own compact SUV. The decisive Automotive Strategy Board meeting rolled around, and both the "globalists" and the "regionalists" recounted familiar arguments.

After much discussion, Rick Wagoner spoke: "In the decades I've been in this company, I've listened, time after time, to reasons why it is critical for this particular vehicle to be totally new and different. And, just as many times, we later ask ourselves why on earth we did that. I'm tired of it, frankly, and we are going to execute the Korean company SUV based on the architecture we already have for the Vue and the Equinox."

And so a key blow was struck for intelligent product sharing across GM's regions. Since I feared he might be stung by what he considered a major defeat, I penned this memo to Henderson:

> Thanks for accepting the decision of the GPDM. I hated the fact that we had a conflict, and felt like a hypocrite because of all the times in my career where I fought hard (and almost always successfully) for the "regional" solution. But, in this case, it was much less about "winning" than it was to really get GM into a global, total-system optimization path, much like Honda. When I look at the golden opportunity GM North America has with the adoption of the Holden VE program for Chevrolet, Pontiac, and Buick, saving us hundreds of millions in engineering and vendor tooling, and, conversely, when I see the relative failure to obtain the synergies we wanted with Epsilon and Delta architectures ("We have to re-tool locally anyway, so why not change it?"), I am convinced that an intelligent global architecture strategy, with flexibility, to be sure, is the way to go. In this particular case, there is no doubt that the GMAP proposal was the best for your region. Yet, I do believe that, for our company as a whole, giving up one inch of width (vs. GMT-1901 Equinox) and losing the availability of the XK6 engine will prove to be small prices to pay for the major downstream and, as yet, unidentifiable savings and synergies. Again, Fritz, I hated the controversy, and I hated disappointing Nick Reilly and the guys. But, as they say, "Nuttin' personal; it's strictly business."
>
> See you soon.
>
> Bob

And thus was launched the first, albeit imperfect, global product program in the modern GM. Two more years passed before the most crucial step: the creation of a centrally administered global product development budget, with attendant capital budget.

Decisions, once the system was fully up and running in 2005, were made at the Global Product Development Council, on which all regions were equally represented. Final authority rested with Rick Wagoner and the monthly Automotive Strategy Board.

This is where I'd wanted us to go, but getting there wasn't easy. Pleased with the success of the compact SUV program, we launched a global program for the next-generation midsize sedans, now finally on the market as the award-winning Opel Insignia, the Buick LaCrosse, and the Buick Regal, with more to come. Even though approved as global architectures in principle, they faced a jungle of regional approvals, questioning, rejection, redos, and more questioning. The problem was that global product development was, by acting globally, essentially spending capital and engineering resources that were still the budgeting responsibility of the regional president.

The number one machete wielder in all this was, once again, Jim Queen. Accepting the physical burden of more international air travel than any human should have to endure, he tirelessly met and negotiated with GM's far-flung engineering teams, working to create a common language, common corrosion standards, common testing methods, and a common global engineering database and CAD system, in record time. Through persuasiveness, logic, persistence, and, when required, sheer strength of his impressive personality, he forged one functional global engineering entity out of four previously very distinct ones.

Once it was done, we could rest assured that cooling tests, durability tests, timing milestones, and everything else engineering organizations do were done one way. Much thought was devoted to how to engineer bodies, for that influenced stamping operations and assembly plants.

While Jim Queen devoted his entire time to the standardization of engineering, Gary Cowger was doing the analogous job for GM Manufacturing. Under uncontrolled regionalism, there was no set GM way to weld bodies, nor was there a process in paint, trim, and final assembly. We decided we needed what Cowger and I called "interbuildability," the ability to take the design of any GM car from any region of the world and very quickly assemble it in any other region. ("Good luck, Bob," Cowger told me. "This is like the tenth time somebody has wanted to do this at GM, but we never got it done.") But that dream became reality with the successful build of the "next-generation Epsilon" (GM architectures were given Greek letters as code names) midsize cars, produced in Europe as an Opel/Vauxhall, and in China and North America as a Buick. This was followed by the new Chevrolet Cruze. GM's global compact became a huge commercial success on every continent and is assembled in GM plants in Korea, Australia, China, Europe, and the United States. This would have been unthinkable ten years ago.

Achieving "interbuildability" around the globe meant not only common engineering and design practices, but also common welding sequences, common methods, common measurements, and common tooling and equipment. A big task, but it got done.

The first really large global program, the "Epsilon" midsize car, was also the first to be assigned to a global vehicle line executive, whose authority and influence would transcend the region where he was based.

Global Epsilon was to replace, with one basic chassis, midsize sedans from Daewoo, Chevrolet, Pontiac, Buick, Opel/Vauxhall, and Saab. Given the spread of price range, some of the executions would be clearly nobler than others. This was achieved by designing various suspension systems of increasing sophistication, but which, as Cowger required for his global interbuildability plan, always bolted up to the underbody in exactly the same way. Whenever we talked about variants of the main theme, we became accustomed to hearing Gary say, "Do anything you want to do, just give me the holes in the same place."

Global Epsilon, carrying behind it the resolve of the corporation to finally engineer a given set of cars once, was an icebreaking ship: it moved forward, slowly edging through an iceberg of regional rules, edicts, requirements, sometimes in direct conflict with one another. Week after week, this process would flush out dozens of issues that had to be resolved in favor of one solution, either by Manufacturing or Engineering, or both.

One such issue involved the location of the central locking control: North American customers expect it on the driver's side door, Europeans on the center console. Neither subsidiary would give, each considering it important for customer satisfaction. In that particular case, we decided we had to do both, even though it introduced different wiring harnesses and interior plastic tooling.

In its early phase, Global Epsilon's vehicle line executive was one Jon Lauckner, a lifelong GM engineer and planner. With a sharp wit, an argumentative nature, and a very un-GM propensity to recognize bad performance and do so out loud, Jon was respected more than loved. Jon never ran in a popularity contest but was always intent on getting the job done for the shareholder. He was later to play a key role in the creation and development of the revolutionary extended-range electric Chevrolet Volt.

Lauckner, as was his nature, was more than pleased to captain the icebreaker as it smashed through oceans of frozen bureaucracy, creating a clear, unencumbered path for global programs that were to follow on Epsilon's heels.

One of the first things Lauckner did was to ascertain the supplier prices for the major components of the then-current Epsilon cars: the Opel/Vauxhall Vectra, the Saab 9-3, the Daewoo Epica, the U.S. Chevrolet Malibu, and the Pontiac G6. Jon's team analyzed the costs for all these cars of such "invisible" things as seat frames, window lift mechanisms, fuel tanks and fuel management systems, heating and air-conditioning, brake systems, and many more. Quite logically, we expected some divergence in the

prices paid for these functionally similar but geographically dispa-
rate and differently engineered and manufactured parts from various global suppliers. Ten percent, perhaps even fifteen.

None of us was prepared for the shock we received when we
saw the results: some seat frames cost three times as much as others.
Heating and air-conditioning was no different: there were huge
divergences in component cost. Lauckner's assigned purchasing
executives immediately went to work, picking the best features
and then dangling a huge prize in front of the global supply base:
instead of 200,000 parts here, 150,000 different parts there, the
supplier companies were now asked to bid on as many as one and
a half million identical parts. Finally, GM was able to tap true economies of scale.

Heating and air-conditioning was sourced at what had to be
a record low price, and other components followed suit. Epsilon
was well on its way to achieving a double-digit cost reduction in
its base architectural components, despite many engineering enhancements and quality improvements. The point was proven:
global engineering saved money.

With global Epsilon (later dubbed "Epsilon 2") solidly on its
way, Lauckner was brought back to the United States from the
architecture team's German home base and was promoted to the
task of overseeing all global vehicle line executives reporting to
me. (With fifty or so Jon Lauckners, I've often observed, GM
would have been a far more stressful and less convivial place to
work. We would also have been far more effective.)

Lauckner was replaced by another of GM's very finest: a superb
engineer and executive in his late forties named Jim Federico.
With a radically bald head, a powerful, swift-moving body, and a
broken-looking, aquiline nose, he could be cast as a successful
prizefighter or, in a black suit and sunglasses, as a Mafia lieutenant
working his way up to don. His piercing gaze missed nothing and
intimidated everyone.

The Epsilon 2 models Federico has brought to market thus far are all resounding market and financial successes. The first was the Opel/Vauxhall Insignia. It quickly became the new standard of German midsize cars, sold extremely well in a weak market, and was named European Car of the Year by a jury of fifty senior automotive journalists from all major countries. The vehicle went on to garner more than 120 major awards.

The Insignia was followed by the larger, longer Buick La-Crosse, manufactured in both the United States and China. It was highly acclaimed in both of the world's largest markets and, in North America, is drawing a new, younger, more upscale set of buyers to the Buick brand. As of this writing, it was America's best-selling large sedan.

A brief digression: Early in the decade, I was asked by the media why GM was keeping the Buick brand. Our intention, I explained, was to make Buick into an American Lexus: elegant, refined, quiet, high-quality, but with better road manners and a lower price. Rarely have I ever made an utterance to the press that was so roundly ridiculed. "Har-har, that'll be the day," about sums it up.

Six years later, thanks to the hugely successful Buick Enclave luxury crossover (not a global program, as vehicles this substantial have little market outside the United States), the LaCrosse, and the smaller Epsilon 2–based Buick Regal (Jim Federico's latest off-spring), few would argue that Buick did not surpass the target. Buick, today, is "the better Lexus."

The outstanding critical and commercial success of Federico's Epsilon 2s (and there are more to come) meant that the icebreaker had, with some delays and minor restarts, vanquished the regional "frozen middles" and had cut a clear channel for the other, equally major global programs to navigate.

The part of globalization that never came about (and still should) is tracking of program cost, investment, and profitability on a global basis. With regional profitability goals superimposed on a global powertrain, product development, purchasing, and manufacturing system, there is much energy still wasted on who pays for what and who has control over "the budget."

For example, if GM North America, under extreme profitability pressure, decides to save fixed costs by reducing engineering and design staff, they run afoul of Global Product Development. Of course, that's exactly what happened. These product development resources, although also (and this is the silly part) in GM North America's cost structure, were really under my budgetary discipline and control.

The company struggled with the concept of global budgets cutting through regional lines. There is still an enormous sense of conflict in knowing there is a tough cost cutter as president of GM Europe, say, who will drive to reduce resources for greater profitability, even if they aren't his (or hers) to reduce. Running a company by region is fine for many industries but no longer optimal for car companies. You have to go global, with the regions reduced to marketing and PR entities, as is the case with the Japanese, Koreans, and Germans in the United States. When is the last time anyone saw published data on Toyota or Honda profitability in the United States? Or BMW of North America? Nobody runs the business that way anymore. Suboptimizing profitability by geographic entity makes about as much sense as declaring every U.S. state a "profit center" for GM North America.

I wish we could have evolved to a global profit and loss method while I was still there. It will ultimately happen, of course, because it has to.

Chevrolet Volt

("I'll Let You Explain It to the Board")

GM WAS LATE TO THE HYBRID PARTY . . . OR WERE WE? AS EARLY AS 1968, GM demonstrated a battery/gasoline engine hybrid, using lead-acid batteries. The company easily had the technological ability. What it lacked was the will.

At several points after my arrival in 2001, the subject of a hybrid vehicle was raised. When we tallied up the engineering expense and the capital required, figured in the cost per vehicle of a gasoline powertrain, plus electric, plus state-of-the-art batteries, and estimated a reasonable list price and sales volume, it was a financial rout. Not only would more than $500 million in capital be squandered on a losing program, but we would actually incur a unit loss per vehicle. That's when Rick Wagoner said, "Who wants to take this one to the board and explain it? I'm not doing it!"

There were no takers.

And here's where a point needs to be made: as senior officers of a large company, our fiduciary duty was to the shareholders of GM stock, as represented by the board. Imagine the leader of a publicly held company going before the board to say, "I'd like to propose a half-billion-dollar hybrid program. Engineering cost will be another $300 million on top of the capital. We think we can sell twenty-five to fifty thousand per year, depending on what fuel prices do. The cost per vehicle will be about $24,000, but we need to sell them for $22,000, so we'll have a contribution loss of $2,000 per unit. Figuring in depreciation and amortization and depending on sales volume, we'll lose between $200 million and $600 million per year. Are there any questions, or do I hear a motion for approval?"

That "motion for approval" would have been highly unlikely in the best of times. And in a period of unsatisfactory profitability or poor "quality of earnings" because so much of the profit came from GMAC, it would have caused the wise heads of the board to shake in profound disbelief. Neither the board nor the management, in our system of governance, is empowered to spend the shareholders' substance on what they know in advance to be a loss-making project.

So, how did Toyota, then, get it done and successfully launch the now-famous Prius? It's simple: Toyota still bears all the earmarks of a privately owned company. The Toyoda family still runs it, selects the top leaders, and anoints one of its own as the CEO of the corporation.

"I think we should create a hybrid car," the founding family and principal shareholder says. "It will cost us money, but so what? We need to demonstrate our ability to master advanced, fuel-saving technology. What if it loses $300 million per year? Isn't that worth it in terms of good publicity? Compared to the billions we pay globally for conventional advertising, it's a drop in the bucket, and it's way more effective." End of discussion. The founder and principal shareholder has been heard from, and everyone turns to act. There is decidedly something to be said for the swifter, more authoritarian corporate governance resulting from someone's name being on the building!

And so, we watched as Toyota launched the Prius in the United

States to huge acclaim from the nation's media. The future of the automobile is here, thanks to the brilliant engineers at Toyota! While America's "dinosaur Big Three" continued to foist over-sized SUVs and pickups on the hapless American public (and, at $1.50/gallon at the time, roughly one-quarter of what the rest of the industrial world was paying for motor fuel, that "hapless" public was buying every big V8 truck we could produce, while small, fuel-efficient vehicles were left to decompose slowly on dealer lots), the wise, omniscient Toyota company, ever attuned to the needs of society rather than financial gain, was creating the vehicles that would save us from both the oppression of foreign oil and the inevitable CO_2-caused planetary meltdown.

Talk about cloaking themselves in virtue. We stood by, nearly speechless with envy over the countless billions Toyota reaped in terms of corporate reputation for the measly three hundred million the initial Prius may have lost them. (Those figures are my conjecture, based on what our loss would have been. It might have been more, might have been less. But we do know it cost them money.)

But for every savior (Prius), there must also be an Antichrist, and the mainstream media found it in the Hummer H2, GM's smaller, "civilized" version of the legendary military vehicle. Heavy, rugged beyond any known requirement, master of any terrain, it also used a lot of fuel. And so, with a well-dressed, blonde, suburban housewife at the wheel, gliding up to a parking space at Neiman Marcus, the Hummer H2 became the detested symbol of a "let them eat cake" insouciance displayed by a moneyed upper middle class. What a fat, irresistible target for the left-leaning media: class warfare and defense of our beleaguered planet, all enabled by vitriolic attacks on the Hummer H2. It was a perfectly good vehicle that consumed no more fuel than a large Mercedes sedan, a Lamborghini Murciélago two-seater, or the much smaller Porsche Cayenne twin turbo sport-utility (and not much more than the virtuous Toyota's own Land Cruiser, Sequoia, or Lexus 470). And so, we were daily bombarded by salvo after salvo of "GM bad, Toyota good" or "GM dumb, Toyota brilliant."

Easily forgotten in the mad virtue versus evil media feeding frenzy was the fact that the real pioneer in fuel-free automobiles was none other than diabolical old GM itself.

At huge investment, and at a time when "advanced batteries" really were at the limits of known chemistry, GM, in 1996, launched the revolutionary EV1, a composite-bodied, suppository-shaped two-seater, crammed with lead-acid (later nickel-metal-hydride) batteries and capable of a range of up to 50-60 miles between charges. Expensive to produce and impossible to sell, the 1,200 or so built had to be leased at derisory rates to get them into the hands of customers. Many of the latter were Hollywood personalities who deeply believed that their use of EV1 (in addition to three Ferraris and S-Class Mercedes V12s) would help atone for America's social and environmental sins: it felt so good to drive one.

But it was costing GM a fortune to keep the EV1s on the road, and so we advised the lessees (all the cars remained the property of GM) that we would not be renewing the leases. Against massive protests from the small but vocal lessee base, we pulled the EV1s from the roads.

And then, in a PR blunder of truly gargantuan proportions, based on legal opinion designed to eliminate product liability risk from any EV1s getting back on the road, we crushed them. If GM had bombed churches and hospitals, the outcry could not have been more negative. And, of course, conspiracy theories abounded, giving rise to Chris Paine's cult classic documentary *Who Killed the Electric Car?*, in which it is broadly hinted that GM somehow received massive financial inducement from Big Oil to eliminate this menace to the petroleum companies' future profitability. Yet another reason to praise the benevolent Toyota Motor Company while vilifying the greedy, Hummer-producing, EV1-killing, planet-destroying GM.

The fact that GM was the absolute world leader in the development of the hydrogen fuel cell vehicle—basically an electric vehicle that creates its own electricity from compressed stored hydrogen—was undeniably true, but failed to resonate with the media or public. We had exciting prototypes, one after another. We had press conferences and press drives, with a focus on Southern California, the hotbed of environmental consciousness. We poured countless billions into fuel cell research. We built a fleet of production-like Chevrolet Equinoxes with fuel cells as their power source. We lent them to influential personalities (no more leases that would give the user a sense of entitlement to permanent ownership).

None of it really worked, because the timetable we (and everyone else working on hydrogen fuel cells) stated for the beginning of full-scale commercial production was a rolling ten years. That time frame is clearly too long for the instant gratification mind-set of the media and environmentally conscious portion of the public. Besides (and this is a legitimate concern), where does the hydrogen come from? How is it produced, distributed, compressed, and filled into the hugely expensive tanks at ten thousand PSI?

Gas stations, on the other hand, were at virtually every corner, and electrical outlets were abundantly available in every house, condo, garage, or place of business. "We will work with the energy companies to create a viable hydrogen infrastructure" was a very tough sell.

In about 2005, I had the thought of creating a fully electric prototype as a show car. It would be an aerodynamic four-seater using very advanced (but unproven) lithium-ion batteries, giving it a claimed range per charge of roughly two hundred miles. A

California high-tech idea and prototype company by the name of Applied Minds assured me it could build a running car. Excitedly, I shared this idea with my peers (and Rick Wagoner) at an Automotive Strategy Board meeting, only to be cruelly shot down.

First, it wasn't known, feasible technology. Second, it would send mixed signals: did GM believe in fuel cells, or did we believe in EVs? Third, our prior experience with EV1 should have convinced us that no market exists. And, finally, the dreaded legal advice: we were engaged, along with most other car producers, in a lawsuit against the State of California over that state's "EV mandates," which were to force a certain percentage of vehicles sold in California to be electric. How could we fight the mandate and dangle an EV in front of the public at the same time? Sadly, I saw logic in that one and gave up.

Meanwhile, faced with the pressure of hybridization, GM did commit the massive sums required to engineer and produce our very sophisticated, ultracapable two-mode hybrid system for full-size trucks and sport-utilities. Our thinking was that if you're going to spend thousands of dollars per vehicle to save 25 percent on fuel, why not do it on the large vehicles that consume a lot of fuel (and that the public wants to buy) rather than on a less-desirable small vehicle that doesn't use much fuel in the first place?

That sounded convincing to us, but while getting a V8 SUV from 14 mpg in the city to 22 mpg might be a phenomenal technical achievement—it equaled the city number of the much smaller Toyota Camry four-cylinder—it was not dramatic enough to cause the skeptical, stridently anti-GM publications to say anything more than that we had gone from "wholly unacceptable" to merely "awful." So, the two-mode hybrid system, jointly developed with such industry stalwarts as BMW and the then-DaimlerChrysler, didn't do much to move the reputational needle out of the red zone either.

Here we were, the company with the best of intentions, vilified for killing EV1 while producing the Hummer H2, seen as pulling the wool over people's eyes with the fuel cell ("a science project they'll never put into production, there to make us think they're doing something"), blessed with merely scant praise for the two-mode hybrid, and all the while compared against wonderful, altruistic Toyota and their "fuel-sipping offerings." The degree to which Toyota benefited is beyond quantification. The mantle of impeccable greenness that was ceremoniously draped over them had a positive effect on all their vehicles, even the ones that demonstrably consumed way more fuel than the equivalent GM product.

I recall one gas station incident where I asked a woman why she had purchased a new Toyota Sequoia. Her answer was all about fuel economy. The family had considered a Chevrolet Tahoe, but as everyone knew, those were guzzlers. I asked her what her highway mileage was, and she replied, "Oh, about fifteen mpg." When I told her the V8 Chevrolet Tahoe was rated at twenty-two mpg highway, it was in such conflict with her established belief system that she simply shrugged it off as an obvious fabrication. Thus, the so-called upper funnel measures, as divined by monthly rounds of research (such measures as "familiarity," "favorable opinion," "purchase intention"), continued to rise for Toyota, while ours shrank at the same rate. Clearly, something needed to be done.

I was convinced that, following on the heels of the Prius success, Toyota would next stun the world with an all-electric prototype, to be built "some time later." If they did that, I didn't see how any competitor could ever make up the resulting reputational hit.

At the Automotive Strategy Board, where the Toyota juggernaut was a routine topic, I again suggested a leapfrog strategy. We could match them on hybrids, but who cares about catching up? We would merely be validating their strategy and technology. GM's leading fuel cell advocate, Dr. Larry Burns, who believed in that technology with something akin to religious fervor, believed we needed more PR, more fuel cell promotional activity. And I once again advocated that we create the world's first practical electric car, a four-seater, using lithium-ion, the latest in battery chemistry. Only that way, I argued, could we blunt the relentless reputational rise of Toyota, coupled, of course, with the "gang that couldn't shoot straight" yoke around our neck.

There was much discussion. The fuel cell people said it was the wrong time to switch horses. If we suddenly went with batteries, people would see it as an admission of the fuel cell's shortcomings. "No batteries, no EVs. We need more money on fuel cell programs." The technical community (primarily Powertrain) weighed in with the fact that lithium-ion, while storing more than twice as much energy as the next best chemistry, was better suited to long, slow drain, as in laptops and mobile phones, than "power" requirements, as in cars or cordless power tools. Finally, CEO Rick Wagoner weighed in: "Bob, we lost over one billion bucks on EV1. How much do you propose we lose this time?" I did not "win" that meeting, and the specter of Toyota domination over GM continued unabated.

I brought the idea up several more times, and was always silenced primarily by the argument that lithium-ion would not work. Powertrain and GM Research sent a series of battery engineers to my office to explain to me in no uncertain terms the severe limitations of lithium-ion chemistry. They just about had me convinced when the California start-up Tesla Motors announced the creation of a Lotus Elise–based two-seat roadster, powered by 6,835 laptop batteries, with a top speed of 140 mph, acceleration time of zero to sixty in four seconds, and a range of two hundred miles.

Naturally, this gave me the lever I needed. Armed with the Tesla press clips, I once again harangued the ASB, arguing that somebody out in California with far more battery experience than we had obviously decided that lithium-ion *would* work and was betting a lot of money on it. How could we, the world's largest and, arguably, most technologically capable car company in the world, declare the lithium-ion battery not feasible for motor vehicles when some outfit run by a couple of dot-com billionaires was making it work?

This time, the meeting got me very tentative permission to investigate a lithium-ion EV as a concept. It was, in retrospect, less permission than absence of prohibition. Whatever . . . I ran with it. This might be called the germination of the Volt.

Hours after the meeting, I sat in my office with Jon Lauckner, now overseeing all VLEs globally. We schemed about creating the GM "reputational shock therapy" vehicle we had both sought after for so long.

Lauckner listened, not so patiently, to my all-electric dream. When Jon has a thought that simply has to get out, he starts banging his knees together repeatedly. Banging them now, he said, "Look, I know you've got your heart set on an all-electric, but let me show you why that's a bad idea. With lithium-ion, you get, assuming an efficient car, five miles per kilowatt/hour. So, to get a hundred-mile range, you need twenty kilowatt/hours. But since you never want to drain the whole battery because it impacts battery life, we'd want a thirty-kilowatt battery. That's huge. And even if we got the world's best price on a lithium battery, you'd be talking a thousand dollars per kilowatt, or a thirty-thousand-dollar battery pack. And you don't even have a car around it. And you'd still only have a hundred-mile range on a good day!" He paused, and then continued: "Now, here's *my* idea."

With that, on a lined pad and using his expensive, gold-nibbed fountain pen, Jon laid out what was to become the Chevrolet Volt. Pushing that abused pen against the rake of the nib when necessary (resulting in a spray of ink droplets), Jon sketched the chassis. "The sixteen-kilowatt battery goes down the middle and out like a T under the back seat. That's nominally good for eighty miles, but we'll only use eight kilowatts; that'll make the battery last forever. This way, it's good for forty miles, and then we'll cut in this little 1.4-liter engine, which will drive a generator to keep the battery supplied with juice for another, say three hundred miles."

Jon knew the statistic: 80 percent of America's daily trips are forty miles or less; the fuel economy would be infinite. A sixty-mile round trip would require burning gasoline from the tiny engine for twenty miles: the rough calculation for a trip that size would be 150 mpg! The smaller, less expensive battery pack, coupled with the overall range of three hundred miles or more, would make this vehicle ideal: fuel-free for most daily trips, coupled with the ability to go long distances at any time, just like a conventional gasoline-powered car. I was sold. I wish I had Jon's original, ink-spattered drawing. It is truly a piece of automotive history.

The next step was to share the concept layout with Ed Welburn, vice president of global design. The car's layout would provide the designers with potentially heroic proportions, and Ed quickly decided the Volt concept would be as arresting visually as it was innovative technologically. We were on the way.

With huge pride and enthusiasm, I told Rick Wagoner that we were creating a vehicle with a goal of 150 mpg on sixty-mile trips. His reaction was muted at best, but again, no "stop work" edict. Part of the vast GM empire did, however subtly, begin to strike back. I was subjected to one PowerPoint presentation after another, presided over by learned hybrid engineers, explaining why Volt was a dumb idea. In the final analysis, they said, it's a sequential hybrid (meaning that the second power source only comes in when the first is exhausted) as opposed to a parallel hybrid (like Prius) where the two power sources, gas and electric, constantly work together for optimal performance. Sequential hybrids, they argued (correctly), are less efficient than parallel.

However, if we insisted on the Volt sequential concept, they, the hybrid engineers, knew how to make it much more efficient: we'd program it to run the gas engine every ten minutes or so, to keep the battery optimally charged, and with the resulting gain in efficiency, we could squeeze out more ultimate range. "Stop, stop!" I cried. "This isn't about absolute, terminal efficiency. This vehicle is about giving the lover of electric vehicles a pure electric battery-powered driving experience 80 percent of the time. They don't want to hear a gasoline engine cutting in all the time. It ruins the whole experience." Undaunted, they droned on about "maximum efficiency," thus demonstrating yet another instance where extremely intelligent people could not grasp a very simple concept: the customer wants forty full miles of blissfully silent, fuel-free electric driving.

More presentations would follow, most showing some huge flaw in the concept. I always had Jon Lauckner at these; the engineers could razzle-dazzle me, a simple marketing MBA, but they couldn't stand up to Jon Lauckner's rapierlike analytical skill. "Aha!" he would shout. "You're forgetting [such-and-such]. Let me just quickly rerun those numbers with the proper inputs this time. . . . Ah, yes, just as I thought, you're wrong, and I'm right! But thanks, guys. This has been really interesting."

The organization, more comfortable with what I call "the oily bits," i.e., complex mechanical assemblies like transmissions and hybrid drive systems, gradually accepted the reality that we were planning to execute a Volt concept car for the 2007 Detroit auto show.

Meanwhile, in Design, Ed Welburn turned the Volt project over to his best advanced teams for both exterior and interior. A substantial number of alternative themes were imagined, sketched, and sculpted in 1/8-scale clay models. Some had a flamboyantly "European" flavor, others were more distinctly American. All were unconventional, and some were shocking.

Since GE Plastics was working with us on modern automotive composites, Design felt empowered to expand their explorations into shapes that could not easily be produced in metal, but which would be feasible in composites. This held especially true for the glass surfaces, which, assuming successful substitution of polycarbonate for glass, could make some unheard-of shapes possible. A transparent roof was to be part of the theme as well.

This was precisely the type of design we selected for the initial show car: bold in proportion, with a long hood and a compact, compressed passenger compartment. Glass on the doors actually followed the shape of the doors in a way that would have engineers scratching their heads for a way to actually make it work. Inside, the design theme was even more unusual, and while visually dramatic and appropriate for a show car, we knew it would never translate into production. The interior space was more or less dominated by a large rectangular tunnel that ran from the front of the passenger compartment all the way to the back seat, where it branched out, T-shaped, under both rear seats. The team had guessed fairly closely on the size of the individual battery cells and the overall configuration of the battery pack; that was one element of the show car that was destined to survive the massive reengineering as Volt headed for production.

By some miracle, the feverish work on the Volt show car remained largely hidden from the media during the final months of 2006, as the exotic machine came together. The battery, obviously, would remain a dummy: with no intent for production at this point, we obviously had neither selected a specific cell size and type, nor had we settled on a supplier. Volt was destined to make its appearance under battery power, yes, but they would be two twelve-volt car batteries, sufficient to move it on and off the stand at low speed. This later caused one journalist to publish an exposé (shock, horror!) to the effect that Volt was a fake. The power came from conventional batteries. This is, of course, standard practice for just about all concept cars at automobile shows, most of which are mere design exercises with no pretense at reality.

When the big day came at the Detroit show on January 7,

2007, the Volt was a sensation. As I stated in my semiprepared remarks before the assembled media corps from all major nations, the "inconvenient truth" (an unveiled reference to Al Gore's Academy Award/Nobel Prize–winning fictiomentary) was that this unheard-of propulsion system, enabling 80 percent of America's daily trips with no fossil fuel use whatsoever, the most technologically advanced vehicle on the planet, was from none other than General Motors. We received television, radio, Internet, and print coverage of record proportions, handily exceeding the previous high-water mark of the Chevrolet Camaro a year before. Volt was the star of the show, eclipsing anything and everything during the 2007 auto show season.

All of the initial coverage was totally favorable. But beloved Toyota Motor Company soon weighed in with strangely negative comments. They had, in fact, been caught flat-footed. To make matters worse, Toyota had selected the Detroit show for the full unveiling of the monstrously large, heavy, and fuel-addicted full-size Tundra pickup, with emphasis on a long-wheelbase, four-door crew cab with huge wheels and four-wheel drive. In short, their stand largely resembled what GM normally did: it emphasized the big V8 trucks!

Toyota immediately labeled Volt a clever but meaningless PR exercise, using a battery chemistry, lithium-ion, which was dangerous, unreliable, and far from ready for automotive use. How much sounder, they trumpeted, was their own homely little Prius using (now eclipsed) nickel metal hydride batteries in their "tried and true, patented, Toyota Synergy Drive" system. Soon after, Toyota invited the world's media to a technical seminar in Japan, where their senior technical officer took great pains to point out the impossibility of lithium-ion chemistry for the mobile sector.

Their purposeful pessimism was not without foundation. After the lithium-ion chemistry was invented in the United States, it was massively adopted and produced in Japan in small-format batteries for laptops, PDAs, and mobile phones. But this early "lithium-ion cobalt" chemistry would not scale up for larger applications: while its energy storage properties were excellent, it required extreme care in its manufacture. Even the slightest short circuit could result in runaway heating, followed by fire.

The theme of the technical seminar was "Toyota knows best. Toyota is conservative!" And they even made the statement that, unlike "some other" automobile company, Toyota would never, ever place the safety of its customers at risk. It is strange, and a further manifestation of the pro-Toyota bias of the mainstream media, that in 2009 and 2010, the period when ten million Toyotas were recalled for unintended acceleration and failing brakes (on the pious Prius, of all cars), not one journalist ever reminded Toyota, despite thirty or more deaths being blamed on its failed engineering, of its claim never to put the customer at risk.

The conviction that lithium-ion was unsafe was a rare (but not unique) example of Japanese hubris. Since that country was the world's largest producer of advanced batteries, with a seemingly insurmountable lead on everyone else, it never occurred to them that research would accelerate in the United States, France, Germany, China, and Korea, all of whom labored to find lithium chemistries that would match cobalt, but without the downside of thermal instability. In the United States, an MIT-originated start-up developed a very promising chemistry, as did SAFT in France. The leader, though, based on GM's exhaustive analysis of the world's lithium-ion producers, was the Korean company LG Chem, which ultimately was to win the competition to supply cells for the Volt. In this combination, the cobalt in the early "portable device" batteries was replaced by nano-phosphate, a benign and ultrastable compound. There are variations on this theme, and massive research continues, but the salient fact is that the (then) infallible, success-crowned, omniscient, and omnipotent Toyota

Motor Company didn't realize that the rest of the world was moving beyond lithium-ion cobalt!

The press was now in somewhat of a quandary. GM said we were confident it would work while Toyota said it was a PR scam and would never work. Test question for the reader: given the reputations of the two companies in 2007, with Toyota's profits, sales figures, and reputation on a meteoric rise, and bumbling old GM ("The problem with GM is they just don't make any products people want to buy") still struggling, who were they going to believe? You guessed correctly, and so the backlash of "GM will never build it because Toyota says the batteries won't work" became a major, but not fatal annoyance: the fascination with the car was still overwhelming.

The bloggers joined the fray: on the positive side, a New York neurosurgeon and car enthusiast by the name of Dr. Lyle Dennis soon started a Volt fan site and quickly attracted tens of thousands of members. The good doctor's efforts on behalf of Volt were so massive and effective that an official GM site could not have been as effective if, indeed, it could have matched it. Dr. Dennis, or "Dr. Lyle" as we called him, was a tireless advocate and true believer, attending every Volt event we held for the media and adding immeasurable amounts of "third-party" credibility. (One does wonder when he found time to actually operate on patients, though.)

On the negative side, we had a garrulous, cantankerous, heavily opinionated electric-vehicle fanatic from California named Douglas Korthoff. There was nothing about GM, the Volt, lithium-ion, or me personally that he didn't despise. An embarrassment to the entire West Coast electric vehicle fan community, Mr. Korthoff launched one vitriolic attack after another. After we became accustomed to Mr. Korthoff's predictable diatribes, we actually began to look forward to them in a perverse sort of way. We became like the mail carrier who relishes the nasty little dog that barks at him as part of his daily routine—an irritant, but one whose absence would be missed.

The overwhelming public and media reaction to the Volt was much welcomed by the board of directors, many of whom were strong advocates of "technology demonstrator" projects. They were every bit as sensitive to the stereotype of "gas-guzzling, planet-polluting GM" as senior management. The tidal wave of praise was always tempered, however, by "but will they build it?" The GM board, having integrated the lesson of how one marginally money-losing hybrid car, the Prius, could suddenly prove to be the tide that floated all other Toyota boats, and in the process, make Toyota the undisputed darling of the media, was not about to insist that the Volt be a profitable program. But they certainly wanted it produced!

Jon Lauckner quickly gathered a team of unconventional thinkers to create an affordable production car that would fulfill our promise of a forty-mile all-electric range and, more important, meet all global safety standards worldwide. Starting from scratch with an all-new chassis made no sense: engineering and capital costs involved would make it totally unaffordable, even for a company now willing to make some financial sacrifice in the name of green technology.

A quick examination of future GM architectures revealed that the length, width, and wheelbase of the upcoming Chevrolet Cruze would be ideal for the Volt. The only problem was engine placement: the concept Volt had the engine placed off of the electric motor/generator, providing an elegant, long hood. But the platform of the future Cruze called for the traditional, far-forward transverse mounting of the engine. This moved the front wheels aft on the car; a shift that is never popular with designers, who like the look of "long dash to front axle," meaning a long hood, with the front axle as far forward as possible.

There was much hand-wringing over the radical change in proportion: the production "Volt" was decidedly *not* going to look like the show car, which had received raves for appearance as well as technology. The financial reality was overpowering: there was no way we could execute the show car. We would have to do the best job we could with the hand we were dealt. As luck would have it, wind tunnel tests of the original concept design proved we couldn't have executed it anyway: despite a svelte and slippery-looking shape, the Volt concept had the aerodynamic qualities of a rough-edged brick.

Aerodynamics is an important element in the quest for fuel economy: at speeds above 30 mph, air resistance is a far greater factor in "resistance to forward motion" than rolling resistance. It's important in conventional vehicles, but absolutely essential in electric vehicles, which, with fully-charged batteries, only have the equivalent of 1½ gallons of gasoline. And when we put that Volt concept car into the wind tunnel, the effects of its shape on its aerodynamics became all too clear. Upon seeing the results, some of the guys wondered if we had put it in backward by mistake.

Using its high-drag design, attractive though it was, would have reduced the electric range from the promised forty miles to something more like thirty-two, if that. We all suffer for beauty, but this was too much. Clay models of the Cruze-based production Volt were soon created and given as many show car design cues as possible. It's doubtful that any GM production car ever spent as much time in the wind tunnel as did the Volt—it was practically designed there. To average forty miles of electric range using 50 percent of our sixteen kilowatt/hour battery, we needed a drag coefficient of 0.27. It was a struggle, involving many small surface adjustments, some of only a few millimeters, but we finally arrived at a body shape that would seat four, house the battery and all mechanical elements, protect its occupants, fuel, and high-voltage components in case of a crash, meet the aerodynamic drag target—all while looking pretty attractive. But we fretted over public reaction on the day we lifted the veil: "Here's the final production Volt. We know it's changed quite a bit, but . . ."

The initial, small Volt team was soon replaced by a large, formal one featuring the finest minds the corporation could muster. Some were veterans of the now-defunct EV1. They brought huge value in their wealth of experience and practical wisdom on this kind of project. Others were new hires: we had been producing gasoline- (and diesel-) powered cars for nearly a century, so there was little in-house expertise in the company when it came to electrochemistry or dealing with the management of several hundred volts of electricity. It was here that I finally appreciated all of GM's fuel cell work (which I often had derided as "nice to have, but hardly essential"): the "power electronics," or high-voltage energy management system, differs little between a fuel cell vehicle (essentially an EV that produces its own current) and a vehicle that stores its energy in batteries. Between the old EV1 veterans and the fuel cell team, we were able to quickly assemble more electric vehicle expertise than any other car company that I am aware of. Still, we needed to hire many young (and old) engineers to work in areas we'd simply never had to focus on before.

The Volt team, now numbering several hundred, was led by Frank Weber, a six-foot-five German vegetarian and one of GM's foremost engineers and leaders, transferred to Detroit from Opel. His unique combination of dynamic, no-nonsense leadership and technical acumen gave wings to the Volt program.

Despite Frank's drive and optimism, he (correctly) saw the "productionizing" of Volt as a multiyear program, with a launch date of late 2012. This, for all kinds of reasons, was unacceptable, and over anguished protests we forced a production date goal of November 2010 onto Frank and the team. Frank simply said, "We will try."

"No," I replied, "you will succeed."

"Yes, we will certainly *try* to succeed."

"No, you *will* succeed."

This exchange continued over weeks and months until Frank and the team, somewhat amazed at the lack of any major disasters with early batteries and prototype hardware and software, began to accept the timing.

The battery was clearly the big risk and the big unknown. It was the industry's first foray into a lithium-ion battery designed specifically for automotive propulsion. A very careful screening of all global producers of lithium-ion batteries, measuring such parameters as engineering capability, quality, production capacity, safety, and the energy storage capacity of their particular chemistry, resulted in the selection of LG Chem. With their vast experience and well-funded research program (with a lot of financial support from the Korean government), along with their expressed willingness to establish a cell manufacturing facility in the United States, they seemed to be the logical partner. And we were not disappointed. From the initial, cobbled-together prototype battery, through a series of iterations involving changes to chemistry for better energy storage and life, LG Chem always met or exceeded expectations. The confidence level in the LG Chem cell technology was so high, in fact, that GM made history of sorts by announcing, in July 2010, that the Volt battery pack would carry an eight-year, hundred-thousand-mile warranty.

On September 16, 2008, the centennial of General Motors, Rick Wagoner, Fritz Henderson, and I rolled out a full-size, realistic mock-up of the production-intent Cruze-architecture-based Chevrolet Volt. Both old and new media gave the event extensive coverage, and not surprisingly, much of it was negative: the Volt enthusiasts, as well as the detractors, were understandably shocked at the amount of change from the original daring but hopelessly impractical design.

But the practical arguments of space and efficiency won out, and over time the public became more comfortable with the Volt's new four-door sedan shape. In short, the much dreaded change in exterior design quickly became a nonissue.

Both the mechanical and the electric portions of Volt proceeded with only minor speed bumps. Changes were made to the battery chemistry with the goal of optimizing the trade-offs between vehicle range, battery life, reliability, and cost. Production facilities were put in place at GM's Detroit-Hamtramck plant, which was soon producing high-quality preproduction vehicles.

In the summer of 2010, GM announced the price of a base-model Volt: $41,000, or a $350/month lease with a $2,500 down payment.

(The list price, admittedly high for a compact car, reflects the cost of first-generation technology which is bound to become more reasonable as battery manufacturing matures and as specialized electrical components, expensive and produced at low volumes today, become more generalized and benefit from automotive industry economies of scale. Federal credits of $7,500 for early adopters of battery-powered vehicles will, additionally, make Volt more accessible for the average buyer. The $350 lease, however, is exceptionally attractive and reflects the belief that the very small initial production quantities will create a very strong demand for off-lease used Volts which should sell at near the original list price.)

So, with pricing in line with expectations and a surprisingly affordable lease rate, one would expect a generally favorable reaction in the general media. After all, GM had long been criticized for its failure to design technologically advanced, environmentally friendly cars, and for letting foreign competitors take the lead. Logic dictated that all this good news would be applauded.

Sadly, logic was wrong. The Chevrolet Volt, as of this writing, has become a political football, reviled by both the lunatic left and the vocal right. Inveterate GM haters compare it to the all-electric, hundred-mile-range Nissan Leaf, ignoring the fact that Volt's total range is in excess of that.

The *New York Times* featured a guest column by someone named Edward Niedermeyer, who writes for something called "The Truth About Cars"—which turns out to be a Web site that often offers anything but—in which he called the Volt a "lemon" and even attacked the $350/month lease, implying darkly that this is a semi-fraudulent come-on as it limits the lessee to twelve thousand miles per year. He conveniently forgets to mention that this limit is pretty much standard for automotive leases.

Meanwhile, from the right, both Rush Limbaugh and Glenn Beck weighed in, pronouncing the Volt a typical government-directed failure, a $41,000 car that would travel only forty miles, period. Of course, Volt's overall range, with the gasoline-powered generator feeding power to the battery, is in excess of three hundred miles.

One may draw a few conclusions: many people in the media follow the thesis that one must never let facts get in the way of a good, sensationalist story. Second, animosity toward the Obama administration is so intense among the right-wing talk show hosts that any vulnerability, however tenuous, must be attacked and blamed on "socialist influence," with no regard to truth or to the damage these reckless claims can make to GM, an American corporation, to the dedicated and hard-driving members of the Volt team, and to a now-misinformed public that may be steered away from a transportation solution that would fill their needs perfectly.

Will all this damage Volt? My guess is "not at all." The truth about this revolutionary car cannot be suppressed. It embodies the ideal solution: silent, clean electric drive for daily trips of about forty miles, with a seamless transition to a gasoline generator–enabled full range equal to that of the average car.

With the universal drive to ever-higher fuel economy standards (or, as expressed in Europe, ever-lower CO_2 emissions expressed in grams per mile), the Volt concept is the most compelling for the future, for it, uniquely, provides both the desired daily electric vehicle capability as well as the versatility that only fossil fuels can currently provide.

We can confidently expect more of the world's auto producers to move to the Volt-type solution, as neither the optimized internal combustion engine nor a battery-only vehicle lineup will, over the next decade or two, adequately fulfill the conflicting requirements of "range" versus "no CO_2 emissions." The skeptics, the pundits, the GM haters, and those who detest lithium-ion as a chemistry will all be dragged, however unwillingly, to the same conclusion: Volt paved the way, Volt was the first with the extended-range EV concept, Volt demonstrated the will and technological capability of General Motors.

More than any of the other highly successful GM products of recent times, Volt is a shining testimonial to the company's vision and willingness to accept large risk. It is indicative of the new attitude at General Motors. And to all the doubters, opponents, critics, and skeptics, from Doug Korthoff to Glenn Beck, I say, "Eat your hearts out. Volt is the future."

Meltdown and Rebirth

JUST HOW AND WHY DID GM, ON JUNE 1, 2009, SLIP INTO CHAPTER 11 bankruptcy and, as a consequence, into temporary majority ownership by the U.S. federal government and, to a lesser extent, the Canadian government? The reader will be spared the arcane financial details and dates, as they will be of interest to only the most dedicated students of corporate financial history. Instead, I'll touch on the real reasons for the meltdown, what it was like to live through it, and what was different about "federal ownership" and the new top leadership.

The previous year had started out well enough, with a middling economic performance in the United States and, as usual, strong growth in China. At GM, we were feeling optimistic about 2008: many great new products were on the road and in the pipeline, and the newly launched Chevrolet Malibu was enjoying great success after having been named North American Car of the Year, our second in a row after the Saturn Aura won in 2007.

Financially, despite a debt-heavy balance sheet, things looked promising. We had concluded a new contract with the UAW in the latter part of 2007 that would narrow the wage-cost gap to the Japanese transplants operating in the South and, most important, transfer ongoing responsibility for UAW health care from the company to a union-sponsored fund (which GM was to set up), thus freeing the company from a crushing burden amounting to six or seven billion dollars a year. (GM's outlays for worker benefits, of a type not assumed by foreign competition, had amounted to a total of $107 billion over the past fifteen years.) At about 6 to 7 percent of revenue, it was like trying to run a marathon with ten-pound weights attached to your ankles while your international competitors wore lightweight running shoes.

Critically, though, the new union-responsible health care regime was not slated to become effective until 2010, too late to help in the 2008 meltdown, as we were soon to discover.

Things started to turn ugly during the first quarter of 2008. The collapse of the subprime mortgage market and the ensuing financial crisis, bank failure, and home foreclosures sucked hundreds of billions out of the economy almost instantly. Although few economists foresaw it, we had been living a life of false prosperity in a gigantic gossamer bubble, pumped up by fictional wealth in the form of more and more credit which, in turn, was collateralized by assets of an ever-more dubious nature.

We now know that the subprime disaster was as least partially incubated in the late 1990s with a series of congressional acts falling under the umbrella moniker of the "American Community Renewal Act," which had the socially laudable (but economically oxymoronic) objective of putting millions of Americans into homes they could not afford. Banks were required to make a certain percentage of loans to persons not qualified by the accepted financial criteria, this presumably a smoke screen for the supposition that applications for mortgages were being denied on the basis of race or gender.

Subprime mortgages soon became a growth industry, with banks paying "bounty hunters" to bring in hopelessly unqualified prospects to whom they could grant a mortgage. The mortgage business and, with it, housing starts (the number of privately owned new houses beginning construction in a given period) grew at a phenomenal rate in the early years of the century, and GMAC (GM's financing arm), with its "ResCap" subsidiary, was a significant participant. I frequently asked at the Automotive Strategy Board meetings why the mortgage arm was suddenly such an amazing generator of profitability, but was easily persuaded that all was on the up and up and "not to worry." I was more than eager to believe: GMAC (and ResCap in particular) was a welcome contributor to GM's profitability, so much so that I frequently thanked GMAC's CEO for subsidizing the North American vehicle business.

It was too good to last. In 2008, ResCap began to show alarming losses with undefined future "exposure" as the bubble began to burst.

Somewhat worried, I asked our in-house economists what the likely effect would be on the U.S. economy and, by derivation, the automotive market. "A minor problem," they told me. "The financial markets and the U.S. Treasury know how to deal with this sort of thing. It will be a slight shock, resulting in modest reduction of the vehicle market, but it's not a time to worry."

I'm not an economist, but I've developed good intuition, and I didn't like what I saw, nor did I believe what I had just heard. "I don't know, guys," I said. "Seems like a potential for total economic meltdown." This was greeted with another torrent of reassuring economist-speak. (About a year later, these same economists came to see me in my office with just one question, the same one I've been asked many times and can't answer: "How did you know?")

Things rapidly went from bad to worse, with the "black hole" created by ResCap's seemingly bottomless exposure dragging the company's performance to ever greater losses. But we might have survived the losses, the write-offs, the retail credit drought, the loss of leasing, the drop in the overall market, if we hadn't received part two of the "one-two punch." Already stunned by a sharp left jab to the jaw, we were dumbfounded when the roundhouse right connected in the form of rapidly rising fuel prices. The lights began to dim.

The sudden rise in fuel prices was as alarming as it was unexpected. I have often stated that I am an (often vilified, roundly criticized) advocate of higher fuel prices. Higher fuel taxes would generate many billions in badly needed revenues without the counterproductive rate increases. It would increase consumer demand for fuel efficiency, rather than making efficiency a government mandate. It would encourage the buying public to think carefully about the relative economy of their next automotive purchase, and it would lower the break-even mileage of costly hybrid systems, making them more attractive. It would also encourage the creation and use of mass transit systems.

Were I emperor of the United States, I would call for a twenty-five-cent-per-gallon-per-year increase in pump fuel taxes until the prevailing global level is reached, about six or seven dollars per gallon. This is what all of Europe pays; it's been inching toward that level for decades. Far from destroying the automobile business and personal transportation there, it has actually helped. The total vehicle market of Europe, at roughly twenty million units, dwarfs our current eleven million, and Europe's fleet was considerably more efficient than ours even before CO_2/fuel economy regulations. The road infrastructure there is incomparably superior to that of the United States, funded as it is by ample gas tax revenue. And so, when U.S. gas prices suddenly shot from about $2.10 per gallon to a peak of $4.50, those who knew my views said, "What are you complaining about? You wanted higher fuel prices, and you got them!"

Of course, my recipe had called for a gradual rise over time, not an overnight doubling. The gasoline sticker shock (due to the only partially explicable sudden rise in the price of a barrel of crude) had an even more profound effect on our fortunes than the financial crisis, because GM's buyer group was hit the hardest. With Chevrolet and GMC, we were the nation's leading producer of full-size pickup trucks (GMC and Chevrolet combined usually outsell Ford, which always and correctly claims to be the number-one single brand), and the market was imploding. Pickups are the preferred vehicles of tradesmen such as carpenters, plumbers, and electricians, and their work had evaporated along with new housing starts.

Between Chevrolet, GMC, and Cadillac, GM was (and still is, albeit in a now-smaller market) the dominant player in full-size V8 SUVs, commanding a share consistently over 50 percent. These had become the family vehicle of choice for many American households as they combined space, comfort, performance, and suitability for many sports and lifestyle activities, all in one vehicle. Decried for decades by the environmental left, they had emerged, in Darwinian fashion, as a powerful species, boosted by economic well-being, the large distances endemic to the United States, and, of course, the omnipresent low fuel price.

The latter ensured a booming market for used Tahoes, Yukons, and Escalades, most of which were snapped up by less-affluent families who still had the same transportation wants as the more fortunate new SUV buyers. As always, good resale value fueled demand for GM's used SUVs, creating a highly profitable, virtuous cycle. GM's and, to a lesser extent, Ford's huge success with large SUVs prompted the Japanese to enter the segment with the monstrous Toyota Sequoia and the Nissan Armada, both of which had fuel-guzzling thirsts that would have caused GM to blush. Neither ever achieved meaningful volumes for the simple reason that American SUVs were the best: better styling, more rugged, longer lasting, more powerful, and offering the best fuel economy to boot. As written earlier, the "truck cultures" at Ford, GM, and Chrysler had, over the decades, managed to avoid the catastrophic loss of customer focus that their car-creating brethren had somehow fallen victim to. You can't convince an owner of a U.S. truck that he or she should "go import" with their next truck purchase; they are delighted with their vehicles. And GM was delighted, too, because the full-size SUVs and pickups were the overwhelming source of automotive profits, more than covering the losses stemming from the heavily incentivized sales of the less-compelling passenger car lineups.

When gasoline prices doubled, SUV resale values tanked. Families on strict household budgets saw their monthly outlay for fuel double, and they scrambled to get out from under their purchases. The resulting glut of used full-size SUVs caused a plummeting of their value, and lease rates had to increase to bridge the growing gap between "new" and "three-year-old coming back off lease."

GM's results took a dive. While our overall sales were down no more than anyone else's, the disproportionate drop in SUVs and full-size pickups made the total damage worse for GM and Ford than for the Japanese producers who, despite decade-long efforts to achieve a meaningful presence in the full-size truck market, were still predominantly selling small SUVs, crossovers, and passenger cars.

This is what we called "luck." But, to the ever-import-focused U.S. media, it was skill, virtue, and prescience.

Every U.S. business journalist in print and television soon jumped on the new bandwagon: the far-seeing wisdom of the Asians had caused them to eschew big trucks and focus, instead, on what the media likes to call more efficient offerings. In contrast, dumb, shortsighted, insensitive, and greedy GM had "persisted" in creating and selling full-size SUVs and pickups despite the "clear signals" that fuel prices were going to rise and favor smaller vehicles. Night after night, the talking heads on TV pontificated on the GM plight, stating that it was "of GM's own doing" for having pursued a "failed product strategy" and having bet on the wrong horse, again unlike the virtuous Asian producers.

As if anyone could have foreseen an artificial and, as it turned out, temporary doubling of fuel prices. Lost in the maelstrom of exaggerated praise for Toyota, now elevated to the position of World's Smartest Car Company, was the fact that they had just spent a staggering $1.3 billion on an all-new super-big family of full-size pickups and equally monstrous SUVs, the Toyota Tundra and its eight-passenger sibling, the Sequoia SUV, as well as the sprawling Texas assembly plant to produce them. The volume target was an initial 300,000 per year; the plant, when I last checked, was operating at less than half that number.

So, GM was officially stupid for having 50 percent of the most profitable segment of the market, the one that was in heaviest demand by customers, the one almost every other producer (including Mercedes-Benz) was eagerly trying to penetrate. Nobody ever "forces" the U.S. public to buy anything: at two dollars a gallon, these were the vehicles that sold, whether the leftist, elitist media or the proponents of global warming liked it or not. Imagine, therefore, the collective glee when that market collapsed, essentially leaving GM with its pants around its ankles.

Pundit upon pundit crucified GM for its "shortsightedness," arguing that it would have been prudent to hedge the bet by also producing some small, fuel-efficient vehicles. Somehow, these simplistic scribes and TV superbrains forgot that GM offered the Malibu with a class-leading 32 mpg, a compact Cobalt at 37 mpg highway, an even smaller, more frugal Chevrolet Aveo, not to mention the Chevrolet HHR small crossover. All of these actually sold well during the gas price shock, but the profitability was low, and the loss of SUV and pickup sales could not be compensated for by the small end of GM's lineup.

By fall 2008, it was obvious that we were going to run out of cash, as was Chrysler and, as they themselves thought at the time, Ford. Clearly, the U.S. auto industry was going to need additional loans to get through the crisis, but after numerous initiatives which proved to be false starts, we had to conclude that the U.S. banking sector, in turmoil after the subprime meltdown, was in no mood to lend billions to car companies. Even if they had viewed it favorably, they didn't have the cash to spare.

And so the U.S. government was approached, and at the worst possible time. The Bush administration was a lame duck, on the way out and awaiting President Obama's inauguration. They were most reluctant to engineer an auto industry bailout and, probably wisely, considered it the job of the next administration.

In mid-November, the nation witnessed the infamous congressional automotive hearings, during which the three domestic CEOs, Alan Mulally of Ford, Bob Nardelli of Chrysler, and Rick Wagoner of GM, were publicly humiliated by a series of grandstanding elected congressmen and senators who, clearly, were not out to help the domestic auto industry but instead displayed truly epic levels of ignorance and holier-than-thou arrogance. Accusation after groundless accusation rained down on the three CEOs, who sat silently, staring at the floor or their shoes like guilty schoolboys receiving a dressing down from a stern teacher. Not a single outrageous statement was even slightly challenged. I couldn't believe my eyes and ears; it occurred to me that if abject portrayal of silent guilt was the order of the day, it was a good thing I hadn't been invited to go along.

Later, when I told Rick Wagoner that I was dumbfounded over the failure of the CEOs to intervene politely and insert some reality into the congressional diatribe, he informed me that high-priced PR consulting help had urged the CEOs to sit through it, don't talk back, don't be defensive. The congressional public flogging and grandstanding by a bunch of politicians who knew little about our business and cared even less was the price they had to

pay for a minimum infusion of federal cash. The visible cause cé-
lèbre triggering the avalanche of congressional indignation was
the use by the CEOs of their company jets to come to Washington, D.C. I won't go into a defense of corporate jets here, but I do
believe that maximum mobility for the most senior people in a
global company is essential. Having said that, I will point out that,
upon discovering the corporate jet use, the noble congressmen,
well-known for their unwillingness to accept favors and perks,
were fuming with righteous wrath. How could these fat-cat CEOs
have wasted money flying to D.C. by G-5 when they could have
flown Northwest? The now defunct—or, rather, corporately absorbed—Northwest happened to be notorious for its unreliable
schedule. (A favorite practice was to cancel half-full flights for
"mechanical problems" and consolidate them with a later flight to
the same destination, but now with a much better load factor. The
number of international connections out of New York and Boston
I have missed due to this practice is astounding. "What is there
about the words 'scheduled flight' that you folks don't grasp?" is a
question I frequently asked of Northwest's terminally surly counter personnel.)

Imagine, if you will, what could have happened if the three
CEOs had been on a cancelled Northwest flight and missed the
hearings. Our elected officials would have been apoplectic with
rage! "These insolent CEOs don't place enough priority on congressional hearings to use their safe, secure, and reliable jets," they
would declare. "Instead, in a grandstanding, penny-pinching move,
they placed their fate in the hands of an airline known for its numerous cancellations. Ladies and gentlemen, citizens of this grand
land of ours, I hope you share my outrage over their failure to
appear due to their cavalier attitude toward Congress, the representatives of the American people . . . blah, blah, blah!" The
three CEOs were wrong no matter how they might have traveled
to D.C.

I have a feeling that, after the first unjust humiliation, Alan Mulally of Ford told himself, "I don't need this," and asked his finance people if they were *sure* Ford couldn't squeak through without government money. Turns out, in their case, they could. A year earlier, Ford, after years of financial stress, had essentially mortgaged every hard and soft asset in the company, including the iconic Ford Blue Oval logo, for north of $30 billion. We, at GM, thought that rather odd at the time: why would anyone want to securitize the whole company when, say, $15 billion in cash should be enough to get through any reasonably foreseeable downturn?

Maybe Ford knew something that we didn't. Maybe they had a crystal ball. Maybe (my theory) it was dumb luck (which is, actually, the best strategy of all).

At any rate, in the months post-financial-meltdown and post-fuel-price-doubling, when all auto companies, foreign and domestic, saw sales decline by 40 to 50 percent, cash was pouring out of the large companies at about the same rate, roughly $5 billion per quarter, whether at Toyota, Ford, or GM. Simple math dictates that, at that rate, the tank at GM would be empty in three quarters, and it was.

Ford, starting with about twice our cash pile, could last six quarters, which was enough to get them through the worst. Toyota, with cash estimated at $100 billion, barely felt it, although the company slipped into severe losses for the first time in its long history. (Today, Ford is the darling of the conservatives, the plucky, brave American company that stood on its own two feet and refused federal assistance. The company has been wallowing joyfully in those accolades ever since, and the goodwill it has brought them vis-à-vis "Government Motors" has benefited their sales way beyond that merited by their admittedly decent product lineup. Whether by luck, chutzpah, or skill, Ford is the new darling of the nation, somewhat replacing the recently fallen idol, Toyota. But GM will get over it!)

Before the second set of hearings, I urged Rick Wagoner to stop playing the role of the puppy caught with a mess on the floor and set some of the record straight. What would be so terribly wrong, I asked, in saying, "With all due respect, sir, I cannot let that accusation stand, for it is profoundly untrue, and I don't want the public to get the wrong information"?

I reminded Wagoner of Lee Iacocca back in the late 1970s, when Chrysler wanted federal loan guarantees. Iacocca faced congressional hostile questioning. One inquisitor asked (this isn't an exact quote, but a reconstruction from memory), "Mr. Iacocca, why should we ask this of the American taxpayer? Wouldn't the money be better allocated to new rail systems and subways? Those, Mr. Iacocca, are affordable transportation for the masses!" In one nanosecond, Iacocca shot back, "And what the hell do you think the Chrysler Corporation is?" That shut that congressman and others up, and the tone of the questioning became much friendlier. Chrysler got the loan guarantees, paid everything back early, brought a return of over $40 million to the U.S. taxpayer, and went on to decades of success.

But my argument was to no avail. The December 4, 2008, hearings were, if anything, even worse. Senator Richard Shelby (R-Ala.), in particular, spewed venom at the domestics, his state being the location of major Mercedes-Benz facilities which he mistakenly believed to be immune to the crisis. (After all, the foreigners are so much smarter.) I was hard-pressed to suppress a feeling of immature glee when, months later, Mercedes-Benz announced the layoff of a shift and other drastic production cuts at their Alabama facility due to the stalled sales of the vehicles produced there.

The low point for me came when Wagoner cast his gaze downward and mumbled an abject apology for having overemphasized the production of full-size trucks to the detriment of small cars. Here then was the spectacle of a browbeaten CEO apologizing for building the vehicles the public wanted. Vehicles that filled the coffers. Vehicles that, several years earlier, the pundits had criticized GM for not creating to the successful degree that Ford and Chrysler had ("GM misses market trend toward SUVs and trucks!"). Vehicles that European and Asian customers didn't want because their governments had had the courage to raise fuel prices gradually to over six dollars per gallon.

Let me assure the reader of one thing: even at gunpoint, nobody could have gotten me to make that false admission. I might have blown the temporary loans we ultimately received. I might have drawn down the wrath of the entire Congress, even been cited for contempt. But my profound awareness of the injustice being heaped on the company simply would have prevented me from uttering those words. I might even have found myself saying, "I'm sorry we produced so many SUVs the American public wanted due to unreasonably low U.S. fuel prices, and then suddenly stopped wanting when pump prices more than doubled."

The hearings, mercifully, ground to an end. I suppose the majority of the uninformed public saw them for what they were intended to be: our elected representatives beating on the greedy CEOs of America's failed automotive industry. Anyone with even a scant knowledge of the facts saw them as the sorry, demeaning spectacle they were. Maybe humility, silence, and abject apologies were the right strategy, but I would have been incapable of executing it. I believe that those hearings caused profound and widespread damage to an American industry that still employs more people, directly and indirectly, and adds more value, than any other in the country.

But the worst was yet to come: Without my knowledge or consent (not unusual, since I was, at the time, not in charge of marketing, external communications, or government relations), GM produced a full-page print ad in which we, as a company, once again apologized for our failed product strategy and our emphasis on full-size trucks, accompanied by a promise to do better in the future.

Disgusted, I found my enthusiasm, which had never failed me before, flagging. Why work for a company that is continually vilified in the media? Why struggle to contribute to America's most important industry when it is despised by our own government, with many advocating the disappearance of both GM and Chrysler ("And good riddance")? Why, if we were to receive government money, produce the "ecologically correct" econo-boxes the media and environmentalists think we all should drive, but that the bulk of the American public doesn't want? (There were rumblings from prominent Democrats that "if they get our money, they're going to produce the kind of vehicles we want them to produce.") I knew we would have no more corporate aircraft, and I knew pay would be cut to levels far below those normal for industry. I could live with that, but a life in a company absorbed into the warm, fuzzy matrix of the federal bureaucracy was not one I wanted to live.

That's why I announced my decision to retire . . . a decision I reversed when the new course of the company became clear. (Happily, my unusual pessimism later proved to be unfounded, except for the company planes and the pay!)

Despite the confusion and hot-potato tactics evident during the transition from the Bush administration to that of President Obama, GM received, in various forms, enough to see the company through until the hoped-for upturn in the spring of 2009. Soon after his inauguration, the new president appointed an Automotive Task Force to investigate the plight of the industry and to suggest courses of action. It was headed by Steven Rattner, a somewhat controversial financier; Ron Bloom, a former investment banker and United Steelworkers negotiator; Larry Summers, a noted economist; and Harry Wilson, a youthful and successful private equity executive. These four, with the analytical assistance of BCG (Boston Consulting Group), which provided the necessary "arms and legs" for countless interviews, analyses, and reports, soon sifted through every aspect of General Motors with a fine-tooth comb.

Many of their preconceived notions were understandable, given the slant of the U.S. media over the decades: They expected a product development activity devoid of great designers and engineers and a tendency toward comfortable, safe mediocrity. In other words, they were expecting the situation that I had found seven years earlier. Happily, they were amazed by the spirit, skill, dedication, and speed of GM's product creators and our laserlike focus on developing best-in-class vehicles. The future product program, when shown to the task force, impressed them with its audacity and excellence. (Behaving like the wealthy individuals they were, the task force exhibited the most admiration and lust for the now-launched 550-horsepower Cadillac CTS-V Coupe, while the more politically correct future small SUVs were praised at a more rational level.) Contrary to the task force's fears, Product Development turned out to be a bright spot, an area of true excellence, and one which almost certainly helped in the later recommendation to engineer a rescue of GM.

The other area of unqualified excellence was manufacturing. Lingering in the minds of the general public are outdated images of dark, rundown, smoky Detroit factories, peopled by lazy, alcoholic, or even drug-abusing workers who, rather than pursuing quality, would actually sabotage the product in order to hurt their employer. (We've all heard tales of Coke bottles being deliberately left in doors to produce a severe rattle later on.) I suppose some of this existed in the bad old days many decades ago, but today's reality is the exact opposite: gleaming buildings, well-landscaped grounds, brilliantly lit inside, with a level of cleanliness that would rival many hospitals. All of the fabled "Toyota Production System" methods were learned and incorporated over the years. Modern equipment, a positive change in union–management working relationships, a union–shared focus on quality, a massive investment in ongoing training, and a relentless drive for greater efficiency had made GM manufacturing in the United States as good as, and often better than, the best of the Japanese automotive manufacturing facilities. The task force, amazed but somewhat skeptical, asked to see our *oldest* plant. It was duly inspected and, other than the bricks and mortar, found to be as clean, bright, modern, and well-maintained as the newest facilities.

What emerged in the opinion of the task force was that GM was a company of basic operational excellence, hampered by a sales and marketing activity that lacked focus and supported too many brands with too many dealers. Finance, accounting, general management, and the apparently ritualized culture of the company's basic way of operating came in for criticism as well.

GM, in the opinion of the task force, was deemed to be a company that knew how to design, engineer, and build great cars and trucks, including those of advanced alternative drive technology, but was sorely lacking in its ability to market them, the totality wrapped in a culture that did not exude urgency or recognize the right priorities.

Once the task force got to work, so-called Viability Plans were developed. Basically, these were largely arithmetic exercises to see at what total North American market size and what market share GM could survive and prosper, assuming fixed costs were cut sufficiently to permit survival as a smaller company. Viability Plans 1 through 3 were rejected by the task force and the U.S. Treasury as too optimistic, so in VP4, active to this day as the commitment against which GM's performance is measured, total market size was cut pretty much to what it is today, and GM's market share was assumed at below 20 percent. For VP4, with its drastically lower volumes, huge cuts in fixed cost were needed. Plans were drawn up on myriad plant closures and workforce reductions, as well as planning a much lower future debt load and pension/health care benefits.

It was during these first few months of 2009 that plans were drawn up to eliminate Saturn, Pontiac, Hummer, and Saab. (Buick and GMC were also on the list but survived when their profitability became better understood. Clearly, though, the future emphasis was to be on Chevrolet and Cadillac.) Personally, I shed nary a tear for Hummer, as the brand, justly or unjustly, had become a lightning rod for the enviro-left and was taxing GM's credibility as a creator of fuel-efficient vehicles. Saab, a perennial money loser, was a failed son I was glad to see leave home. Again, not a tear from me!

Saturn and Pontiac were a different story. Both now had the best product lineups in their histories. Unfortunately, during the past few years of growing financial stress, both had seen their marketing and communications budgets slashed to the point where even sensational new products like the Saturn Aura and the Pontiac G8 V6 and V8 rear-wheel-drive sedan (a great, traditional Pontiac if ever there was one) were launched with so little advertising and sales promotion that they were what I call "confidential entries"—only the people at GM knew about them.

Still, the task force was right: GM needed to shed brands, with advertising and communication dollars devoted to the four critical ones—Chevrolet, Buick, GMC, and Cadillac—and not peanut-buttered over the original eight. As we reduced dealer count in line with the strong advice from the task force, GM's salespeople did the best they could in applying objective criteria to the cuts, such as sales results, customer satisfaction, and dealer profitability. But it was a hasty job at best, and in many cases the dealers had to be reinstated.

Other mistakes were made as well: in an effort to reduce Cadillac dealer count, many rural dealers who lived off of their Chevrolet, Buick, or GM franchises but who also sold five or ten Cadillacs per year to the local mayor, banker, or physician, were terminated to get the number down. This was counterproductive: a lot of Cadillac's strength lies not in massive urban "Taj Mahal" marble, chrome, and glass palaces like Mercedes, BMW, or Lexus, but rather in smaller, family-owned dealerships where personal relationships and integration into the fabric of the community are key. Cutting those stores got the number of Cadillac outlets down, but it did it in the wrong places. We wound up, later, restoring almost all of them.

Meanwhile, things at GM itself were grim. The market stayed down in the first half of 2009. Cash was running low again, and in view of the still intractable fixed costs, the debt burden, and the ongoing health care contributions, we saw our cash dwindling. Chapter 11 was really the only viable solution, despite the fact that it would destroy the equity ownership of the shareholders as well as a good percentage of the value in the hands of the debt holders. Not sure what the timing or duration of Chapter 11 would be, or what kind of company would ultimately emerge, we were busy reducing future product investment in order to minimize cash outflow. Several near-term launches, like the Chevrolet Camaro convertible, were delayed a year, and engineering effort was minimized, all to save precious near-term cash.

The emphasis was on "shucking the losers," not only in domestic brands, but also in GM's international empire. Thus, the decision by the board to sell the European Opel/Vauxhall operations, wholly owned GM subsidiaries which, although accounting for two million units annually and making high-quality contributions to GM's global passenger car programs, were a perennial money loser. Part of the problem was past mismanagement, and part was due to years of strife between Opel and the Zurich, Switzerland, headquarters of GM Europe. Opel, a proud German company, still considered the 1929 acquisition by GM a historical accident that could somehow be reversed or at least ignored. (In the mid-1990s, there was even something akin to a war of secession, with senior executives openly and publicly siding with an independent Opel. The rebellion was put down, but the operational and emotional damage would linger for over a decade.)

A major issue was the concentration of manpower and production facilities in Germany, possibly the most expensive country in the world in which to manufacture automobiles. Many GM competitors had seen the handwriting on the wall decades ago, moving ever deeper into the former Eastern Bloc: Poland, the Czech Republic, Hungary, etc. GM Europe largely missed that boat, and never did confront its intransigent IG Metall head of the Works Council, Klaus Franz. This gentleman is unique. A crafty street fighter with, I suspect, political ambitions, he enjoys the limelight and never fails to take any internal discussion or restructuring plan directly to the media regardless of potential damage to the enterprise. In fairness, we shall assume that he believes he is doing the right thing, but his strident (and unfortunately effective) defense of German jobs has robbed Opel of the flexibility enjoyed by Ford of Europe, VW, Audi, BMW, and Mercedes, who all benefit from a better balance of German costs versus lower wage facilities in countries as far away, in Ford's case, as Turkey. For these reasons, running GM of Europe was a difficult, frustrating, and thankless task: so many of the levers that an intelligent leader would normally pull were blocked by Klaus Franz and the code-termined (50 percent labor, 50 percent shareholders) Supervisory Board. To be fair, in Klaus Franz's Opel-centric view, the problem was not German cost, but rather the global GM bureaucracy and its sometimes manifested ineptness. His solution would have been "reverse the 1929 acquisition, make Opel independent again." (Given Opel's relatively small size and dependence on GM for much of its technology in engines, transmissions, crossovers, hybrid systems, et cetera, it was not a realistic solution.)

Still, there was a magic, almost fatalistic, convergence of desires: GM wanted to rid itself of the losses. Klaus Franz and a coterie of chauvinistic German executives wanted the divorce. The media, swayed by Klaus Franz, the self-appointed spokesman for Opel, chimed in. And Magna Corporation's (the world's largest automotive supplier) founder and principal owner, Franz Stronach, wanted to own a "real" automobile company. The latter struck a deal with Sberbank, one of Russia's largest, for financing. A team of executives was recruited. The modalities of future cooperation on global vehicle platforms were agreed upon. (Although I believe this would have fallen by the wayside in a few short years.) Price was agreed. GM was to keep a minority share.

Personally, I worried about a future GM without the superb (but expensive) capabilities of Opel's engineering organization, but elimination of the huge annual profit drain and ongoing large capital commitment dictated the choice. European Chevrolet, with production in Korea and the Eastern European countries, was not part of the divestiture, and was to form GM's future in the world's largest car market (Europe). But, while profitable and growing rapidly, it could not hope to compensate, in terms of volume and market share, for the loss of Opel/Vauxhall. The Opel-less GM, losing two million units, would no longer even be a contender among the giants vying for the title "world's largest automotive company." But, having made the painful decision to sell GM's European operations, little did we realize that, a few short months later, the decision would be reversed by the new board, selected jointly by GM's three largest new shareholders, the U.S. federal government, the Canadian government, and the UAW.

That reversal was hastened by the next shock to a now partially numb GM: on March 30, 2009, Rick Wagoner was pressured to resign by the Automotive Task Force, the U.S. Treasury, and, I suspect, the new president himself. The old GM board, still legally bound to defend the shareholders as well as to select or fire key executives, was miffed over the way this was handled, considerably at odds with the law and rules of corporate governance. It was "explained" to the board that, post–the increasingly firmly planned Chapter 11, the government would be the largest shareholder and that understanding and support for Wagoner's "resignation" would be in the best interest of all.

The reaction in the company over Wagoner's departure was one of sadness and regret. Rick was a kind, intelligent CEO of spectacular human qualities. The welfare of the GM family was close to his heart. Much of the progress, ill-publicized and subject to media distortion though it was, must be credited to Rick and his team. Possibly, it was his very concern for people and his unwillingness to take "bet your company" risks that convinced the task force that the cleanup in Chapter 11 and after should be left to a new team. It's hard, when a new owner pays billions for a company, to argue that he or she can't select the players.

Rick Wagoner's last act as CEO was to convince the Automotive Task Force and the board to ask Fritz Henderson to replace him. Initially, Henderson's title was to be preceded by the dreaded "interim." Wagoner, mustering his considerable powers of persuasion, convinced the decision makers that equivocating on Henderson's authority or permanence would severely restrict his ability to get the job done; the adjective was dropped. It soon became obvious in board meetings, however, that "interim" was alive and well: On meeting Henderson for the first time, the new chairman, Ed Whitacre, drawled, "It's gonna be hard for me to be a non–executive chairman. Ah'm used to runnin' things. The job ah really want to do is yours, Fritz." Embarrassed laughter all around.

Still, Fritz, a supremely intelligent executive who had successfully run Latin America, Asia-Pacific, GM Europe, and had most recently been chief financial officer and vice chairman, immediately set to work with a sense of urgency. Meetings were cut to a minimum, executive ranks were reduced drastically through voluntary and less-than-voluntary retirements, product excellence (my role) continued as the highest priority, massive fixed-cost reductions were implemented, and for the first time in years—and with strong encouragement from Chairman Whitacre—advertising and marketing budgets were greatly expanded. In one memorable meeting with Whitacre, Fritz and I suggested a doubling of advertising for the remainder of 2009, from—as I recall—roughly $375 million to $700 million. Ed declared this sum to be penny-ante.

"I want to spend $2 billion between now and the end of the year." Fritz and I gasped in astonishment: it was not in the profit budget! "Wal," he drawled, "the government just gave you fifty billion dollars. What the heck do you plan to spend it on? We've got to let the country know about our great new products!" And so, with this stroke of simple genius that often marked Ed Whitacre, we broke the vicious cycle of "lower sales equal less money for marketing, which in turn drives lower awareness and lower sales."

Soon, profitability and cash flow exceeded the commitments made to the Feds in the benchmark fourth and final "Viability Plan" submitted to the Treasury and the task force. One would have expected approval and support from the board in the face of such demonstrated, unexpected progress but, in fact, the opposite took place. In every board meeting, the slings and arrows flew, with ever more unfounded criticisms, "suggestions," and downright accusations of incompetence. It was clear that the board did not share my enthusiasm for Henderson's leadership. But Fritz, shaken but undaunted, focused on his responsibility and professed optimism that, as results became public and the new board became more familiar with the complexities of our business, approval and support would surely follow. This was to prove a naïve assumption, and on December 1, 2009, the board requested Henderson's resignation.

To the Treasury, the task force, and the board, it was simply unacceptable that a GM "lifer," however successful in his track record and current assignment, should play a key role in the rebirth of the company. At least one board member basically said it: "This team is lousy. If it were any good, you wouldn't have gone Chapter 11!" The expectation was that we were all subpar, and only a clean sweep of all the upper echelons would produce the much-needed change from an underperforming culture into a high-performance one.

In truth, I can conjure up a modicum of sympathy for that view: charged with "changing the culture" as his highest priority, Henderson, to my dismay, went about it the old GM way. The "problem" was discussed, democratically, teams for "culture change" were appointed, and consultants were hired. At several instances, I pointed out that this was emphatically *not* the way to "change the culture." I was, as always in situations of this type, an advocate of a much simpler, stronger, and more forceful management style. "Lead, follow, or get out of the way" (while maintaining an accessible, sometimes humorous, often self-deprecating posture) has always worked for me, and in my estimation, was exactly what was needed. But coming up with that solution, effective though it may be, is simply not what "culture change" teams and consultants do. I now believe that the traditional GM approach to changing the culture—well-intentioned, slow, and democratic—may well have been the one legitimate source of impatience (even exasperation) on the board's part.

Not surprisingly, Ed Whitacre replaced Henderson as CEO and quickly adopted the management style I felt had so long been missing: somewhat authoritarian, but delegating to the proven performers. Results or else. Everybody made to understand the mission and do their job. Cut out the silly "metrics" and meetings dealing with nonessential nice-to-have fluff. In one of his first meetings, Whitacre cancelled the "culture change" initiative, fired the consultants, and declared the culture fixed. And it was! The media correctly summarized Henderson's departure with the words "he never had a chance." But he was a good leader and did the right things overall. Maybe, by inclination and training, he just didn't want to adopt a stronger leadership style.

Let's back up. On June 1, 2009, GM officially declared Chapter 11. The "old GM" could be bankrupt and would be the repository of all the "toxic" assets the corporation needed to shed. Meanwhile, a "new" GM would be formed, free of the untenable burdens that diminished and ultimately sank the company. It was a brilliantly conceived scheme to limit the period of "business interruption" and the loss of consumer confidence. (While customers may buy a $500 airline ticket and care little whether the airline is in Chapter 11 or not, it's understandably a bit different in the case of a twenty- to fifty-thousand dollar durable goods purchase. It was this concern that caused Rick Wagoner to publicly preclude the Chapter 11 option for GM: he didn't believe the company could retain meaningful market share while in bankruptcy and figured the ensuing cash drain would soon create a bottomless hole.)

On June 9, GM got a new board, with the aforementioned Ed Whitacre, the prototypical lanky Texan with a highly deceptive "I'm just a country boy" manner, elected as non–executive chairman of the board. The new board was half experienced, successful executives selected by the federal government (with one member representing Canada's interest), and half more recent appointees to the former GM board—they, presumably, being less culpable in the lengthy decline of the company. It was to prove, initially, a contentious board, with the most aggressive questioners usually being those with the most absurd preconceived notions and the least knowledge of the structure and operation of a car company.

On July 10, barely six weeks after bankruptcy, the "new" GM declared itself open for business, with a new labor agreement; the Automotive Task Force wisely insisted that the UAW eliminate the last vestiges of the cost gap that still existed between the union-ized "Detroit Three" and the nonunion Japanese and German op-erations in the southern states. Moreover, the dreaded "Jobs Bank," the ill-conceived system of paying workers who were not needed in the production process, was abolished as well. The new GM had a low level of debt and a fresh $50 billion in new equity.

The latter caused an uproar among the country's conservative pundits, with terms like "nationalization" and "government take-over" bandied about with reckless abandon. To this day, Rush Limbaugh regularly trashes GM products and suggests they be boycotted in order to preclude any successful outcome for "Gov-ernment Motors."

The granting of financial aid through equity, though, had nothing to do with "socialist ideology," and everything to do with common sense. Harry Wilson, a member of the Automotive Task Force, was the originator of the plan, and he had, reportedly, a dif-ficult time convincing his colleagues (and the federal government, which wanted no part in "owning" a car company) of its wisdom.

Luckily for everyone, Wilson prevailed, GM received over $40 billion in U.S. and Canadian government equity, crushing interest payments were avoided, and to prove the time-honored adage that "no good deed goes unpunished," the Obama administration, a reluctant participant in the equity solution, winds up being pil-loried by conservatives for "nationalizing" GM and "creating Gov-ernment Motors," for the purpose of "building the green cars nobody wants, but which the Democrats think we should drive."

It should come as no surprise that the government wants to shed its ownership as quickly as possible, and environmental ide-ology takes a far backseat when it comes to emphasis on profit-ability leading to a successful initial public stock offering. GM is subject to the same (albeit onerous) fuel economy regulations as every other automaker, but if the company can achieve those numbers while also producing and selling Camaros, Corvettes, Tahoes, and Escalades, that's seen as being to the government's financial advantage, as well.

As of this writing, GM is solidly profitable, with a lineup of well-conceived cars and trucks which the public *wants* to buy, as opposed to being *induced* to buy via profit-sapping incentives. (GM Europe, for reasons mentioned, remains a weak spot. Profitability would be higher without the drain imposed by the European operation, a drain which, happily, is more than erased by the good rest-of-world results.)

Of special note is the source of profitability: it's the car business! This is in sharp contrast to the old days, when vehicle profitability was marginal or negative, and most of the money came from the finance company, GMAC, and the seemingly endless profitability of ResCap, the mortgage subsidiary, in particular.

Weaknesses remain at GM, and they must be addressed: GM has a troubled relationship with external communications, formerly called "PR." Instead of a welcoming, open, "let me help you" attitude toward the press, there remains a level of shyness and caution, an unwillingness to grant the media access to senior leadership who, for the most part, consider it a waste of time and a distraction from their "real job." Rick Wagoner was fond of saying, "All we need are good results, that'll take care of everything." But what if the positive engagement of the CEO and the top people *drives* results? What if the public tends, for equivalent value, to buy from a company they love and trust? I'm convinced that senior leadership has no more important role, beside ensuring product excellence, than constantly and consistently telling the company's story, and explaining, on "background" if necessary, how and why certain actions are being taken. Proof that this works can be found at Chrysler. During the Iacocca era, Lee relentlessly sold the com-

pany and its (mediocre) K-car products to an increasingly ador-
ing media and, thus, public. Chrysler, instead of being vilified for
taking government support and producing essentially one car in
a dozen versions, became the brave, tough little underdog that
wouldn't give up.

Or take Ford today: CEO Alan Mulally and Mark Fields, head
of North American operations, through their accessibility, charm,
seeming candor, and willingness to devote large quantities of time
to explaining and teaching, have become the darlings of the U.S.
media. Consumer willingness to buy, or at least consider, Ford
products is considerably in excess of the actual quality of their
(good) product lineup. Ford has become the brave underdog that
refused government assistance, and they do everything else right,
too. Product flops like the ill-conceived Ford Flex and the monstrously proportioned Lincoln MKT are quietly glossed over and
forgotten. Had they been GM products, they would have been
held up for repeated ridicule as examples of corporate ineptness.
GM, when using the same platform for several brands, usually
provides an expensive, entirely different body for each brand. Ford
spends no such money on at least two major, high-volume platforms, where the differences between Ford, Lincoln, and Mercury
must be discerned in grilles, tail lamps, and ornamentation. Test
question: which company, Ford or GM, is consistently accused
of "badge engineering," i.e., selling essentially the same vehicle
under different brands? You guessed it! In the words of one well-
known scribe, "Ford always gets the benefit of the doubt, because
we know and like them. GM doesn't because we don't."

Ford earned this by regarding the media as an important
factor in corporate success, worthy of the time and intellect of the
leadership. GM's attitude is best described by a comment made by
Ed Whitacre in a meeting. He was angered by some article that
was not entirely positive. "Why do we waste all this time talkin' to
the press? It doesn't do us a bit of good, and it just distracts us

from our job. We don't have to constantly tell these people what we're doing! I think it's better if we're sort of mysterious." Sadly, being "mysterious" is a recipe for disaster. People fear what they don't know, and they *hate* what they fear. Engaging the public, through the media, in an open, supportive, positive manner is something GM needs to learn if success is to be permanent.

Perhaps the elevation of Dan Akerson to CEO, replacing Ed Whitacre, will provide the opportunity to engage the media and the American public in a positive dialogue. Akerson is not shy, and at times is overly forthcoming with strong personal opinions, which I, of course, like. While these traits may occasionally be counterproductive and irritating, they are indicative of a forceful personality with ideas and a sense of direction. Early feedback from members of the media indicates that Dan Akerson is engaging and articulate—two extremely positive traits for effective communication.

Akerson has inherited a company headed for success. The string of product hits, such as the Cadillac SRX, CTS Coupe, Chevrolet Camaro, Chevrolet Cruze, Chevrolet Equinox, GMC Terrain, and a host of others are enjoying high levels of market success and, most important, commanding higher prices than their less-desirable predecessors. General Motors, for the first time in many years, is very profitable in the actual automobile (as opposed to financing) business, both overseas and in North America. Fixed costs are low, production capacity, if anything, is too tight, and profit-sapping interest payments on debt are low due to an equity-rich balance sheet. The fact that GM can be profitable in a total North American market of just 11.5 million units per year, as opposed to losing money in a 17.5-million-unit market as it had been doing a few years ago, speaks volumes about the transformation that has taken place.

Dan Akerson does not have to "fix the business." His role is not to run the operations but to set the overall direction, inspire the troops, and make sure the product development momentum continues. In short, Akerson needs to be the head coach and not the quarterback on the field.

With a new approach to communicating with the public, admittedly a big task given the historic GM reticence to engage in honest dialogue, Akerson's largest contribution could be to become the respected and liked spokesman, the personification, of General Motors. But it will require a fundamental change of direction, a realization that money will need to be spent, senior-most executives must make themselves copiously available, and communication must be genuine, as opposed to distributing a heavily vetted, triple set of "corporate position talking points" to be spouted verbatim by robotic executives.

Making GM more open, more human, more accessible, and thus more likeable is the last, great unfinished task. A CEO who says, "I don't have time for appearances on news or talk shows or for interviews; I have a company to run," simply does not understand that the perception of the company in the collective mind of the public has more bearing on ultimate business results than any set of "operational improvements" a CEO could effect by closing the door to outward communication and focusing internally. Many senior executives experience a sense of guilt about being "media personalities." While such self-effacing modesty may be a commendable trait from a human standpoint, it is, in today's world, wrong from a business perspective. The CEO and his senior people must accept the glare of notoriety and work it to the company's advantage, for like (or dislike) of an automotive brand is based on a complex set of beliefs, right or wrong, about that brand, much as it is with political affiliation.

What Lee Iacocca achieved through his willingness to speak, respond, be filmed, interviewed, or used in commercials, as much as his time would allow, had a transformational effect on the fortunes of Chrysler and is not much different from the astonishing, overwhelming success of Barack Obama in his successful bid for the presidency of the United States in 2008.

Rational executives err when they look at public exposure as "style" and "fluff" over substance. But the change of beliefs about and feelings toward a company wrought by an engaging charismatic leader *are* "substance." Naturally, the rest of the company's work has to "cash every check the CEO's mouth writes" but, as stated, that's not the problem with GM today.

When a company and its products are vastly better than their reputations, it's time to focus on changing perceptions. I just hope Dan Akerson "gets" it and does not become yet another internally focused, hardworking GM executive who is little known and even less loved by the media and by the general public.

I'll be watching!

What's with American Business Anyway?

(Ask the Dogs!)

GM'S BUSINESS PHILOSOPHY OVER THE PAST THIRTY YEARS HAS BEEN mired in the belief that the power of analytical intellect can solve all business problems as well as create viable strategies for success. This dogma is by no means confined to General Motors or the automotive industry: witness the decline and ultimate failure of many iconic U.S. business enterprises, household names that have gone out of business, been taken over, or shrunk to a shadow of their former selves.

Some will say, "It's the unions; they wrecked it." Others will say, "Government meddling and regulation." As I've said, there's a case to be made for both explanations. But the manufacturers and traders in many other countries deal with unions as entrenched and powerful as ours and are entangled in a web of government-woven regulations that make them envy the U.S. environment, and yet these foreign companies, automotive or otherwise, somehow survive and in many cases achieve excellence in all they do. They sell their wares at premium prices in the United States to a willing public that sees these foreign products as superior.

Warren Buffett, iconoclastic billionaire, once said, "If I had an

IQ of 160, I'd sell forty points." This seems a strange statement, coming as it does from one of the savviest and most successful businessmen ever. But my personal observations over forty-five years in business lead me to conclude that Mr. Buffett, as usual, is on to something.

American business, especially in the service and manufacturing sectors, has become, as the Brits like to say, "too clever by half." (Not quite Warren Buffett's percentage, but close enough.)

The problem lies, as it so often does, in the deliberate intellectualizing of a very simple task: creating and selling a meaningfully superior product or service to the public. It's not rocket science. You design, you manufacture, you sell, you collect money, and you reinvest. With any luck, some of the proceeds will reward the shareholders. Somebody has to keep the books, and someone needs to recruit capable employees and pay them competitively. This was all competently taught by the nation's business schools for decades— until they discovered what I'll call the "Sense of Academic Inferiority."

Bluntly put, in the academic environment, where the "hard" sciences rule, where physicists are pushing the boundaries of knowledge and seeking the elusive "God particle," where chemists use ever more sophisticated means to explain the complexities of the stuff all things are made of, the "professor of business" gets no respect! No "business researcher" can be identified as "pushing the boundaries of accounting" (although, arguably, many businesses have tried of late). There is nothing mysterious or arcane about design, customer delight, quality, or an efficiently run personnel department. Business educators, for the most part, felt like the cleaning and maintenance crew in an art gallery: necessary, yes, but hardly the main attraction. But how to emerge from these nonintellectual shadows, how to garner the respect of the "true" academics?

The answer presented itself at the close of World War II, when

Robert McNamara (later to become president of Ford Motor Company) and his "Whiz Kids" attained notoriety through their use of mathematical optimization concepts on behalf of the Defense Department. Mathematical modeling, quadratic programming, dynamic programming, game theory, and more were used to improve logistics, schedule bombing raids, and generally bring order to a fairly chaotic environment. (Of course, there was no "end customer.")

The world of business academe snapped it up, wolfed it all down, and made it its own. No more inferiority complex on campus. We're scientific now! We use math. We generate "optimization models" and use computers with the best of them. Masters and doctoral theses were soon riddled with mathematical formulae, and a sophisticated jargon was born to give the whole thing a lustrous veneer of intellectual respectability.

Only students of surpassing intelligence could understand it all ("Whatever happened to just setting a budget and figuring out how many better widgets we need?") and only a very few could actually contribute to advancing the art of "business as a science." They were the A-students, the sought-after cream of the crop, able to pour out a never-ending stream of phrases like, "We'll need to get the data, analyze it at a granular level, prepare a set of possible alternative approaches, weigh them against probable future scenarios, and then stress-test each for the downside ramifications." Who wouldn't want to hire men and women who could produce such verbal pearls at will?

Thus, the American business sector went into the IQ accumulation business. If you're not brilliant, don't have an MBA, and didn't graduate with at least a 3.5 GPA, we're not interested, thank you.

For the better part of my career, I have seen what these bright, analytical, dispassionate, data-driven geniuses have done to our country's industry and commerce. Through a relentless pursuit of "winning strategies" and elaborate "Missions, Values, and Goals" statements—which, incidentally, consume vast amounts of non-value added time—these modern MBA graduates reject the obvious as being "simplistic," and believe that elaborate alternative scenario planning and "test wells" will provide a better (if not logical) answer.

Read any business school case study (as I have, by the score), and you'll find reams of data in the form of words and tables. Somewhere in that thicket of information lies the key to renewed financial success: "Grant easier credit terms." "Reduce the complexity of the product assortment." "Close a plant." "Consolidate freight into car load lots." "Stop selling in Canada due to low margins." It's useful, and they're good exercises. But here is the fatal flaw: the customer is never discussed. She is taken for granted. Continued sales volume is simply assumed, no matter how much "optimization for margin improvement" is done!

Why does a celebrated American hospitality school call the course "Food Chemistry," when Europeans call it "Gastronomy"? Why did GM produce generations of automobiles that met all internal targets yet fell wide of the mark in sales? Why are America's most prestigious hotel chains, the ones renowned for superior food and service, foreign-owned? Why do most of us prefer to fly the Pacific on Singapore Airlines or JAL, and the Atlantic on Lufthansa or SwissAir, as opposed to Delta or American Airlines? Why did the eccentric, disruptive, and incorrigibly right-brained Steve Jobs (who, I am sure, is totally perplexed by phrases like "a probabilistic, resource-optimized potential future product portfolio") have to come back to save Apple after those who ousted him, boasting that "Apple would now be run soundly, by business professionals," promptly ran it full-speed into the ground? Why did Sir Richard Branson, with no higher education at all, succeed so brilliantly in both the airline and music businesses? The simple answer is: they have a blissful lack of awareness of the analytical science of business. Uninfected by the MBA virus, they simply strive to offer a better product, one that delights the customer. They control costs, of course. And they tolerate a necessary level of bureaucracy. It's essential. But the *focus* is on the product or service . . . thus, the customer. American business needs to throw the intellectuals out and get back to business!

While I was vice chairman of GM, I had the opportunity to visit a nationally celebrated engineering college from which GM often recruited graduates. I was invited to speak to the student body, did so, and later visited with the dean. There was something he needed to get off his chest: "You know," he said, "GM is missing out on some of our very best students because you won't interview anyone with a grade-point average below 3.0. In fact, you select the highest GPAs you can find. Quite often, I encourage your recruiters to look at an exceptionally gifted, creative young man or woman with a GPA of 2.7 or even 2.5. These are passionate students who work on aerodynamics or suspension systems, or who create their own hybrid cars because they love getting their hands dirty. Unfortunately, the book work sometimes takes a backseat, but they pass. It's not uncommon, on the other hand, for us to produce a 3.8-GPA graduate whom I would not hire, because all she did was study, study, and memorize for the tests. But you hire her, and leave the real hands-on engineers by the wayside. Couldn't you make some exceptions and occasionally, at my specific recommendation, hire a student of exceptional capability who doesn't meet the 3.0 GPA minimum?"

Sounded logical to me, so upon my return to GM I immediately and enthusiastically repeated the message from the dean. I met a stony reception. "Yes, we've heard all that before, and we're not buying. We have a *standard*, and it's called 'the 3.0 GPA.' There are plenty of students who are both hands-on and get their academic work done. Anyway, you have to draw the line somewhere, and a 3.0 GPA is where we drew it years ago!"

"But surely," I countered, "we would consider an exception in the case of a sub-3.0 student who is personally and highly recommended by the dean himself?"

"Well, no, we would not. Our insistence on academic excellence is a long-standing policy, and it has served us well over the years." Oh, really?

The highly creative 2.5-GPA hands-on candidates then find employment with smaller companies, foreign and domestic, where the emphasis is on creating hardware and inventing new solutions as opposed to looking and sounding brilliant while essentially tackling nothing. Small wonder that many new automotive technologies and components are brought forward by suppliers to the large automotive companies: the supplier companies had to "make do" with all those "dumb" 2.5-GPA engineering graduates. I will bet that the two young engineers at Chrysler who (without authorization) tinkered with a company car over several weekends and, at low cost, created the first U.S. manual-shift feature for automatic transmissions were *not* 3.5-GPA intellectuals.

Thus, as is so often the case, we see quantified "rules" overwhelming common sense. The result, ultimately, is a failure to achieve excellence. Thanks to a pervasive bias toward an ever more analytical, intellectual approach to business as taught by America's esteemed graduate schools of business, we are churning out armies of bright young executives, all skilled in numbers and business-speak, all eager to reduce cost and game the system for ever-greater short-term benefit. (After all, we *do* get measured every quarter, and we *do* have stock options that we want to see "in the money.")

But where, I ask, is the business school that preaches, above all, acceptance of the obvious, simplicity, and that uncommon virtue, common sense? Where is the business school program tailored to the highly intelligent, creative, right-brained individual who *senses* rather than analyzes, whose mind skips countless spreadsheet analyses and sees right to the solution? Where is the business school course entitled "Customer Delight as a Key Factor in Business Success?" Maybe there is one. I surely haven't heard of it, and I can vouch for the fact that GM didn't hire any of the graduates. I'd like to teach such a course, but it would not be popular in the school, because my basic and simple lesson would be this:

If you're running a dog food company, your "food chemistry" can be brilliant, the ingredients healthy and procured at an optimized low cost. Manufacturing and canning can be done on the latest, low-labor equipment. The young, motivated workforce can be nonunion. Marketing and advertising can be researched, focus-grouped, and tested to perfection. The balance sheet and accounting practices can be the envy of the category. Logistics and distribution can have been computer-modeled for just-in-time replenishment of excellently placed store shelves, access to which was skillfully gained by a world-class sales force. And the management ranks can be filled with 3.5-GPA MBAs from the nation's finest business schools. However, as the old joke goes, it's all for naught if the dogs don't eat.

If dogs don't like the end product, the dog food company is sunk. . . . It's a very simple maxim that is blissfully ignored by higher business education, which teaches all of the "techniques" but fails to train people in the importance of "the dogs." Rather than bask in the false belief of the superiority of American business education, the big business schools should be asking themselves how and why it all went wrong. They have produced generations of number-crunching, alternate-scenario-loving, spreadsheet-addicted idiots-savants. They should be ashamed.

Of Management Styles

I AM FREQUENTLY ASKED, ESPECIALLY IN LIGHT OF HAVING EXPERIENCED four different CEOs at GM over a period of sixteen months, what kind of leadership style is the "correct" one for an automobile company. And while many of the principles may be universally applicable, the direction of a large car company is distinctly different from, that of say, GE. The latter is a conglomerate comprised of wildly different companies, most completely unrelated to one another, with their own priorities, problems, products, and customers. "Running" this conglomerate in detail is clearly beyond the capability of any one man: the fields of action are too scattered and too diverse. What leadership does in a conglomerate like this is set the goals, the measurement criteria, and the overall governing policies; select the right leaders for the individual businesses; measure progress; and sell underperforming units while adding new, promising entities to the portfolio.

A car company, on the other hand, is one enormous, hugely complicated organism that has many moving parts, all closely interrelated and interdependent. Many of the company's activities are day-to-day: running the plants to produce components and assemble cars, procuring supplier parts, moving the finished vehicles to the dealers, billing same, and booking the revenue. The operations portion of the automobile business has been thoroughly optimized over many decades, doesn't vary much from one automobile company to another, and can be managed with a focus on repetitive process. It is the "hard" part of the car business and requires little in the way of creativity, vision, or imagination. Almost all car companies do this very well, and there is little or no competitive advantage to be gained by "trying even harder" in the procurement, manufacturing, or wholesale area.

Where it suddenly turns complex, and where the winners are separated from the losers, is in the long-cycle product development process, where short-term day-to-day metrics and tabulation of results are meaningless activities. Despite the advent of many new computer tools to speed engineering, testing, and certification, the "initial idea" to "first unit off the line" time is still, depending on the complexity of the product, about three and a half years. (Most of the compression has been eaten up by vastly more stringent safety, emissions, and fuel economy requirements.) It is here that the recipe of the dog food is determined.

Astonishingly, in this critical product creation area, where the future of the car company hangs in the balance, the much-scorned autocratic style of management works well, and numerous success stories confirm it. The big proviso, of course, is that the autocrat must be so steeped in the car business, and have so much taste, skill, intuition, and sense for the customer, as to be nearly infallible. (I shall eschew discussion of the less-than-knowledgeable autocrat: delving into things he or she knows little about and ordering, demanding that it be done this or that way, is a near-infallible recipe for disaster. According to many, the former chairman of Daewoo many years ago fit this mold, and he destroyed the company while making sure all his employees treated him with due reverence.)

A prime example of a "highly skilled autocrat" is Dr. Ferdinand Piëch, grandson of the original Dr. Porsche, former CEO of VW, and, I take it, chairman of their supervisory board for as long as he elects to stay. With a self-confidence bordering on and perhaps crossing into arrogance, Piëch ruled VW with an iron fist, listening to few and firing many who dared question his supreme wisdom. Cowed and fearful, giant VW was run by one man. He made portfolio decisions; he insisted on cars with advanced technology; he made design decisions, often ordering a redo shortly before production if he spotted an interior detail he didn't like, such as an air vent in a poor position. And, while his stubborn sense of infallibility led to one or two colossal blunders (such as the beautiful but failed VW Phaeton, a $100,000 luxury car that was doomed by its VW badge), Piëch's strong direction and insistence on excellence made the VW Group, including Audi, Seat, Skoda, Lamborghini, and now Porsche and Bentley, into a global automotive powerhouse and currently the largest car company in the world.

But does the autocrat, no matter how gifted, create sustainable success? Or does his style drive away other, capable leaders who would form a leadership *team* after the great man's departure? Time will tell. But, like him or not (and I would personally prefer not to work for Dr. Piëch), reputation, market share, profitability, and shareholder value all increased dramatically under the my-way-or-the-highway style of the good doctor. The future is another matter, but if the purpose of leadership is to drive results, chalk up one major victory for the supremely skilled autocrat.

Contrast this to the benevolent, thoughtful, sharing, "respect other people's emotional equity" approach that so long characterized GM. Everything was laboriously studied and restudied; personal opinions, as in "I think we should do *this* and not *that*," were discouraged. Open verbal disagreements were rare. It was hoped that "the data," generated by swarms of analysts and planners (to say that the plans and analyses were often slanted to coincide with leadership's prejudice would be belaboring the obvious) would send a clear message, the unequivocal numbers on the screen assuring everyone that this, indeed, was the only right course. No need for an acrimonious discussion. Just everybody nod and then go complain bitterly in the sanctity of your own office. Above all, GM leadership sought stability, balance, and equilibrium. No traumatic shake-ups, no nasty exchanges at high-level meetings. Small wonder I often irritated the assembled group when I said, "I see the numbers, and I know who put them together and why, and I don't believe any of it!" More than once I was told, more or less politely, that "we" preferred to run the business based on "hard data" rather than "Bob's hunches." And, again more than once, "Bob's hunches" ultimately turned out to be correct and the dispassionate analysis dead wrong.

The main victim of vague direction, though, was Product Development, which ran as a reliable, predictable machine, turning out products of perfect mediocrity. It was here that I took an approach more like that of Ferdinand Piëch, in that I articulated a clear vision of what I wanted in design, visual quality, and driving characteristics. Unblinded by thirty or forty years of loyal GM service, I saw what was wrong with the system and its output, and I knew I had to change it if we were to be successful. But in an American corporate environment much attuned to "mutual consideration and respect," I could not be *quite* like Dr. Piëch. Where he could order others around under threat of dire consequences, I had to demonstrate, argue, persuade, field counterarguments, and compromise, only to find that what I thought had been understood was not what people "decided" I had meant, and so the loop began all over again. It was time consuming. Piëch would have done it faster, but he was CEO, and I was only a vice chairman. Still, I often ask myself if the company could have achieved the turnaround in product excellence faster if I had been less patient and more brutal in my approach.

One of the things I found I had to do was teach the basics of what constitutes a beautiful interior, beautiful paint, and superb fits of outside sheet metal. Friday after Friday, I was in one engineering shop or another, surrounded by midlevel engineers, designers, manufacturing execs, going over a future model in tiny detail, showing everyone how the same part looked on an Audi or Lexus (we always had one of each for comparison), then asking why we couldn't execute it like that, and listening to more or less valid answers.

I had to ask myself, and still do today, if it is the proper role of a vice chairman of a $200 billion revenue company to get down in the trenches for hours on end, teaching the love of perfection in the smallest details when perhaps a more impatient autocrat would simply have ordered—nay, demanded—that it happen, laying down a deadline and then firing masses of people if the deadline came and the results weren't there.

The fact is, though, that my effort to instill into the organization a drive for perfection and customer delight in all things was successful. And still I wonder—was I right? Did I change the core of the product development culture by teaching, or did I rely too much on my own will and my considerable influence to get what I wanted? If the latter, excellence will soon be lost again, and "value engineering" and "Let's see how much we can cut before the customers start complaining" will rear their ugly heads again. Death by a thousand small cuts, because anytime the company loses the focus of providing the very best it can, delighting the eye, ear, butt, and wallet of the customer more than the competitors do, the inevitable decline sets in.

That's what happened at Chrysler after I left in 1998. I'd thought the culture had absorbed, permanently, the lessons I had so passionately taught during my stint as president of the company. But the Germans were obsessed with the belief that a mass-produced U.S. Chrysler or Dodge had to be much cheaper to produce than an equivalent Mercedes, and so every bit of customer-perceptible "worth" and "goodness" was stripped out, with disastrous consequences. (This is a mistaken belief: any U.S. midsize car contains the same parts count, the same engine and transmission technology, the same safety equipment, the same ABS brakes and traction control, the same or similar seats and interiors, much of it from the same suppliers. A Chevrolet Malibu's material cost is within a couple percent of that of a BMW 3-Series.)

I obviously failed to create a sustainable culture of customer focus and product excellence at Chrysler. But I believe the lesson will "stick" at GM.

But now contrast the highly effective "brilliant despot" approach of Dr. Piëch with that of Ed Whitacre.

Whitacre, of the friendly smile and the deceptive "only a country boy" demeanor (but watch the steely eyes that never really smile) professed no knowledge of the automotive business whatsoever. Furthermore, he didn't see why he should acquire any. In his eyes, his job at GM was to simplify, to weed out decades-old processes, reports, meeting structures, and approval paths. He correctly concluded that the "long-cycle" part of the company, namely Product Development, was in good shape—no sense tampering there. In other areas, he made a series of senior-level personnel and structural changes that would have been unthinkable in the old GM.

Whitacre was focused on results, and more than any GM CEO before him, on sales results. Complicated, softcover-bound reports containing arcane financial detail were held up to scorn and ridicule, and eliminated. He wanted, and soon got, the "Dick and Jane" version of everything. These very simple, very basic reports gave him all the information a CEO would need to guide the company, without being distracted by minutiae better left to the lower rungs of the organization. This left Whitacre's mind clear to focus on the mission, "to design, build, and sell the world's best cars and trucks." He didn't feel he had to know *how* to do that himself (whereas I always thought it was my *role* to know how); he just had to have the right people in the right places and make sure they fully adhered to the mission.

Note the purity of that mission statement: Most of the ones you see include something about "serving the communities in which we work" (goal conflict: how much money and time gets deflected for that?), "protecting our environment" (ditto the goal conflict), "treating our people as our most valuable resource" (so, no firings, layoffs, demotions, or early retirement? No salary cuts in hard times?), and, of course, the perennial, all-time sine qua non: "create shareholder value." That one is almost guaranteed to drive bad behavior on the part of a significant minority. If "shareholder value" is as important as "great product," why not squeeze a tiny bit of goodness out of the vehicles, reduce cost by a few hundred dollars, improve the margins (before the customers catch on), and have a blowout quarterly result that drives the stock up?

It is really only the simple purity of the mission statement "to design, build, and sell the world's best cars and trucks" that can be conveyed internationally, all the way to the hourly workers in Korea and China. In an unequivocal fashion, it sanctifies the customer and the product. And, of course, if the company gets *that* right, all of the other desirable "goals" evolve naturally from the market success of the products. (During Chrysler's success in the 1990s, the mission statement was "It is the mission of Chrysler to design and build cars and trucks that people want to buy, will enjoy driving, and will want to buy again." I doubt that that mission statement survived the acquisition by Daimler.)

Understanding the beauty and efficiency of the simple message was Ed's genius. Whitacre is much smarter than he wants you to believe, but in a battle of IQs, I'm sure he, as almost all of us, would succumb to the intellectual powerhouse that resided in Rick Wagoner. Who has the better leadership style? Who was a

more effective CEO? Whitacre's term was too short to draw any
meaningful conclusions. But I'll offer one tiny nugget.

While in the graduate school of business at UC Berkeley,
I was a pilot in VMA-133, or Marine Attack Squadron 133, a
Douglas-A-4-equipped reserve unit flying out of Naval Air Sta-
tion Alameda, near Oakland.

We were advised that the squadron would be receiving a new
commanding officer. Rumor had it that he was a modest man,
with much to be modest about. He was already older and had received his commission in World War II, on the battlefield. He had
no higher education. And, to top it off, his "civilian" occupation
was "Hoseman Number 2" in the San Francisco Fire Department.
He had almost no jet time! The lieutenants and captains in the
squadron, all ambitious graduate students at Cal and Stanford, were
shocked: the Marine Corps was giving us an uneducated, elderly
fireman as a leader.

At the change-of-command ceremony, we discovered that our
new CO, Art Bauer, was also of modest stature. Truly, an unin-
spiring sight. After the formal ceremony, Lt. Col. Art Bauer called
the twenty-odd junior officers together and gave the following
talk, as I remember it:

> Gentlemen, I don't know why the Corps chose me to lead this
> unit, but choose me they did, and we're all going to make the
> most of it. I know my education is far below yours, and my ci-
> vilian profession, although I'm proud of what I do, is humble.
> All of you have recent active-duty experience, and all of you are
> more skilled pilots and know much more about today's Marine
> Corps than I'll ever know. So, I'm not going to run this squad-
> ron. You each have your squadron roles, be it Intelligence Of-
> ficer, Operations Officer, Safety Officer, Maintenance Officer,
> or Administration. I want and expect you to each do your jobs;
> talk to each other, be a team, and help each other. I'm going to

stay out of your way, because you're all more capable than this old officer. I don't expect you to respect me for my flying ability, because it's not at your level. But I do want and demand your support and respect, not for me, but for the uniform I wear and the rank that's on it. You, gentlemen, not I, are going to run this squadron, and I don't want you to let me down.

The doubts and secret snickering soon stopped. Within eighteen months, VMA-133, under the command of Art Bauer, was rated the number one reserve squadron in the Marine Corps Reserve, with the highest operational readiness, the highest scores in Inspector General inspections, and the highest scores in ordnance delivery. Those responsible for senior officer selection in the Marine Corps must have been as surprised as we were that this modest, self-effacing man, of limited skills but the right leadership touch, had attained such a level of success. But perhaps they weren't surprised at all. Maybe they knew that a leader like Art Bauer was exactly what this squadron of self-assured and cocky aspiring doctors, lawyers, and business professionals needed.

The parallels with Ed Whitacre are obvious. In leadership, as in all things, less is often more. I hope and trust that GM's new leader Dan Akerson will achieve the right balance.

If I Had Been CEO

THIS CHAPTER IS HIGHLY CONJECTURAL FOR, AS I STATE FREQUENTLY, boards of directors usually don't appoint creative right-brainers to the CEO post: there is just not enough predictability, not enough respect for carefully crafted "future scenarios" (which, due to their numerical precision, provide the faint of heart with a false sense of stability and order), too many changes of course, too much emotion and communication. Not only do boards not *select* people like me, they actually get rid of them when they have them. The fact that the most remarkable business successes were produced by individuals like Bill Gates, Steve Jobs, and Sir Richard Branson does nothing to alleviate the anxiety over their boldness in seeking new products and services. No board was ever going to confer the ultimate responsibility on me, but it's *fun* to go down the list and see just what I might have done differently had I come in as CEO in 2001 instead of as vice chairman.

I am not even tempted to claim that the final outcome, Chapter 11, could have been averted. The corporation was so overextended, so heavily in debt, so burdened with a drain of $6 to $7 billion per year for so-called legacy costs, that the double whammy of the spring 2008 subprime mortgage meltdown, coupled with the unpredicted (and unpredictable) jump in fuel prices to well over four dollars a gallon, would have overwhelmed even the best-managed company.

There are, however, many areas where I would have acted differently.

The Lutz regime would have been focused on product first and foremost. In terms of capital and engineering budgets, I would have spent more, rather than less. Believing as I did that alternative fuel vehicles like Volt represented an opportunity to change the public's (erroneous) perception of GM as a reckless producer of gas guzzlers, I would have accelerated the creation of hybrid vehicles as well as all-electric prototypes and auto show concept cars. It's not that there was, or is today, a huge market for the things. It's just that the media praise those who make them and smother them in superlatives for their environmental correctness. Those who eschew them are greedy, shortsighted, or technologically incompetent.

In fairness, we *did* have one such program that received a huge amount of annual research budget and which GM hyped to the limit of its communications skills: the hydrogen fuel cell.

The problem with our fuel cell program was that, despite GM's best efforts, the world saw it as "vaporware." Aided, no doubt, by some of our esteemed competitors, the media's general conclusion was that, with our dearth of fuel-efficient vehicles and our failure to produce hybrids, we were dangling the sugar plum of a carbon-free future in front of the nation in an effort to draw attention away from our current perceived shortcomings. The fuel cell program was just too easy to attack: production was too many years away, deadlines for initial production came and went, and it was all too easy for detractors to point to the absence of a distributed hydrogen infrastructure (we have only a handful of experimental hydrogen fueling stations in the whole country).

And then there were the issues of cost. Despite the best efforts of GM's highly talented hydrogen fuel cell team, which achieved breakthrough after breakthrough in terms of performance and reliability, material cost of a fuel cell vehicle, at any realistic near-term production volume, remained many multiples higher than a conventional gasoline drive system and a couple of multiples higher than a battery-powered vehicle like the Chevrolet Volt.

I frequently attacked what I considered to be the single-minded, heavy financial commitment to fuel cells, feeling they were too far out on the time horizon and robbing us of the research funds needed to create more viable near-term solutions. But it was always for naught: the internal fuel cell "lobby" had the ear and heart of Rick Wagoner, who let himself be convinced that a few years of additional effort would make GM the reinventor of the automobile, that we would be producing vast fleets of carbon-free vehicles, and that costs would actually be below those of a conventional car. It was a noble vision but a big bet.

I would have dialed the research program way, way down and perhaps sought joint ventures. Support for our maximum-effort fuel cell program within the company was mixed, at best. Most shared the public's (and my) misgivings about cost and the low probability of convincing oil companies to spend billions on high-cost hydrogen fueling stations all over the country, along with the high pressure tankers needed to resupply them. And the dirtiest secret about fuel cell vehicles is that, despite the hype, the mileage is not infinite. As near as anyone can reasonably calculate, the total consumption of carbon fuel for a fuel cell vehicle, from "well to wheel," as the phrase goes, is only a bit more than double that of a very efficient internal combustion car, or about 80 mpg. That figure, it is generally acknowledged, is about what can be attained using a small diesel engine in conjunction with a battery hybrid system. An emission-certified diesel hybrid is also an expensive proposition, but far less than half of even the most optimistic fuel cell projections. I would have kept it going as a long-term project with modest funding and would have reallocated the money! And we would have stopped talking about it.

My main focus, however, would have been the elimination of superfluous activities, committees, and non-value-added work. When hour upon hour was spent arguing at the most senior corporate meetings about whether potential future managing director candidates are "functionally specialized" or "general management" in their capabilities, my eyes glazed over. What difference could it possibly make? Are they aggressive, smart? Are they leaders? And this "planning" was done so far in advance that so much would change, personnel-wise, in the interim, that most of the "good work" was for naught anyway. I would have summarily scrapped the hallowed, enormously time-consuming "Performance Management Process" system, with its dozens of interlocking "functional" versus "geographic" goals, all "box-balanced" by region and function for absolute precision, eliminating any inconsistency in goal setting. The worst thing about the PMPs was that, when the laborious process of goal setting and metrics was finally complete, after months of work by the HR department, it was already out-of-date. The fast-shifting world saw to it that major economic and market functions had changed enough to render pursuit of the original goals meaningless. The elaborately prepared, earnestly negotiated and discussed sheets of goals remained tucked away in file cabinets and drawers, never to be consulted until midyear review time, at which point all agreed that, given the new circumstances, we were working on the right things.

The excuse given for the PMP process is that it provided "general corporate alignment on objectives." In my view, that would have been accomplished by a short memo from the CEO. I'd much rather have a group of executives who know the overarching goals, and know in a fast-changing environment what they should be working on. The PMP process added nothing except, once again, that analysis-derived comfort level. Out with it!

I would have attacked what I considered to be our weak, sometimes close-to-clueless marketing activities. GM had precious little in the way of gifted marketing executives—men and women with an innate feel for the product and the best ways to convey its advantages to the public. Our longtime ad agencies would have had to go. It's not that they were bad agencies—they did good work for other clients. It's just that we have had them way too long, some for over seventy-five years. The benefit of this long-standing relationship was that agency and client were intimately familiar with each other's foibles. That was also the main weak point. We took each other for granted; there was no "tension" in the relationship. The agencies made themselves useful by assuming much of the workload of our internal marketing people. Whether it was "brand boards," presentations, marketing proposals, or whatever—the agencies did it. In essence, we were paying, in many cases, twice.

Further, the agencies knew exactly what kind of advertising would be "acceptable" to the client: safe, uncontroversial, not too product-focused, and it had to tell some sort of heartwarming story, as opposed to focusing on reasons why the customer should pay $35,000 for this particular product. I proposed changing agencies once and was told this was "unthinkable." Too much agency change promotes turmoil and inconsistency. Too little promotes complacency, mutual tolerance, and the production of an ineffective stream of inoffensive advertising that does not sell cars and trucks.

During my reign, I would have sharply trimmed the scope and power of Product Planning. My experience at each of the Detroit Three has taught me that, far from being inspired "car guys" (includes females), most product planners are highly analytical left-brainers, often of exceptional intelligence, and many are recycled finance executives with the same fondness for and faith in highly detailed quantitative analysis—the farther into the future, the better. Product planners will often use statistical data to come to highly improbable conclusions, and since they are there to plan "new entries," there is a pronounced tendency to identify ever more "segments," or pockets of demand, and "subsegments" within the segments. And, each time a "segment" is "discovered," a certain percentage of it is assumed for the GM brand in question. Adding all that up theoretically results in more market share, but in the real world, it does not. The consumer does not think by "segments" or even categories, and two vehicles of the same brand, but of differing "segments," sitting in the same showroom, will not result in two sales. The customer believes them to be much the same, and selects one. Thus, the Chevrolet Equinox laid waste to the slightly larger Trailblazer, and the Ford Escape dispatches the Explorer.

"No, no, you foolish customers! You're not supposed to do that!" the product planners cry. "The Equinox and Escape are small front-wheel-drive car-based utilities. The Trailblazer and Explorer are midutilities, with real frames and rear-wheel drive. They are different products!" The customer, however, sees in each case, a fairly large, box-shaped, four-door sport-utility that will carry five people in safety and comfort. "Which one is cheaper? I'll take that one." Many product planners have little or no understanding of the real world as it unfolds in a dealer's showroom.

At Chrysler, I once had to address an auditorium full of product planners who wanted to know why I hated them. I explained that I liked *them*, but disliked what they did—and I had plenty of examples to make the point. To me, the proper role of Product Planning should not be to have full responsibility for the product program. That, in a car company, is the role of senior management (hopefully automotively enlightened), with input from Design, the more savvy marketing people, and Product Development. That's where the overall character and scope of the portfolio have to come from; Product Planning can then "run the numbers" to see if it makes business sense. They should be the analysts, checkers, keepers of order. They should not try to be the originators of new product ideas, because most planners are congenitally incapable of right-brain thought.

At some point, starting in about 2005, and looking at the amount of money the "legacy costs" would siphon away, advertising budgets began to be progressively cut back. The argument was that the smaller sums would be adequate if the advertising could be "more effective," and while there is nothing too wrong with that view, the fact was that our presence in print, on TV, and on the radio began to fall below the levels needed for public awareness. When you launch a Saturn Aura midsize sedan, and it is named "Car of the Year" by a jury of fifty North American auto journalists, and in 2009, the public is still asking "a Saturn *what*?" you know you haven't spent enough.

It's true that if you took the budget's revenues and costs as gospel, we could not afford more advertising. But the derisory levels of advertising begat lower revenue which, in turn, dictated ever lower advertising budgets. We were trapped in a vicious circle. I would have busted out and started spending in the belief that the revenue would grow fast enough to offset it. It might have been a colossal mistake, but the way we were going, we were like the mythical bird that flies in ever smaller circles until it disappears into its own rear end.

Earlier, I would most likely have cancelled the so-called "Alliance Strategy," whereby GM owned minority shares in Isuzu, Suzuki, Fuji Heavy (Subaru), and, for a time, Fiat. Not being present when it was conceived, I never really heard a coherent explanation of why we would benefit from owning portions of other automobile companies, especially when there was precious little to be gained from "product synergies." Importing Japanese cars and rebadging them with domestic GM nameplates had stopped being profitable years ago, and there was really no way that we would share meaningful amounts of product with Subaru or Fiat.

Yes, we benefited in diesel engines from both Isuzu and Fiat, and there were countless other small benefits along the way, but nothing to justify the management distraction, the constant effort to make the Alliance Strategy look smart, not to mention the very costly penalty GM had to pay to back away from our Fiat commitment.

As stated earlier, I liked the Saab cars themselves but not how we were permitting Saab to continue as a money-losing, quasi-independent entity. I would have thoroughly consolidated it into GM Europe and eliminated all of the unique fixed costs associated with the brand. In 2006, I was a strong advocate for the brand's sale to whomever, but the general consensus was that it could be "made profitable," a perennial hope that never materialized. Love the brand or not (and I do), from a business perspective, GM should never have purchased it. In retrospect, I see not one single scrap of evidence that GM ever benefited in the least from the ownership of Saab.

When Rick Wagoner was focused on buying the ultrabankrupt Korean carmaker Daewoo, I was afraid we were purchasing another bottomless pit to be filled with money, although the purchase price was ridiculously low and involved next to no cash. I was concerned over our intent to own a minority piece (again!) of yet another Asian car producer, and this one was in the most abysmal financial state possible. If I had been CEO, it might well have been impossible to convince me that this was a smart move. And that would have been a colossal mistake: Daewoo, with a bit of assistance from GM, proved to be a highly capable enterprise once freed from the strictures of bankruptcy and the fatal idiosyncrasies of their past chairman. The restructured GMDAT (General Motors–Daewoo Automotive Technologies) today forms the backbone of GM's Asian strategy under the Chevrolet brand, is a highly capable design and engineering source, and is the key element of Chevrolet's rapid global growth to well over four million units per year. Turning this one down would have been a very serious mistake on my part.

I'll tell you one company I *would* have bought but we didn't, and that's Chrysler. In 2006, when Daimler wanted to divest itself of Chrysler (after having thoroughly messed up the product program), I urged Wagoner and Henderson to take a look at it in the hopes that we could take it all off Daimler's hands for next to nothing and merge Chrysler into GM.

Why would this have made sense? Because, operating in the same geography, same union environment, in the same legal and regulatory climate, the consolidation savings would have been huge. We could have, in all cases, collapsed two finance departments, two design groups, two engineering organizations, two human resources departments, two legal, two tax . . . into one of each, perhaps 10 percent larger than GM's former entities. As in the case of Chrysler's acquisition of American Motors Corporation, maker of Jeep, in 1987, a careful sifting would have taken place, keeping the best and brightest of both companies and retiring the "bottom halves." We would have acquired Jeep, Dodge Trucks, the minivan architecture, and a good rear-wheel-drive sedan architecture. Longer term, huge capital and engineering savings were in the offing, through consolidation of truck chassis, drive-lines, and passenger car platforms. Fritz Henderson was enthused: a simple analysis showed a savings potential of $7 billion in the first year. Roughly 1.5 million more units, but with only a bit of added fixed cost, would have diluted GM's fixed cost per unit to the point where we would have been hugely profitable. Daimler's Dieter Zetsche liked the idea (they would have gotten an equity stake), but they also talked to other suitors and in the end, Cerberus offered more, and that's where the ill-fated Chrysler Corporation and Chrysler Credit went.

In the middle of 2008, it became clear that Cerberus was desperate to unload Chrysler. Henderson and I looked at the idea again and were convinced that time was running out for both companies. Something dramatic needed to be done, if only to show Washington that the automotive CEOs were "doing something." The consolidation savings were still there. The new and by far world's largest car company would have enjoyed unprecedented leverage with the UAW and suppliers. Fritz and I were excited. Rick Wagoner took it to the board several times. Alas, that's where it stopped. Several influential board members were almost paranoid about the UAW ("Why would we want to compound that problem?"). Arguments about urgently needed consolidation savings fell on deaf ears. Rick heeded the board's advice. I would have fought on. At that point, the CEO's job was in peril anyway. May as well go down swinging!

And then there's the issue of GM's brands: While we successfully absorbed Daewoo, a brand we really didn't need, into Chevrolet, globally we still had too many. Oldsmobile had been terminated prior to my arrival. My problem was that, basically, I loved them all, especially the traditional five in the U.S. market: Chevrolet, Pontiac, Buick, and Cadillac, and in light trucks the increasingly respected and highly profitable GMC. I was a bit less "emotionally committed" to Saturn, feeling as with Saab that it was an experiment GM should never have undertaken, but now that we had the brand and a loyal (bordering on the fanatical) customer base, I was a strong advocate of providing the brand with world-class products. Sadly, while the new product generation of Aura, Vue, Outlook, Sky roadster, and Europe-sourced Astra were very well-received by the media, the lack of advertising available for the brand resulted in disappointing volumes, and the handwriting was on the wall. But in view of state-by-state dealer protection legislation, it would have cost a major fortune to cancel the brand. Chapter 11 was the real enabler here.

Hummer turned out to be a colossal mistake, although coming on board in 2001 I was a major proponent of feeding its growth. Those were the heady times of economic expansion, and with a complete line planned down to small but capable off-roaders with four-cylinder engines, the brand had the potential to challenge Jeep as the dominant American "rugged, capable, off-road" brand. Unfortunately, the increasingly strident anti-CO_2 forces created an environment (eagerly seized upon and magnified by the media) where the large Hummer H2 became the poster child for upper-class greed, insouciance, and environmental irresponsibility, poisoning the whole brand. The fact that many European luxury sedans and sports cars routinely suck more fuel than a Hummer H2 was lost in the hysteria.

In retrospect, GM should never have launched Hummer as a brand. In the early 2000s, we should have launched the H2 as "the Hummer by GMC" and sold it through GMC dealers. That would have vastly reduced our financial commitment, permitted us to drop it quietly when the heat came on, and avoided the massive legal exposure to an entire, newly created retail structure. But, as with Saturn, the cost of exit was too great and only Chapter 11 was able to create the conditions that permitted shedding the brand. I was no smarter than anyone else, though, when the Hummer brand was hot.

Buick and Pontiac were frequent nominees on Rick Wagoner's "reduce brands" list, but I felt very strongly that each had its legitimate place in the lineup and that they were not "superfluous" as much as they were victims of parental neglect. Buick was ultimately saved because of the importance of the brand to China, as well as by the current resurgence thanks to hugely successful products like the Buick Enclave luxury crossover and the spectacular new LaCrosse.

I personally would have fought to keep Pontiac. Research

showed it to be one of the brands most coveted by Generation Y, the youngest identifiable demographic group, and despite endless interference and attempted direction changes from a rapidly rotating set of Pontiac marketing heads, we had finally managed to develop a unique, plausible, complementary product philosophy for Pontiac: sporty, entertaining, high-performance cars with rear-wheel drive, like BMW at much lower prices. Two of the foundation stones were in place: the Pontiac Solstice roadster and coupe and the highly acclaimed G8 rear-wheel-drive sedan, which, despite practically no launch advertising, soon began to sell well to exactly the type of customer we had always envisaged.

Next up was to be a smaller rear-drive sports sedan, a value-oriented car sharing its basic layout with a future smaller Cadillac. Alas, there was no "China factor" to argue in the case of Pontiac; it was, as a brand, not (yet) profitable. Because the "new" Pontiac was not as far along as the "new" Buick, it was cut. If it had been my choice, I would have kept it. My decision may well have been proven wrong. The numbers said drop it; my gut said keep it. We'll never know.

What would I have done about the UAW and our legacy costs? I wish I could claim that I would have tackled the problem head on, with boldness. The truth is, I would not have done anything differently. In the 2007 negotiations, under the leadership of Rick Wagoner (and thanks to a growing sense of reality on the part of the UAW under Ron Gettelfinger), GM successfully negotiated a solution to the crushing, multibillion-per-annum funding of UAW health care costs. The irony is, the savings were not to become effective until 2010 . . . exactly two years too late to save us from the "perfect storm" of the 2008 mortgage and car market meltdown.

A tough approach, often advocated by outsiders unfamiliar with the situation, of "Here's the new package, take it or leave it" to the UAW would have resulted in a lengthy, crippling strike, one which would have seen GM out of cash and bankrupt before the UAW exhausted their strike fund.

Cooperation, education, careful reduction of unneeded capacity, and gradual elimination of uncompetitive work practices while waiting for 2010 to roll around was the right approach. Without the 2008 meltdown, it would have seen us through. Once again, the radical cleanup, the dramatic UAW reductions, the numerous plant closings, and the elimination of any residual wage gap to the Japanese transplants operating in America's nonunion South, was ultimately enabled by Chapter 11 and the strictures laid down by the Automotive Task Force, which did not spare the UAW from further concessions.

It is predominantly in the area of management style that I would have acted in a manner commensurate with my nature. Like Ed Whitacre, I have a strong tendency toward simplicity. Open discussion among a seasoned, aggressive group of doers (as we had at Chrysler) is more productive in arriving at solutions than endless scenario-studies and useless projections of the future (with a near-zero batting average) created by legions of MBAs. I view this business as fundamentally simple: get the product right, advertise it well, and everything else will fall into place. I have always encouraged a substantial degree of irreverence in meetings, using humor to allay fear and encourage more junior people to speak up. I have always been a great slayer of sacred cows and believe that to take one's history and internal institutions too seriously is to impede speed and progress. It goes without saying that we had an excessive number of senior executives, many of whom looked good, spoke well, and didn't drive change. Many were "boss watchers" without any convictions of their own.

I believe in strong direction, in unmistakably conveying what I believe should be done. I will listen, but if convinced of the rightness of my views, I will ultimately, with ever less gentleness in the suggestions, get it done. I don't believe large organizations will "move" adequately without a degree of forcefulness from the leader.

Finally, I would have changed GM's historic reticence when it comes to telling the truth about the company to the public. I don't believe that "hoping it will blow over" or "it's only a one-day story, don't dignify it with a response" is a good long-term strategy. As CEO, I would have had myself scheduled on every major network and cable show imaginable and would have worked tirelessly to tell our story and stamp out misconceptions. Many CEOs see this as a waste of the top person's time. I don't. The job of the CEO is, in large part, making sure the company is seen in a favorable light. False beliefs and unjust accusations need to be tackled, not left to fester in the files of the media, to be pulled out when another negative story is due. I do not see the media, or media exposure, as a negative. A frank, open, and candid approach, with lots of easy access to the CEO, is a winning strategy.

It comes naturally to me; I should probably have been a teacher or preacher. Even the occasional gaffe is excused if the media senses an underlying respect for their profession and a desire to communicate honestly. Lee Iacocca is the role model in this area, and it worked well.

So there you have it: my hypothetical tenure as CEO. Some hits, some misses—who knows what difference a more open, less formal, less reverential leadership style might have made. In all probability, given the intractable nature of GM's legacy cost problems, the damage done in generations past by a combination of failed government policies (fleet average fuel economy standards, a Japan-biased exchange rate), an overly analytical, non-product-, non-customer-focused series of CEOs, a UAW that couldn't, politically speaking, adjust downward, a retiree-to-active ratio approaching ten to one, all culminating in the "perfect storm" of the spring of 2008, Chapter 11 would have been the ultimate result no matter who was in charge. My mistakes, though, would have been in the category of "errors of commission" rather than "errors of omission." And we would have entered Chapter 11 with less public hostility and better understanding.

But we'll never know for sure.

And in Conclusion . . .

IN A SENSE, THE DECLINE, FAILURE, AND REBIRTH OF GENERAL MOTORS is simply a metaphor for what is happening to the whole United States. The days of absolute industrial and economic dominance that we took for granted and assumed would go on forever are over. They have been over for some time; we just didn't notice it. They were over the day the Asian producers cleaned out our home electronics industry, camera industry, small-appliance industry, and many others. They were truly over when Japan, Korea, and others demonstrated they could produce and ship vehicles as good as ours or better. "Superior technology," that old fallback, was no longer a reliable U.S.-only weapon, as technology transfer is quasi-instantaneous in today's world, where everyone can know everything. The minute we concluded that industrial products made elsewhere could be imported and sold at prices well below what it took to make them here, we began to lose our industrial preeminence. Following the dictates of classical economics, we followed the money, and in the quest for greater profitability (after all, the purpose of business), the nation soon imported everything and paid for it with IOUs called "Treasury bills."

Sure, it worked for a while: nonindustrial activity, financial markets, the odd "bubble" here and there, like the ephemeral "dot-com boom" and the later "subprime lending housing boom," masked the underlying problem that, internationally speaking, we were not competitive. "What a great world," I liked to say. "We pay each other high salaries, wages, and benefits, and then we go to Wal-Mart and buy a nineteen-dollar CD player from China."

To me, it was evident (although a lot of economists disagreed) that it was not sustainable. A country can no more consume beyond what it produces in value-added goods than an individual family can spend more than it makes. The trouble with that rule is that, at both the macro and micro level, it can be violated with impunity simply by "maxing out the credit cards." Then, after a lag, the real disaster sets in.

Whether it's residential foreclosures, military cutbacks, renegotiated wages, benefit cutbacks, budget shortfalls in many states, countries, and communities on the verge of bankruptcy and unable to pay their employees or retirees, school systems going under from the burden of excessively rich contracts and ridiculous teacher "tenure" negotiated by the teachers' unions, the signs are everywhere that the days of "What the hell, we can afford it! After all, we're the richest nation on the planet!" are over. Everyone was slow to recognize it, because it crept up on us. But now it's here, and one of the reasons an almost trillion-dollar stimulus is not "stimulating" as much as hoped is that the natural objects of stimulation, namely manufacturing jobs, are largely elsewhere: China, India, Indonesia, Vietnam, you name it.

As a country, we need to go through this painful collective Chapter 11–like experience. For a time, we need to put the "American Dream" of ever-more, ever-bigger, ever-richer on hold as we grapple with the reality that we are, on balance, far less competitive than we need to be. We need lower salaries, less obscene bonuses (especially those derived from toying with financial instruments, or "smoke-and-mirrors value," as opposed to real value added). Worker wages and benefits should not rise; if anything, future workers may need to enter the industrial workforce for less compensation than their fathers did.

The reality that the USA has been charging prosperity to the credit card and the realization that it's high time to "get real" needs to sink in everywhere.

I sense the "adjustment" taking place. With a devalued dollar and more competitive wages, it's a time for *in*sourcing back into the United States. Industrial jobs *can* be created again, and Americans *can* once again aspire to middle-class jobs through actually making things. We need to remember that economic value is basically created only one of three ways:

- Mining the material from the bowels of the earth

- Growing food and wood on the surface of the earth

- Manufacturing and distributing the products of the first two

Everything else is simply trading "value" that has already been created. And issuing mortgages, for high profit, to home "owners" who manifestly don't qualify for homeownership is about as economically useful as a Ponzi scheme, which, now that I think of it, it resembles.

GM will come back. The people, the skills, the desire to succeed are all there. The competitive "killer instinct" is at a higher pitch than at anytime in the last fifty years. The burdens of the past, which so shackled the company, and hangovers from the parties of better days, are gone. Unfortunately, many investors, including the author, lost a lot, but that's what Chapter 11 does: it assures a new beginning, but with new owners.

I would hope that the mistakes and the sense of "we're too

big and too powerful to fail," all the things that marked the last four decades at GM, are duly noted. The resurgence of the focus on the customer, the mission of "designing, building, and selling the world's best cars and trucks," the replacement of arrogance with a new sense of reality and a determination to succeed, to reconquer, to prove the naysayers wrong are all lessons imparted by the last ten years of dramatic change at GM.

Restructuring and rebirth are possible, but not without self-recognition, pain, and hardship.

Let us hope that the United States, challenged as never before, finds the path to renewed industrial competitiveness and, thus, wealth and influence. We do not want a national "Chapter 11" and, subsequently, a change in ownership of the country!

Acknowledgments

COUNTLESS PEOPLE HELPED IN WRITING THIS BOOK, SOME WITH VALU-able information, some with encouragement, some with examples of excellence, and some who provided graphic examples of how *not* to succeed in a customer-focused business. (I'd like to say "You know who you are" but I doubt if the benighted ones are aware of their limitation.)

On the positive side, the main contributors are:

Andy Norton, who provided valuable insights into the bad old days of GM's disregard for the voice of the customer.

Jack Hazen, that rare blend of bean counter by profession, car guy in his soul, and his soul always won out.

Ed Welburn, GM vice president of global design, who provided me with historical perspective on GM Design's ups and downs.

Betty Gonko, ace administrative assistant, who provided me with the freedom from trivia that allowed me to conceive the book.

Mark Walkuski, intrepid driver, sounding board, and huge saver of my time.

Tony Posawatz, the soul of the Volt team, for providing some valuable insights into the creation of the world's first extended-range electric vehicle.

Nancy Breedlove, typist, who deciphered hundreds of my handwritten pages and, being the first reader of the book, wrote "Thanks! I enjoyed it!"

Amy King, home administrative assistant, who has picked up the load created by literary endeavors since my retirement.

Much appreciation goes to my patient wife, Denise, who spent entire Caribbean vacations looking at her husband filling pad after pad (and also providing motivation when I didn't).

Dee Allen, formerly with GM Communications and now adviser and counselor, for his hints and suggestions.

And last but certainly not least, my long-standing speechwriter and editor John Cortez, whose literary skills vastly exceed mine but who can change and improve so it still sounds like me!

Index

Also by Bob Lutz

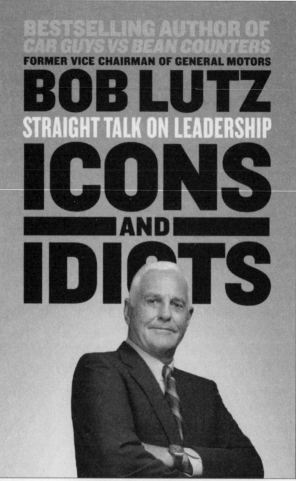

ISBN 978-1-59184-604-8

Now in hardcover wherever books are sold.

PORTFOLIO
PENGUIN

Portfolio/Penguin
A member of Penguin Group (USA) Inc.
www.penguin.com